THE COMPLETE
OPERAS OF
PUCCINI

THE COMPLETE OPERAS OF PUCCINI

A CRITICAL GUIDE

BY CHARLES OSBORNE

DA CAPO PRESS

Library of Congress Cataloging in Publication Data

Osborne, Charles, 1927–
   The complete operas of Puccini.

   (A Da Capo paperback)
   Bibliography: p.
   Includes index.
   1. Puccini, Giacomo, 1858–1924. Operas. 2. Opera—History and criticism. I. Title.
   ML410.P89O8 1983   782.1′092′4   83-10142
   ISBN 0-306-80200-7 (pbk.)

10   9   8   7   6   5

Da Capo Press books are available at special discounts for bulk purchases in the U.S. by corporations, institutions, and other organizations. For more information, please contact the Special Markets Department at the Perseus Books Group, 11 Cambridge Center, Cambridge, MA 02142, or call (617) 252-5298.

This Da Capo Press paperback edition of *The Complete Operas of Puccini*
is an unabridged republication of the first edition published in New
York in 1982. It is reprinted by arrangement with Atheneum Publishers.

Published by Da Capo Press
A Member of the Perseus Books Group
http://www.dacapopress.com

Manufactured in the United States of America

To
Ken Thomson

CONTENTS

LIST OF ILLUSTRATIONS

following page 124

The composer's father, Michele Puccini

The Composer's mother, Albina Puccini Magi

Giacomo Puccini as a student

Water-colour sketch by Frederick von Hohenstein for Act II of *Le villi*

Puccini and Ferdinando Fontana, librettist of *Le villi* and *Edgar*

Puccini at the time of *Le villi*

Water-colour sketch by Giuseppe Palanti for Act II of *Edgar*

The original costume designs for Edgar and Tigrana in *Edgar*

Left to right: Verdi, Puccini, Boito, Mascagni, Leoncavallo and Giordano

Sketch by Ferruccio Pagni of the hut used for meetings of the *Club la Bohème*. The cabin is no longer standing, and the lake frontage has changed beyond recognition

Page from the autograph score of *La Bohème*, Act I

Cover of the earliest English vocal score of *Madam Butterfly*, published by Ricordi (design by Leopoldo Metlicovitz)

Enrico Caruso

Caricature of Caruso of a rehearsal of *La fanciulla del west* at the Metropolitan Opera House, New York

Puccini at the time of *Turandot*

INTRODUCTION

As with my earlier critical guides to the operas of Verdi and Mozart, this is a book on the operas of Puccini as works of musical theatre. It is not a full-scale biography of the composer, though a biographical thread links one chapter to the next, nor is it the kind of music criticism to which Bernard Shaw used to object, and which he satirized in a famous passage in which he subjected Shakespeare's 'To be or not to be' to the method of the musical analyst: 'Shakespeare, dispensing with the customary exordium, announces his subject at once in the infinitive, in which mood it is presently repeated after a short connecting passage....'

That was Shaw's satire, but this is a passage from a volume on Puccini's operas published in 1958: '...there is an example as early as *Edgar* of diminished seventh chords side-slipping in parallel and in the same opera a similar set of parallel chords of the thirteenth. By *Manon Lescaut* Puccini was prepared to be more daring than this with a set of chords of the seventh so disposed that bare augmented fourths follow the melodic line in parallel.'

This book is addressed to the opera-lover who may not find any use for information as specialized as that above but who wants to know the background of the operas he enjoys, to have the works set in their historical context and the music discussed in terms reasonably free of jargon — remembering that operas are not abstract symphonies.

A list of books I have consulted will be found at the end of this volume. Unless otherwise stated, quotations from the letters of Puccini come from Giuseppe Adami's edition of *The Letters of Giacomo Puccini*, translated by Ena Makin (London: Harrap, 1931), though I have indulged in a little 'touching-up' here and there.

C.O.

I

Le villi

an opera in two acts

Dramatis personæ:

Roberto	(tenor)
Anna	(soprano)
Guglielmo Wulf, Anna's father	(baritone)

LIBRETTO by Ferdinando Fontana

TIME: The Middle Ages
PLACE: The Black Forest

FIRST PERFORMED, in a one-act version, at the Teatro dal Verme, Milan, 31 May, 1884, with Antonio d'Andrade (Roberto), Regina Caporetti (Anna), Erminio Pelz (Guglielmo Wulf), conducted by Achille Panizza. The revised, two-act version was first performed at the Teatro Regio, Turin, 26 December, 1884, with Filippi-Bresciani (Roberto), Elena Boronat (Anna) and Agostino Gnaccarini (Guglielmo Wulf)

Le villi

UNLIKE MOST OF the other great composers of opera – Wagner, Strauss, Verdi – but like Bach and Couperin, Giacomo Puccini came from a long line of musicians. His family, first heard of in the tiny village of Celle in the Apuan Alps of Tuscany, established itself in the city of Lucca early in the eighteenth century. The first of the musical Puccinis, one Giacomo Puccini and the great-great-grandfather of *the* Puccini, was born in Lucca in 1712, studied in Bologna either with the celebrated Padre Martini whom he certainly knew or with Martini's colleague Giovanni Caretti, and became organist and choirmaster at the cathedral of San Martino in Lucca. Giacomo Puccini was a prolific composer of masses, oratorios, cantatas and other music for the church and for civic occasions. He died in 1781 at the age of sixty-nine.

Giacomo's son, Antonio Benedetto Maria Puccini, was born in Lucca in 1747, studied music at first with his father and later in Bologna, and at the age of twenty-four became a member of the distinguished Accademia dei Filarmonici of Bologna. He may well have been present at the ceremony at which the fourteen-year-old Mozart, visiting Bologna with his father, was received into the Accademia. In 1772, Antonio became his father's assistant at San Martino, and in due course succeeded him as choirmaster. He too composed a large number of works, among them a Requiem Mass on the death of the Austrian Emperor Joseph II in 1790. Antonio died in Lucca in 1832, aged eighty-five.

The first of the Puccinis to compose full length operas was Giacomo's son, Domenico Vincenzo Puccini, who, after studying at first in Bologna and then with Paisiello in Naples, became his father's assistant at San Martino. Born in 1771, Domenico was appointed director of Princess Élise's court orchestra at Lucca at the age of thirty-four, and made a more than local reputation with his comic operas and with an *opera seria*, *Quinto Fabio*, which was staged at Livorno in 1810. Domenico died suddenly in 1815, at the early age of forty-four; it was rumoured that, suspected of harbouring anti-Austrian ideas, he had been poisoned at a dinner party. He left a widow and four young children one of whom, Michele, became the father of Giacomo Puccini.

Michele, born in Lucca in 1813, studied music with his grandfather and subsequently in Bologna and in Naples, where his teachers were Donizetti, and Verdi's rival, Mercadante. He then took up the family position of organist and choirmaster at the cathedral of San Martino, composing secular and religious music, and two operas, one of which, *Giambattista Cattani*, was successfully staged in Lucca in 1844. He was also highly regarded as a teacher, and the author of two textbooks on harmony and counterpoint. Michele married Albina Magi, the sister of one of his ex-pupils. Of their eight children, five were girls and three boys, one of whom died in infancy. The fifth child, born on 22 December, 1858, at home at 30, via di Poggio, a narrow street in one of the oldest parts of Lucca, was Giacomo Antonio Domenico Michele Secondo Maria Puccini, who was destined to bestow a fame considerably more than local upon the family name.

Giacomo was only five when his father died at the age of fifty-one, but it was clearly assumed in the Puccini family that, if not immediately, then at some time in the future the son would succeed his father as organist and choirmaster at the cathedral. This assumption was shared by the Lucchese authorities, who, in appointing Michele Puccini's brother-in-law, Fortunato Magi, to the vacant position, inserted a clause in his contract which required him to 'hand over the post of Organist and Maestro di Capella to Signor Giacomo, son of the aforementioned defunct master, as soon as the said Signor Giacomo be able to discharge such duties'.

Magi, in fact, became the first teacher of his young nephew Giacomo, giving him organ lessons and coaching him in singing. But Giacomo was by all accounts a lazy and apparently untalented pupil, though he began to make more progress when his mother found a new teacher for him, one Carlo Angeloni, at the Istituto Musicale Pacini. At the age of ten, Giacomo became a choirboy at San Martino, and by the time he was fourteen he was occasionally playing the organ at services, not only at the cathedral and at his neighbourhood church of San Michele but also at churches in the vicinity of Lucca. And not only at churches: Giacomo was also in demand as a pianist in the local taverns and, it was rumoured, in a brothel in the via della Dogana. He played, too, at the near-by fashionable resorts of Bagni di Lucca and Lerici, thus supplementing his mother's inadequate pension of 75 lire a month (the equivalent then of £3 or 12 dollars). Giacomo kept back part of his salary, however, in order to buy cigarettes, for he had begun to smoke while still a child. He was also not averse to stealing organ pipes, enlisting his younger brother Michele and other friends as accomplices, to keep himself in cigarette money; he was able to prevent immediate discovery by playing the organ in such a way as to avoid the notes of the missing pipes. A more respectable source of income was his one and only pupil, Carlo della Nina, a lad of his own age whom he taught for four years.

Puccini's earliest compositions, some of them organ pieces for his pupil to play, were written when he was sixteen. Many are based on the improvisations which were expected of a church organist, especially at the end of the service as the congregation was leaving. Puccini's improvisations occasionally shocked the pious, for he would insert into them lively folk songs or snatches from popular operas. 'You are trying to outdo the theatre,' said his elder sister, Iginia, who was about to take the veil as an Augustinian nun.

Giacomo was, of course, already interested in the theatre, especially in opera, for his teacher Angeloni had introduced him to the scores of *Rigoletto*, *La traviata* and *Il trovatore*, the middle-period masterpieces of Italy's greatest living composer, Giuseppe Verdi. Verdi was at that time in his sixties, and had recently composed *Aida*. When the opera was performed at Pisa, about twenty miles from Lucca, on 11 March, 1876, the eighteen-year-old Giacomo and two friends walked there and back to hear it. 'When I heard *Aida* at Pisa', Puccini said later, 'I felt that a musical window had opened for me.'[1]

It was after he had heard *Aida* in Pisa that the young Puccini began to turn away from composing solely for the organ. He produced the somewhat melancholy but attractive and confidently scored *Preludio Sinfonico*, a work for orchestra lasting about ten minutes, and in the following year, 1877, entered a competition with his setting of the patriotic poem *I figli d'Italia bella* – only to have his manuscript returned by the judges who had found it virtually illegible. (Puccini's musical script remained difficult to decipher throughout his entire life.) A Motet and Credo in Honour of San Paolino, which he composed in 1878 at the age of twenty for the annual Feast of San Paolino, Lucca's first bishop and the city's patron saint, was successfully performed on the saint's day, and two years later Puccini incorporated its two movements into a Mass for Four Voices and Orchestra (*Messa a quattro voci con orchestra*), which was praised by his teacher Angeloni and also performed in Lucca. The music critic of the local newspaper, *Provincia di Lucca*, thought that the work contained 'extremely noble ideas', was well harmonized and well developed. The Mass, which remained in manuscript until 1951 when it was published as *Messa di gloria*, is a full-scale work in five movements, which owes a great deal to Verdi's great *Messa di requiem*, composed only six years previously. But if Puccini's Mass looks back to Verdi, and to earlier Italian operatic style, it also looks forward to the Puccini of the theatre: indeed, the composer was later to plunder it when writing his second and third operas.

At the end of Puccini's time at the Pacini Musical Institute, means were found to enable him to continue his studies at the Milan Conservatorium. His mother appealed to Queen Margherita, who administered a scholarship fund for talented students from poor families; as a result, the Queen's fund offered a one-year scholarship, while an

[1] Quoted in Mosco Carner, *Puccini: a critical biography* (London, 1958).

uncle of Puccini's mother guaranteed the remaining two years of Puccini's three-year term at the Conservatorium. Neither the town of Lucca nor the ecclesiastical authorities contributed, although Albina Puccini more than once appealed to the Lucchese Council, and Puccini himself applied to the Mayor of Lucca for a grant at the end of his second year in Milan. Puccini's application was not even acknowledged.

Arriving in Milan in the autumn of 1880, the twenty-two-year-old Puccini submitted himself to the Council of the Conservatorium for a preliminary examination. This he passed easily, which meant that he was admitted as a student for a probationary year. He had his first lesson on 16 December, and on 18 December wrote home to his mother:

Yesterday I had my second lesson from Bazzini. It is going very well. That is the only lesson I have so far, but on Friday I am beginning aesthetics. I have made myself this time-table: in the morning I get up at half-past eight, and when I have a lesson I go to it. If I have no lesson I practise the piano a little. I don't need to do much, but I have to practise a bit. I am going to buy a very good 'method' by Angeleri, the sort of method from which one can learn a lot by oneself. I go on till half-past ten; then I have lunch and go out. At one I come home and work for a couple of hours preparing for Bazzini, then from three to five at the piano again for some reading of classical music. I'd like to take out a subscription for music, but I haven't enough money. At the moment I am reading the *Mefistofele* of Boito, which a friend of mine, Favara, from Palermo, has lent me. At five I go to my frugal meal (special emphasis on the frugal!), and I have Milanese broth which, to tell the truth, is very good. I have three plates of that, then some other mess, a bit of Gorgonzola cheese, and half a litre of wine. Then I light a cigar and go off to my usual walk up and down in the Galleria. I am there till nine o'clock and come home dead tired. I do a little counterpoint, but no playing: I am not allowed to play at night. Then I get into bed and read seven or eight pages of a novel. And that's my life! . . .

The teacher mentioned by Puccini was Antonio Bazzini (1818–1897) who had begun his career as a violinist and later turned to composition. His only opera, produced at La Scala in 1867 without success, was *Turanda*, based on Gozzi's *Turandot*, a subject to which his pupil was to turn many years later. Bazzini had joined the staff of the Milan Conservatorium in 1873 as professor of composition, and during Puccini's time there he was to become director of the institution. Puccini's other principal teacher at the Conservatorium was the successful opera composer, Amilcare Ponchielli, of whose five operas one, *La Gioconda*, is still quite frequently performed in Italy.

Especially after his first year, when he was joined in his lodgings by his younger brother, a cousin, and the nineteen-year-old Pietro Mascagni, future composer of *Cavalleria rusticana*, life in Milan was enjoyable for Puccini. Money was in short supply, however, and landlords, restaurant proprietors and other creditors had to be outwitted whenever possible. His general surroundings seem to have been very similar to those of the first two acts of *La Bohème* which Puccini was to compose fifteen years later. Mascagni would inform importunate creditors that Puccini was out, while that young man hid in the wardrobe; Puccini would play the piano noisily to drown the clatter of utensils when a meal was being cooked in the room; and he once pawned his only overcoat, admittedly not to buy medicine for a dying seamstress but to take a ballet dancer from La Scala to supper. He spent as many evenings at the opera as he could afford, discovering and enjoying such works as Thomas's *Mignon*, Verdi's *Simon Boccanegra* in its revised version, Bizet's *Carmen* and Catalani's new opera, *Dejanice*.

For his final examination at the Conservatorium in July 1883, Puccini composed a large-scale ten-minute orchestral piece, *Capriccio Sinfonico*. 'I felt inspired and composed it at home, in the street, in class, at the Osteria Aida or at the Excelsior of good old Signor Gigi where one ate without the silly pretence of being able to pay for it; I wrote on odd sheets, bits of paper and the margin of newspapers', the composer later told his biographer Arnaldo Fraccaroli. The *Capriccio Sinfonico*, a one-movement piece in a-b-a ternary form, and full of melodic charm, was played on 14 July by the student orchestra conducted by Franco Faccio, the leading Italian operatic conductor of the day; it was Faccio who had conducted the first Scala performances of Verdi's *Aida*, and who four years later was to conduct the première of *Otello*. The day after the concert, the Milan newspaper *La Perseveranza* published a review by the leading critic, Filippo Filippi, who referred to Puccini's 'decisive and very rare musical temperament, one that is specifically symphonic', and asserted that there was more 'unity of style, personality and character' in the *Capriccio Sinfonico* than in the work of most living composers. Faccio conducted the work on at least two later occasions. After that Puccini forbade further performances or publication; he even borrowed the score from the library of the Conservatorium and neglected to return it, probably because he had used passages from the work in two of his operas and did not wish the fact to be generally known. He may have forgotten that an arrangement of the *Capriccio Sinfonico* for piano duet had been published, a year after he left the Conservatorium.

Armed with his diploma, in the summer of 1883, Puccini now had his professional future to consider. He could have returned to Lucca to take up the traditional family occupation of organist and choirmaster at San Martino; he could also have accepted an offer to teach at the Pacini Institute in Lucca. He chose, however, to stay in Milan and attempt to make his way as a composer of opera. His teacher and mentor Ponchielli helped by mentioning Puccini to Giulio Ricordi, director of the famous publishing firm, and also by putting the young composer in touch with a librettist when Puccini decided to enter for a competition which he had seen announced in the *Teatro illustrato*. The competition, sponsored by a wealthy Milanese industrialist and newspaper proprietor, Edoardo Sonzogno, was for a one-act opera, and the prize was 2,000 lire (about £80 or 320 dollars). The Sonzogno prize, initiated in this year, was awarded occasionally until 1904: in 1889 it was won by Mascagni with *Cavalleria rusticana*. It was open to composers from all over Italy, and even to foreign composers, so the chance of an inexperienced newcomer carrying it off was remote. Puccini recognized this, but it seemed as good a way of beginning as any.

The librettist Ponchielli had in mind for Puccini was a thirty-three-year-old writer and journalist, Ferdinando Fontana (1850–1919), to whom he broached the subject when they were both staying with Antonio Ghislanzoni, Verdi's *Aida* librettist, at Ghislanzoni's hotel, Il Barco, in the country outside Milan. A few days later, Ponchielli followed up his verbal request with a letter, to which Fontana replied:

> I should be very happy to be of use to Maestro Puccini, but you know that I am always sailing in shallow waters. So far I have managed to keep the wolf from the door without resorting to the tedious task of writing libretti, and if I write one now I expect at least to make a profit. So I shall not write libretti for less than 300 lire per act.
>
> However, I consider myself an intelligent and pleasant young man, and, as you know, by no means intransigent. The fee I quote is the minimum within reason, and much less than I would earn from some other chore, albeit a less glamorous one than writing a libretto. Writing a libretto, however, is an appealing and amusing occupation, and more in keeping with my intellectual tastes. I propose, therefore, to do as you suggest, and I ask for 100 lire to be paid on completion of the libretto, with an additional 200 lire to be paid if Puccini wins the competition. Surely this is not unreasonable![1]

Many years later, Fontana described the circumstances of his first collaboration with Puccini:

> It was in August of 1883. One fine morning when I had gone to Lecco, from Ghislanzoni's retreat at Caprino Bergamasco, I fell in with the summer colony of artists from Maggianico. Among them were Ponchielli, Dominicesi, Saladino, and other distinguished men. Puccini also was there. We did not know each other well, but a strong current of sympathy had passed between us on those few occasions when we had met. I entered the same carriage as Ponchielli, who spoke to me of his pupil's intention of entering for the Sonzogno competition and suggested that I should write his libretto. There and then, with the memory fresh in my mind of the *Capriccio Sinfonico*, I felt the necessity of an imaginative subject for the young musician, and I outlined for him the story of *Le villi*. He accepted it. The libretto was ready at the beginning of September . . .[2]

[1] Quoted in Arnaldo Fraccaroli, *La vita di Giacomo Puccini* (Milan, 1925).
[2] Quoted in *Letters of Giacomo Puccini*, ed. Giuseppe Adami (London, 1931).

Puccini wrote to his mother that he liked Fontana's idea for a subject 'very much, there being ample scope in it for the descriptive, symphonic kind of music, which attracts me particularly because I think I ought to succeed in it'.[1] A week or two later, in September, he returned to Lucca with Fontana's libretto, to live at home while he worked on the opera. His method was to compose the vocal line and sketch its harmonic implications first, and then to elaborate and expand while he was orchestrating. For four months he spent several hours of each day at work on the opera which, at this stage of its life, was called *Le willis*. He also earned a little money by giving music lessons: one of his pupils was Elvira Gemignani, a young married woman whom he had probably known when they were children.

Puccini only just managed to complete the opera by the closing date of the competition, 31 December, and had to send off his virtually illegible manuscript without having had time to get it copied. When the results of the competition were announced early in 1884, *Le willis* was not even mentioned. The prize was shared between *Fata del nord* by Guglielmo Zuelli and *Anna e Gualberto* by Luigi Borelli, neither of whom was to achieve any lasting success as a composer. It was thought at the time – certainly by Puccini and his friends – that the judges may not have tried very hard to decipher Puccini's manuscript scrawl.

The two winners had their operas produced within a few months at the Teatro Manzoni in Milan. Puccini's librettist Fontana was determined that their opera would also reach the stage, and to this end he arranged for Puccini to be invited to the salon of Marco Sala, a wealthy dilettante whose house was frequented by a number of influential writers, artists, musicians and patrons of the arts. There Puccini played and sang excerpts from the opera, to such effect that the assembled company immediately agreed to raise funds to have *Le willis* staged. Giulio Ricordi offered to publish an edition of the libretto without charge, and Arrigo Boito, Verdi's librettist, who was then working with the great composer on *Otello*, persuaded the manager of the Teatro dal Verme to allow *Le willis* to be performed there.

Puccini took the opportunity to make a few changes to his score. 'As you will have heard', he wrote to his mother on 13 May,

> I am giving my little opera at the Dal Verme. I had not mentioned it to you because I was not sure. The expense of production is being shared by many gentlemen of Milan, and also some people of importance like A. Boito, Marco Sala, etc., who have pledged themselves each for a certain sum.

Le willis, described on the playbills as an 'opera-ballo' in one act, was given its première on 31 May, 1884, in a triple bill in which it was preceded by *Ruy Blas*, a popular opera by Filippo Marchetti, a middle-aged composer whose fame was short-lived, and followed by a 'grandioso ballo' called *La Contessa d'Egmont*. There were three performances in all, on consecutive evenings.

The press announcement of the première stated: 'Tonight at the Teatro dal Verme will be given the first performance of another of the operas submitted to the competition of the *Teatro illustrato*, one of the works that received neither a prize nor an honourable mention.' This might not seem the most likely way to entice people into a theatre; nevertheless, the first performance played to a capacity audience, who gave the work an enthusiastic reception. The singers were excellent, though they were not famous names – the tenor was a brother of the celebrated baritone Francisco d'Andrade. The conductor was not, as some reference books state, Ettore Panizza, who was to have a distinguished career at La Scala, Covent Garden and the Metropolitan Opera: Ettore Panizza was only nine years old in 1884. The Panizza who conducted the première of Puccini's first opera was Achille Panizza, already an elderly man.

Not only was *Le willis* warmly appreciated in the theatre – the symphonic intermezzo had to be played three times, and two other numbers were encored – it was also praised next day by the music critics, one of whom wrote of the young Puccini as 'una delle più brillanti e più promettenti speranze dell' arte' (one of the most brilliant and most promising hopes of art). Filippo Filippi in *La Perseveranza* referred scathingly to 'that wretched competition jury which accorded Puccini not even an honourable mention', and the *Corriere della sera* found the composer's craftsmanship so elegant and complete that 'we seem to have before us not a young student but a Bizet or a Massenet'. 'We believe sincerely', the critic concluded, 'that in Puccini we may have the composer for whom Italy has long been waiting.' It is interesting to note that Puccini's use of the orchestra is singled out for special mention, and that he is considered to be a modern 'symphonic' composer rather than a traditional 'vocal' one in his approach to opera.

Puccini's mother had been in ill health for some months. Now bedridden, she was unable to witness her son's triumph in Milan, so he sent her a telegram: 'Tumultuous success. All hopes surpassed. Eighteen calls. First finale encored three times. Am happy. Giacomo.' Six weeks later, in Lucca, Puccini was at his mother's bedside when she died.

Within days of the première of *Le willis*, the great master of Italian opera himself commented upon Puccini. In a letter to his friend Count Arrivabene, on 10 June, the seventy-one-year-old Verdi wrote:

I have heard the composer Puccini well spoken of. I have seen a letter in which he is highly praised. He follows the modern tendencies, which is natural, but he adheres to melody, which is neither modern nor antique. The symphonic element, however, appears to be predominant in him. Nothing wrong with that, but one needs to tread cautiously here. Opera is opera, and the symphony is the symphony and I do not believe it's a good thing to insert a piece of a symphony into an opera, simply for the pleasure of making the orchestra perform.[1]

Verdi would have been told of the first performance of *Le willis* either by Boito, who was seen to applaud vigorously from his box, or by Giulio Ricordi. Four days after he had witnessed the success of the opera in the theatre, Ricordi offered Puccini a contract, under the terms of which the firm of Ricordi acquired world rights in the opera, which the composer undertook to recast in two acts; moreover a second opera was commissioned from Puccini and Fontana, for performance at La Scala. Ricordi was moved by practical considerations in asking for *Le willis* to be revised: a full-length opera would be easier to place in the larger, more important opera houses than a short, one-act work.

Puccini completed his revision by the end of October, and, with a slight change of title by which the foreign word 'willis' became Italianized as 'villi', the two-act opera was produced at the Teatro Regio, Turin, on 26 December. The singers were Elena Boronat, sister of the more famous Olimpia Boronat, as Anna, Filippi-Bresciani as Roberto, and Agostino Gnaccarini as Guglielmo Wulf; they and the opera were applauded although Puccini and Fontana did not think highly of the assembled forces. On the day of the dress rehearsal, Fontana wrote a letter to Ricordi which was signed jointly by Puccini and himself:

> There is no doubt that the performance of *Le villi* at the Regio will be not only very far from what we wished, but also very inferior to that which it could have been in a first-class theatre.
>
> The singers are a lot of old crocks. The orchestra is weak and lifeless, and even the baton of the valiant Bolzoni is powerless to infuse any spirit into it. . . . I may add that Puccini, who is really very patient in his criticisms, does not dare to make any more, because the only suggestion which he made last night was received with scant courtesy.
>
> The choruses are lamentably weak. At times they are simply not heard. And you know that the acoustic properties of the Regio are of the worst. I say nothing of the staging. We have not yet been allowed to see the scenery!
>
> Puccini has little hope. I, on the other hand, believe in spite of everything that it will be a success. . . . The less said about the ballet the better. They have foisted a third-rate dancer on us as ballet master.[2]

Four weeks after the Turin production, on 24 January, 1885, *Le villi* was staged at La Scala, Milan, the leading Italian opera house. It did not repeat there its earlier successes, although Puccini himself supervised the staging and the opera was conducted by the distinguished Franco

[1] *Letters of Giuseppe Verdi*, ed. Charles Osborne (London, 1971).
[2] *Letters of Giacomo Puccini*, op. cit.

Faccio, chief conductor of La Scala. The singers were Romilda Pantaleoni, who two years later was to be the Desdemona in the first performance of Verdi's *Otello*, Andrea Anton (Roberto) and Delfino Menotti (Guglielmo Wulf). Despite being officially a 'full-length' work, *Le villi* still contained no more than an hour's music, so that even with a long interval, it played for less than two hours. At some of its thirteen performances at La Scala, the evening was filled out with a ballet, *Messalina*.

In the spring of 1885, *Le villi* reached Naples, where it was received at the Teatro San Carlo with catcalls and hisses. It was performed abroad, notably at Buenos Aires in 1886; in German translation at Hamburg, conducted by Gustav Mahler, in 1892; in Warsaw, in Polish, in 1893; and in English, by the Carl Rosa Company, at Manchester in 1897. At the Metropolitan Opera, New York, in 1908, it was glamorously cast with Frances Alda, Alessandro Bonci and Pasquale Amato, and conducted by Arturo Toscanini. There no pretence was made that it was a full-length work: it shared the bill with Mascagni's *Cavalleria rusticana*, in which Emmy Destinn and Enrico Caruso sang.

Gradually, the work fell out of favour. Vienna saw it in 1938, and Mannheim in 1940, and there have been occasional productions of *Le villi* in more recent years, in Siena, Spoleto, Florence, Treviso and elsewhere in Italy. Amateur and student performances were given in London (in 1955 and 1960), New York and Philadelphia, and a couple of complete gramophone recordings were made.

II

The title of Puccini's first opera does not translate easily into English. Balletomanes will know what a 'willi' is: others may not. 'Wraiths' will not do, 'witch-dancers' comes closer, but the willis are really creatures of Central European legend, spirits of maidens who have been betrayed by their lovers. Now turned into vengeful, vampire-like creatures, they appear to their faithless lovers in the forest by night, forcing them to dance until they die of sheer exhaustion. Giselle, in Act II of the popular ballet of that name, becomes a willi, and the eponymous heroine of Lehár's *The Merry Widow* sings a song about a willi or 'Villia' ('Vilia, o Vilia, the witch of the wood'). Puccini's librettist Fontana obviously was fascinated by this un-Italian folk legend, and was presumably fluent in the German language, for he was later to translate *Die lustige Witwe* (The Merry Widow) for its Italian première in 1907.

The opera is in two acts, and the action takes place in a village in the Black Forest of Germany, at an unspecified time presumably in the middle ages.

Act I. Guglielmo Wulf's cottage occupies a clearing in the woods. A path leads over a small bridge and into the forest. It is springtime, and the cottage wears a festive look, for the betrothal of Guglielmo's daughter Anna to Roberto is being celebrated. A table with food and drink is set outside the cottage. Mountaineers and villagers assemble not only to congratulate the young couple but also to say goodbye to Roberto, for he has inherited a large fortune from an elderly female relative and is leaving that day for Mainz to claim it. Anna's father, Guglielmo (baritone), joins in the dancing and festivity, but Anna (soprano) is understandably sad at her fiancé's departure. She places a bouquet of forget-me-nots in the valise Roberto is to take with him. Roberto (tenor) attempts to dispel her fears that he will forget her, and promises to return soon. Guglielmo leads the assembled company in prayer, and Roberto then sets out for Mainz.

Act II. It is now winter. The act begins with two orchestral interludes, each preceded in the score by a short poem which should either be declaimed from the stage or printed in the programme when the opera is performed, for the poems contain information necessary for one's understanding of the plot. The poem of eight lines which precedes the first orchestral interlude reveals that, at Mainz, Roberto fell victim to the wiles of an adventuress who fascinated young and old alike, drew Roberto into 'obscene orgies' ('Ella trasse Roberto all' orgia oscena') and caused him to forget Anna who, after waiting for several months for his return and hearing nothing of him, died of a broken heart at the coming of winter. ('Ed al cader del verno / Ella chiudeva gli occhi al sonno eterno.') One is momentarily reminded of Tannhäuser, Venus and Elisabeth. As the curtain rises, behind a gauze Anna's funeral procession is seen.

A second poem of eight lines now introduces the Black Forest legend of the willis, the spirits of betrothed maidens deserted by their lovers. At night they are said to haunt the forest, waylaying their betrayers and forcing them to dance until they drop dead. Roberto, abandoned by the evil temptress of Mainz, has made his way back to the Black Forest and to Anna's village. It is a cold winter night, and the willis are abroad in the forest. To the music of the second orchestral interlude, the willis perform their dance of vengeance, and depart.

Guglielmo emerges from his cottage, mourning the loss of his daughter. He calls on her spirit, if the legend of the willis be true, to take revenge on Roberto. As he enters his cottage, the willis return and lie in wait for Roberto who, when he arrives, expresses his longing to see Anna again, and curses the beauty of the 'cortigiana vil' (vile courtesan) who had detained him. Anna's spirit appears to him with the other willis, but thinking she is still alive he embraces her. 'Non son più l'amor, son la vendetta!' (I am no longer love, I am vengeance), she exclaims as she draws him into the fatal dance. When Roberto falls dead at her feet, Anna cries 'Sei mio!' (You are mine), as she and the other willis disappear. A triumphant cry of 'Hosanna' is heard from the willis.

Fontana's plot, such as it is, clearly derives from the old folk legends of vampires and revenging spirits which were prevalent in Central and Eastern Europe. The ballet *Giselle*, first produced at the Paris Opéra in 1841, with music by Adam and a scenario described as being adapted from Heine by Théophile Gautier, uses what is basically the same plot, and so does the English opera, *The Night Dancers* by Edward Loder, first performed at the Princess's Theatre, London, in 1846. An effective opera libretto could certainly have been written on the subject of the willis, but Fontana's is rendered inept by its matter-of-fact brevity and, at moments, absurd by the turgidity of its verse. There are no subsidiary characters, only a wronged heroine, a repentant hero and a grieving father, all of whom are completely unconvincing. Two of the few potential dramatic highlights of the story, Roberto's debauchery and Anna's death, are not shown on the stage but merely narrated in the explanatory verses preceding the orchestral interludes.

Even had the libretto been competently written, it would have remained unsuited to the nature of Puccini's talent or to that of Italian opera in general, for the libretto's world of Germanic myth is one in which Weber, Wagner, Lortzing, Spohr, Marschner and Humperdinck move easily, but not Bellini, Donizetti, Verdi, Mercadante, Puccini, Ponchielli, Giordano, Mascagni or any other Italian composer. The influence of Wagnerian Romanticism was strong at the time in Italy, however, and a number of composers temporarily succumbed to it, among them Alfredo Catalani with his *Loreley* and *La Wally*. The inexperienced Puccini, in a hurry to meet the competition deadline, appears to have accepted Fontana's libretto without question; in later years, he was to be extremely exacting with his librettists.

The legend of the willis, which first found its way on to the stage in *Giselle ou Les Willis*, was discovered by Théophile Gautier in Heinrich Heine's essay, 'Über Deutschland II: Elementargeister und Dämonen' (On Germany II: Elemental Spirits and Demons) which appeared in 1834. Fontana no doubt knew the ballet *Giselle*, and had probably read Heine, who says that the legend, though Slavonic in origin, was familiar in certain parts of Austria. It has affinities, too, with the German legend of the water nymph, the *Lorelei*, which attracted a number of composers. One must, however, regret that Puccini was led to it by the not very talented Fontana.

III

Le villi begins with an orchestral prelude. The earlier nineteenth-century Italian composers, Rossini, Bellini and Donizetti, had favoured full-scale overtures, but with Verdi the shorter orchestral introduction began to replace the usual overture. No Verdi opera after *La forza del destino* has an overture. Puccini, therefore, was following the Verdian pattern, though at the time his use of the prelude was considered to be an indication of Wagnerian influence. Oddly, since Puccini is the least Wagnerian of composers, the prelude to *Le villi*, a graceful, confidently scored piece of no more than 43 bars, does in its final bars sound rather like *Parsifal* taken at a brisk Italian tempo. Wagner's final opera had been performed for the first time the previous year, and the cadences of Wagner were in the air, not only of Germany but of northern Italy, the country in which most of *Parsifal* was composed and in which its composer had died. That said, this little *andante mosso* remains Italian, indeed already Puccinian in the personality of its melody.

After the prelude, the curtain rises on a conventional opening scene to the music of a conventional chorus, a lively *allegro* with which the villagers sing and dance their congratulations to Anna and Roberto, and also dispense to one another the information that Roberto is about to leave to claim his rich inheritance. The second part of the chorus is an attractive waltz, its gaiety interestingly clouded by its being in a minor key, during which Guglielmo is introduced and utters a sentence or two in tempo before being swept into the dancing. The music of the waltz dies away as the villagers dance their way out of sight, and the stage is left empty for the entrance of the prima donna.

The prima donna: one calls her that, rather than 'Anna', because it is not easy to believe in this character who seems a wraith well before she becomes one, despite the fact that Puccini has composed for her music of some delicacy and charm. The aria, 'Se come voi piccina io fossi, o vaghi fior' (If I were tiny like you, o pretty flowers), which Anna coyly addresses to the bunch of forget-me-nots she is about to place in Roberto's valise, is interesting because, in addition to its being sweet and graceful in character, we can now hear in it something of the voice of the mature Puccini, the composer of *Madama Butterfly*, with whose eponymous heroine the less individual Anna shares a touching vulnerability. The chord progressions, the repetition of short melodic phrases, these must have stood out, when the opera was new, from much in the score which derives closely from Verdi, and proclaimed that here was a new, fresh voice. The singer should end the aria on a sustained B, ignoring the optional invitation to skip up to G above the stave which is, both musically and dramatically, one of Puccini's errors of judgement.

In the love duet, 'Tu dell' infanzia mia le gioie dividesti e le carezze' (You who shared the joys and caresses of my childhood), the tenor is first given the broad C major melody, a tune which would not sound out of place issuing from the larynx of that future Puccini anti-hero, Lieutenant Pinkerton [Ex. 1]. It is then sung by the soprano, to whom it is less well suited, for it is really a typical Puccini tenor aria in disguise. The mature Puccini, however, would have been less likely to take his tenor up to G

Ex. 1

and A in the first few bars: he would have saved the high notes for the climax. Already noticeable in the recitative leading to the duet is Puccini's development of Verdian arioso. He had learned from *Aida*, and no doubt from Verdi's other 'third period' operas, how to give melodic and harmonic interest to passages of recitative, to such an extent that, even in this, his first opera, there are very few bars in the music linking the separate musical numbers which reach the ear simply as 'recitativo accompagnato'. If this is not Wagnerian endless melody, it is at least arioso, and as full of musical interest as an egg is of meat.

A distant bell tolls four notes at the end of the duet and again after a few bars of stealthy *allegro*, after which the music becomes more open and extrovert as the chorus of villagers reassembles to see Roberto off on his journey. Roberto asks Guglielmo for a blessing, and Guglielmo begins the Act I finale with his prayer, 'Angiol di Dio, che i vanni rivolgi al ciel stasera' (Angel of God, who spreads wings to heaven this evening). Anna, Roberto and the chorus join him, and what begins as middle-period Verdian cantilena turns into middle-period Wagnerian ensemble, with a liberal use of the melody from the prelude as well as specific echoes of *Lohengrin*. At the conclusion of the prayer, farewells are said swiftly, and if the soprano has a high C, she will use it to cut through the chorus on her final Addio instead of the C an octave lower which, though offered as an alternative, would not make itself heard. Echoes of Wagner, as well as of Roberto's C major tune from the love duet, are heard again in the 16 bars of orchestral tumult, the brass much in evidence, which accompany the final tableau and the fall of the curtain. The effect again is of a speeded-up *Parsifal*.

Whether the eight lines of verse printed in Puccini's score at the beginning of Act II should be declaimed from the stage by a speaker, or simply printed in the programme, is perhaps not the weightiest of questions, but is nevertheless one which has to be considered when the opera is being staged. The appearance of a dinner-jacketed actor would surely be inappropriate, but a director might decide to dress him as one of the villagers, or perhaps have this and the subsequent piece of verse delivered by Anna's father, Guglielmo, the only one of the principals to survive at the end. An anonymous voice amplified to the audience might provide the most satisfactory solution.

The orchestral movement which begins Act II is given in the score the title, 'L'Abbandono' (The Desertion). The orchestra begins quietly, joined by distant female voices singing a 'Requiescat' for Anna, then surges to a more passionate section, nervous triplets giving an urgent pulse to the grief it expresses. When the curtain rises, Anna's funeral procession is glimpsed obscurely through the veiled mists of night, and the music becomes calmer, the voices repeating their prayer, 'O pura virgo, requiesce in pace' (O pure virgin, rest in peace). That Mascagni, who played in the orchestra at the première of *Le villi*, remembered this orchestral intermezzo when he came to write his *Cavalleria rusticana* five years later can hardly be doubted, for the celebrated Intermezzo from *Cavalleria* is strongly reminiscent of Puccini's 'L'Abbandono'. (Puccini, a good ten years after the première of *Le villi*, claimed bitterly in a letter to a friend that '*Le villi* initiated the type [of opera] that is today called "Mascagnian", and no one gives me credit for it.')

The curtain is lowered and, after the second poem, is raised again as the orchestra begins another intermezzo, 'La Tregenda' (The Witches' Sabbath), with an explosive chord in G minor. The scene is now a winter night, and the willis dance to the accompaniment of Puccini's very lively and harmonically inventive tarantella which, however, can hardly be said to sound particularly menacing. The menace has to be provided by the choreographer.

Mosco Carner, in his masterly critical biography of the composer, describes Guglielmo's recitative and aria, 'Anima santa della figlia mia' (Blessed soul of my daughter), as being in close proximity to Verdi's dramatic style. To the present writer's ears, the aria sounds Germanic, though one cannot help being reminded (by the dramatic situation) of the father–daughter relationship which ran through Verdi's *œuvre*. Verdian, too, is the emphasis on the upper notes of the baritone's range: the climactic phrases of both recitative and aria take the singer to his high G, though in both instances he is also offered lower alternatives.

Considerably more imaginative and original is the following number, an extended *scena* for the tenor, Roberto, which Carner suggests is 'possibly the longest solo scene in all Italian opera'. It is hardly that, for it takes less than ten minutes to perform, whereas *Lucia di Lammermoor*'s Mad Scene, to select only the first solo *scena* to come to mind, takes rather longer. However, it is certainly the longest such scene in Puccini, who in his later years did not go in for this kind of number, frequently found in the older Italian operas. If any of the characters in *Le villi* comes alive, it is Roberto in this *scena*, which, though not typical of the mature Puccini, is certainly worthy of him. It is preceded by an agitated orchestral passage and the off-stage voices of the willis warning Anna of Roberto's arrival, as he appears on the bridge. Roberto's distraught recitative ranges over a wide spectrum of moods, as does the orchestral comment. His aria in B flat minor, 'Torna ai felici dì dolente il mio pensier' (My sorrowful thoughts return to those happy days), may be modelled on an aria from Catalani's opera of the previous year, *Dejanice*, but it is nevertheless distinctly Puccinian in temperament, and in its tendency to luxuriate in masochistic self-torment – a characteristic of Puccini's tenors which is shared, we shall find, by Rodolfo, Cavaradossi, Lieutenant Pinkerton and Dick Johnson in later operas.

After the aria, an orchestral postlude of ten bars leads to further recitative and to Roberto's *andante religioso* prayer, 'O sommo Iddio'. (O great God), whose sweeping phrases, which have already been heard in the prelude to the opera and in the choral finale to Act I, almost constitute a leitmotif or motto for the opera. His prayer interrupted by the sound of the willis' voices, Roberto breaks into anguished recitative again, cursing the temptress of Mainz. Puccini's masterly use of the orchestra for expressive purposes is revealed in the final ten bars of postlude in which Roberto's wild despair has turned into numbed resignation.

The composer's inspiration, which has been intermittent throughout *Le villi*, deserts him in the opera's finale. When Anna appears as a willi, she addresses Roberto reproachfully in music from their love duet in Act I, after which they combine in an unmemorable duet before the willis begin their fatal dance, to music which we have heard in the 'Witches' Sabbath' interlude. This time, they sing as well as dance, and there is a certain dramatic irony in their use of the words 'Gira! Balza!' (Whirl, dance) which were used joyously in the peasants' dance at the beginning of the opera, but are now addressed to Roberto as a baleful imperative. This episode is a somewhat mild adumbration of the torture scenes which feature in the later operas, *Tosca* and *Turandot*. With the willis' triumphant 'Hosanna', as Roberto falls dead, the opera comes to an abrupt end.

Though there is no likelihood of *Le villi* joining the mature Puccini operas in the international repertoire, it is well worth occasionally reviving, perhaps under festival conditions but also in student performance, for it is an entertaining and enjoyable work and, lasting for no more than an hour or so (Act I slightly less than a half-hour and Act II slightly more), is in no danger of boring its audiences.

Throughout his career, Puccini habitually continued to alter and revise his scores, so that editions, especially of the vocal scores, tend to differ from one another, sometimes significantly and sometimes not. (Unless expressly stated to the contrary, it is Puccini's final versions, as performed today, that are discussed in these pages.) The original one-act version of *Le villi* remained unpublished, and there are minor differences among the four vocal scores issued, in 1885 (twice), 1888 and 1892. After the last date, Puccini abandoned *Le villi* to its fate. No full orchestral score has ever been published.

II

Edgar

an opera in three acts

Dramatis personæ:

Edgar	(tenor)
Gualtiero	(bass)
Frank, his son	(baritone)
Fidelia, his daughter	(soprano)
Tigrana	(mezzo-soprano)

LIBRETTO by Ferdinando Fontana, based on Alfred de Musset's play, *La Coupe et les lèvres*

TIME: 1302
PLACE: Flanders

FIRST PERFORMED at La Scala, Milan, 21 April, 1889, with Gregorio Gabrielesco (Edgar), Aurelia Cataneo (Fidelia), Romilda Pantaleoni (Tigrana), Antonio Magini-Coletti (Frank) and Pio Marini (Gualtiero), conducted by Franco Faccio

Edgar

I

PUCCINI AND ELVIRA Gemignani, his pupil in Lucca, had probably become lovers before the death of the composer's mother. Now they decided to live together openly, and Elvira left her husband and joined Puccini in Milan, taking with her the elder of her two children, a girl named Fosca. This caused much excitement in Lucca, where Puccini's behaviour was denounced by almost everyone, including his own relatives, as having brought shame upon the respected and honourable name of the Puccini family.

They were a handsome young couple (though something in the severity of Elvira's features might have warned Giacomo of the unhappy, suspicious, self-destructive woman she would later become) and in their first years together they were happy. Puccini was still busy with the composition of his second opera, *Edgar*, when, in 1886, two years after they began living together in Milan, a son, Antonio, was born to them.

Puccini was never to be a prolific composer, but few of his later works were created with such difficulty as *Edgar*, which took him more than three years to complete. To a large extent, the difficulty was caused by the libretto which Fontana had foisted upon him. Based upon *La Coupe et les lèvres*, a play in verse by Alfred de Musset, Fontana's libretto, originally in four acts, was even more inept than the one he had produced for *Le villi*. But the composer appears not to have complained; he merely toiled away at the music, slowly but stolidly.

During this time, Puccini lived on his royalties from *Le villi* and also on a small monthly income provided by Ricordi. His publisher had agreed to advance this monthly sum for one year, but at the end of the year Puccini had to ask for an extension, which Ricordi granted. 'A work of such importance and of such difficulty', Puccini had called the opera in a letter to Ricordi. Clearly it was difficult, and important in the sense that it was being composed for performance at La Scala; but can Puccini really have thought it a worthwhile venture? Either his critical faculties were not fully developed, or he was blinded by his loyalty and gratitude to Fontana who had, after all, been largely instrumental in getting their first opera on to the stage.

When his brother Michele, after an unsuccessful attempt to set up as a music teacher, emigrated to South America, Puccini was forced to send him money occasionally, which he could ill afford to do. The more he realized how important it was that he should finish *Edgar* quickly, the less easily did the music flow. It is usually said that Fontana refused to make any changes in the libretto, but this apparently was not the case. When the composer asked for certain changes before proceeding with Act II, Fontana provided them. Meanwhile Puccini and Elvira had moved back to Lucca from Milan, but they left Lucca again when her pregnancy became noticeable. He worked on the orchestration of *Edgar* in San Antonio d'Adda, a small town not far from Bergamo, and finally completed the opera in September 1887 at Ghislanzoni's establishment at Caprino Bergamasco.

The première of *Edgar* was scheduled to take place at La Scala on Easter Sunday, 21 April, 1889. Puccini had hoped that Francesco Tamagno, who in 1887 had been Verdi's first Otello, would sing the title role, and at as late a date as two months before the première, he was still attempting to secure the famous tenor: '. . . to live in hope is already something, at least it's better than a certainty that is lousy. There comes in the life of every man a decisive moment, and that is for me the good success of *Edgar*. I cling to him who can save me, as one who has suffered shipwreck clings to the last plank. And that plank is you! . . .'[1]

It does not sound as though the composer was at all confident of the worth of what he had composed. In any event, the last plank floated off to lucrative engagements in America, and Puccini had to rest content with a Romanian tenor, Gregorio Gabrielesco.[2] The two female roles were sung by the sopranos Aurelia Cataneo and Romilda Pantaleoni (Verdi's Desdemona in 1887), though Pantaleoni's role of Tigrana was officially designated as mezzo-soprano. The conductor was Franco Faccio, who had steered Verdi's *Otello* to success in 1887, but who found himself unable to do the same for Puccini's *Edgar*. The opera was politely received on its first night, but only two further performances were given.

Critical opinion of *Edgar* was in general unfavourable. By far the kindest review was that contributed by 'Gramola' to the *Corriere della sera*:

> . . . The curtain rises after a few bars and the chorus sings a rustic song in unison, somewhat in the style of Gounod, which in my opinion is destined to please the public in the future more than it seemed to please them last night. Follows the first song of Fidelia, of which it can be said that it is Italian in its melodic content and *alla* Bizet in its instrumental content . . . The beginning of the scene between Tigrana and the chorus produced in the public a sense of

[1] Quoted in Carner, op. cit.
[2] Some earlier commentators list Giovanni Battista de Negri as the creator of the role. This is an error. De Negri was to have sung in a revival of *Edgar*, but the performances were cancelled.

fatigue, relieved at once by the brilliant close of the same scene with trombone effects which are perhaps a little overwritten but which suffice to let us recognize in Puccini a vigorous artistic temperament . . . The first act ended coldly . . . During the second act Puccini was called three times, but the success of the music as a whole was much inferior to that of the first act . . .

Having invested a considerable amount of time and money in the young composer who now, at thirty-one, was not so young and whose career hung in the balance, Ricordi issued a statement immediately after the première in which he admitted that the critics had been so severe that, 'if the artist in Puccini were made of less stern stuff, he would look for another occupation.' In his view, however, Puccini should not feel discouraged, for 'such passionate and heated discussions, such long and numerous articles, more destructive than encouraging, are not written for mediocre compositions'.

Six days after the première, Ricordi called a meeting with Puccini and Fontana, to discuss what might be done with *Edgar*. The following morning, Ricordi wrote to Puccini:

The long discussion of last night has troubled me much. Because of it I was unable to pass a tranquil night . . . Concerning the modifications which were proposed, except those which are absolutely necessary and which you yourself could make, you have let yourself be carried away by your natural and exuberant musical instinct . . . I doubt that these modifications can be made in time so that *Edgar* might again be given in May on two or three evenings . . . I am wondering how all the changes can be made in so short a time, how the score can be corrected, the parts, the choruses etc. etc. What is the impresario going to say, who will ask himself all these questions? If the opera will not be ready, then trouble . . . protests! – and then it will not be given again.

It is a question here for rapid and feverish labour. I understand that that could cost you a great deal . . . But in God's name, one is not Puccini for nothing. One is not in the flower of life if one fears these problems and problems even more grave . . .

Remember, Puccini, that you are in one of the critical and difficult moments of your artistic life. I say this not because of the idiocies given forth by our famous music critics, but because now we must open a breach, scale it with courage and perseverance, and there plant a victorious flag. I, who am neither a writer nor an artist nor an opera composer,[1] yet sense the worth of this *Edgar*. I read in it clearly all your gifts, all the hopes for the future. But to realize these hopes it is necessary to follow one motto: *Excelsior!*

That interminable discussion of almost five hours! Yesterday it made me fear. Your good Fontana has shown himself to be an eloquent orator but a cavilling one. More of a philosopher-lawyer than a poet: the subtleties of his

[1] Giulio Ricordi was, however, an artist as well as a businessman. Under the pseudonym of J. Burgmein he composed a number of songs and salon pieces for piano, some orchestral music, and an opera which was produced in Turin in 1910.

reasoning are admirable but they do not convince, they do not persuade. He holds to the same ideas as before . . . Yet, after all, it is the imagination and the personality of the musician which are everything. It is the musician who colours the work, who presents it to the public. Without him it is a zero. Please understand, dear Puccini, that I am not in agreement with the systematic belittlers of the libretto of *Edgar*. There are two effective acts: that is something. But it also contains much obscurity, many fallacies which derive from the theories of Fontana, who assumes that everybody thinks with *his* head. What impressed me all the more during the long discourses yesterday is that he will never benefit, not now, not later, from the experience of these days. Let us admit all the exaggerations, all the malice that the cruel critics have expended on the libretto: none the less there is some truth in what they say, and we must reckon with it.

The conclusion of my long letter is this: that before you lay your hands on *Edgar* in order to retouch it, it is necessary that I talk to you alone. It is also necessary that, apart from the artistic part of the work, the material part be stabilized if we are not to make a hole in the water and find ourselves at the opportune moment with empty hands!! . . . It is necessary that we decide *absolutely* if the opera can or cannot be given again, within a few days.[1]

Giulio Ricordi's business associates wanted him to drop the young composer; but Ricordi fought for his protégé, even to the extent of uttering the threat that 'if they wish to close the door to Giacomo Puccini, I myself will exit with him by the same door'. He continued and increased Puccini's monthly stipend, undertaking to repay the money to the firm out of his own pocket should Puccini prove a less than sound investment.

What Ricordi now wanted was for Puccini to abandon *Edgar* and search for a new subject for his next opera. Though he took steps to do this, the composer was at first reluctant to concede that *Edgar* was beyond recovery, and made a great many changes to his score in readiness for further performances at La Scala in the spring of 1890, a year after the non-success of the opera's première. However, the illness of Giovanni Battista de Negri, the tenor engaged to sing the title role, led to the cancellation of these performances.

Meanwhile, Puccini's domestic circumstances were causing him difficulty. It had not proved possible for him to live openly with Elvira in their home town, Lucca, so Elvira and her daughter were living with her married sister in Florence, while Puccini and their son Antonio stayed in Lucca with one of the composer's sisters. Fortunately, Puccini now discovered the small village of Torre del Lago on Lake Massaciuccoli, less than fifteen miles from Lucca, near the resort town of Viareggio. He rented a house there, by the shore of the lake, and he and Elvira moved in with both children.

In the autumn of 1891, *Edgar* was given thirteen enthusiastically

[1] Quoted in George R. Marek, *Puccini* (New York, 1951).

acclaimed performances at the attractive little opera house in Lucca, the Teatro Giglio.[1] These were the last performances of *Edgar* as a four-act opera, for Puccini now set to work at Torre del Lago to make further revisions, in the course of which he reduced the number of acts to three, shortening the first two acts and jettisoning most of the original Act IV, but grafting its final scene – the murder of Fidelia by Tigrana – on to the end of Act III. Years later, he was to use a passage from the suppressed Act IV in Act III of *Tosca*: not for Cavaradossi's 'O dolci mani', as one sometimes reads, but for the accompaniment at the beginning of the Tosca–Cavaradossi duet, 'Amaro sol per te'.

The three-act *Edgar* was first performed in Ferrara on 28 February, 1892, with Puccini in charge of the staging.[2] When the opera's first production abroad, at the Teatro Reál in Madrid, was put in jeopardy due to the defection of the tenor engaged,[3] Puccini again threw himself on the mercy of the celebrated Tamagno. Knowing that he was about to depart for Madrid to appear in another opera, Puccini wrote to Tamagno:

> . . . I take my courage in both hands and make bold to address to you a request – to ask you a very great favour which, if granted, will be of immense advantage to my career . . . *Edgar* should have been given at the Teatro Reál last year, but time and circumstances to do with the repertoire prevented this. At the time I had been given the formal promise by the management . . . that this work of mine would be produced during the current season; rehearsals were already at an advanced stage – we were in fact near the date of the première – when I was notified that Durot had dissolved his contract and so my poor *Edgar* was left without a protagonist and without hope of a performance! Tetrazzini and Pasqua were to have been the other principal interpreters. This was for me a most ruinous disaster, as I had counted on the production of *Edgar* to give me an uplift which I need most direly, morally as well as materially. Hence my request, which I make bold to address to you, to sing the very important part of the protagonist. Courage and audacity is needed, what! But since I know you to be so kind-hearted, I took the liberty of putting this idea to you. Shall I be granted this request? I confess that I hope so. The opera has now been reduced to three acts. Two years ago you saw the music and studied it so that it will not be new to you and give you little trouble to learn it. If you accept, you can be sure of my immutable and unlimited gratitude. Among the many misfortunes that have befallen me, this would at least be my good luck! I'm writing to you just as my heart dictates it, jotting down the words as they leap into my head. I am so excited when I think that perhaps – who knows? – you will sing my stuff!

[1] Marek, op. cit., says the opera house is now called the Teatro Puccini. But when the present author attended a performance of *Tosca* there on 19 September, 1977, it was still the Teatro Giglio.

[2] Some earlier writers on Puccini, among them George Marek, op. cit., and Edward Greenfield in *Puccini: Keeper of the Seal* (London, 1958), have stated that the three-act revision was not made until 1905. This is incorrect.

[3] Durot, who had sung in the Lucca performances.

It took two further letters from Puccini as well as letters and telegrams from Ricordi to persuade Tamagno to sing the role of Edgar in Madrid. He did so, however, and the performances took place, the first of them on 19 March, 1892, in the presence of the composer. Learning that the Queen of Spain was to be present, Puccini composed for the Madrid performances a Prelude which was not used in any later productions of the opera, and has never been published. Even with Tamagno in the title role, Eva Tetrazzini (elder sister of Luisa who was to become the more famous of the two) as Fidelia and Giuseppina Pasqua (who was to be Verdi's Mistress Quickly the following year) as Tigrana, and conducted by the highly regarded Luigi Mancinelli, then Music Director of the Teatro Reál, the performances were not successful.

Puccini made further changes to the score of Edgar in 1901, and again in 1905 when the opera was performed in Buenos Aires in his presence, with Giovanni Zenatello as Edgar.[1]

Of the Buenos Aires production, Puccini wrote: 'Edgar last night only so-so. First act a good success, the second nothing or little, the third a discreet success. It is warmed-up soup. I have always said so. What is wanted is a subject which palpitates with life and is believable – not trash.' In London in the autumn of 1905, Puccini met Sybil Seligman, who became a close friend and was to be his correspondent and confidante for the rest of his life. On a copy of the vocal score of Edgar which he gave her, the composer made a number of annotations, described by her son Vincent Seligman:[2]

> The title itself has been defaced by additions into: 'E Dio ti Gu A Rdi da quest' opera!' (And may God preserve you from this opera!).
> Of the end of the second act he declares: 'This "finale" is the most horrible thing that has ever been written.' In the third act . . . when . . . Edgar dramatically lowers his cowl and cries: 'Yes, for Edgar lives!' Puccini's laconic annotation, 'Mensogna!' ('It's a lie!') shows that he failed to share his hero's belief in his immortality. Only two passages in the whole opera are marked 'this is good': Fidelia's 'Addio mio dolce amor' and her lament beginning 'Nel villagio d'Edgar'; and as the drama moves forward to its unnecessarily bloody climax and the crowd are reduced to repeated and rather naïve exclamations of the word 'Horror!' Puccini is content to add: 'How right they are!'

Thereafter, the composer abandoned the work, and so, by and large, did the world's opera houses. The current Ricordi vocal score (a full score has never been published) is of the opera as performed in 1905. Edgar was staged in Malta in 1920, and Toscanini conducted the Act III Requiem at Puccini's funeral in Milan Cathedral in 1924, after which the

---

[1] But not conducted by Toscanini, as the unreliable Marek, op. cit., states. The conductor was Leopoldo Mugnone.

[2] In Puccini Among Friends (London, 1938).

next complete performance of the opera seems to have been at La Scala in 1944. The British première was in a semi-professional production at Hammersmith, London, in 1967.

II

The opera is in three acts, and the action takes place in Flanders in the year 1302.

Act I is set in the main square of a Flemish village. On one side of the square is Edgar's house. Facing each other across the square are a church and an inn. It is dawn on a morning in April, and the music of the angelus is heard from the church bells while, in the distance, peasants and shepherds can be heard singing. Edgar is seated, asleep, in front of the inn. Fidelia appears and awakens Edgar who appears to be somewhat morose. Fidelia, who is in love with him, breaks off a twig from the almond tree growing in the square, and gives it to him. She runs off as she hears the approach of the shepherds. Edgar attempts to follow her, but is accosted by Tigrana who enters carrying a dembal, a type of lute. Tigrana comments sneeringly on the tender scene she has interrupted, for she too is in love with Edgar.

Edgar brusquely dismisses Tigrana, and tries to silence her when she reminds him that there was once a time when he preferred her embraces to those of the innocent Fidelia. Edgar, in a state of agitation, rushes into his house, and Fidelia's brother Frank appears. He is in love with Tigrana, who was abandoned in the village some fifteen years ago by a band of Moors, and brought up with Frank and Fidelia by their father, Gualtiero.

Turning her back contemptuously upon Frank, Tigrana enters the inn, while Frank soliloquizes upon the hopeless and humiliating love he feels for her. As he leaves, a group of peasants arrive, and approach the church which has been filling up during the preceding scene. Finding no room in the church, the peasants kneel outside to pray. As the congregation both within the church and outside begins to sing, Tigrana emerges from the inn, sits on a table with an insolent and provocative air, and starts up a song of her own, accompanying herself on the dembal. The peasants order her to stop, but she refuses and taunts them with her profane song while they shout sanctimonious abuse at her, calling her such names as 'serpent' and 'vile courtesan'. When they threaten her physically, Tigrana retreats towards Edgar's house.

Edgar appears and sides with her against the villagers. 'Indietro, turba idiota!' (Get back, you mob of idiots), he exclaims, and somewhat extravagantly announces he is leaving the village for ever. He curses his paternal roof, which he says he is about to destroy by fire, and retreats into his house from which a few moments later smoke and flames are seen to emerge. When a few villagers attempt to enter the house to put out the fire, Edgar appears in the doorway with a firebrand in his hand and pushes them away. Turning to Tigrana, he invites her to leave with him and enter upon a new life of voluptuous joy ('Noi pure accenda / Di nuova vita la voluttà!').

Frank now appears and tries to stop Edgar from taking Tigrana with him. Despite the attempts of Frank's father Gualtiero and his sister Fidelia to separate them, the two men fight, urged on by Tigrana, and Frank is wounded. The house continues to burn as Edgar and Tigrana leave, cursed by Frank and the villagers.

The setting of Act II is described thus in the opera's vocal score: 'A terrace, with gardens on the right, and a road at the rear. On the left a few steps lead to the splendidly illuminated hall of a sumptuous palace from which can be heard the dying echoes of an orgy. In the background, a vast landscape is crossed by streams made silvery by the light of the moon.' This is presumably somewhere in Flanders, but distant from Edgar's village.

As a chorus within the palace sings of its devotion to a life of pleasure, Edgar comes out on to the terrace 'con aria stanca e tediata' (looking weary and bored). He sings of his disillusionment with the delights of the flesh, and longs to be back in his native village with Fidelia whose innocent love he regrets having tossed aside so lightly. When Tigrana joins him on the terrace and attempts to rouse him from his gloomy thoughts, Edgar repulses her with a distinctly unaffectionate phrase: 'Taci, demonio, taci!' (Quiet, demon, quiet!). His revulsion from sensual pleasure has, it seems, concentrated itself upon the chief proponent of that way of life.

Sounds of drums and trumpets are heard in the distance, heralding the approach of a platoon of soldiers. When they appear, Edgar greets them warmly, offers them hospitality and asks to see their captain who turns out to be, of all people, Frank. He and Edgar do not take long to resume their former friendship, for, as Frank puts it, 'Your sword cured me of an abject, unworthy love' ('D'un amore abbietto, indegno, / Il tuo ferro mi guari!'). Edgar reveals that he wishes to redeem himself by joining Frank's band of soldiers, and both men turn on Tigrana, reviling her when she attempts to dissuade Frank from this course of action. As Edgar and Frank leave with the soldiers, Tigrana makes a menacing gesture of revenge.

The opening of Act III is described thus in the vocal score:

The bastion of a fortress, behind which in the distance can be seen the city of Courtray [or Courtrai, modern Kortrijk, in Belgium]. To the right, a large tower; to the left, under a canopy of black drapes attached to posts, is a catafalque near a church. The sun is setting, and the flaming sky is furrowed with dark strips of clouds. The distant sound of trumpets announces the approach of a funeral procession. An officer positions sentries near the catafalque, at the corners of which four pages set up candelabra and light the large tapers.

A chorus of boys' voices is heard in the distance chanting a Requiem, and then

the funeral procession begins to file past, led by a squadron of soldiers with a draped flag. Several soldiers follow, carrying on their shoulders a litter on which lies a dead knight, fully clothed in armour. On both litter and corpse are flowers and laurel branches. A monk and Frank follow the litter, the monk's hood pulled closely around his head, while Frank's visor is half open. Behind the monk and Frank are several friars. Following them, among the crowd of people, are Fidelia and Gualtiero. The litter is placed on the catafalque.

We are to understand that the great hero who has died in battle is Edgar, for Fidelia grieves for him: 'Non basta il pianto / Al mio dolor, / O Edgar, Edgar, Edgar, / Mio solo amor!' (My tears are not sufficient to express my grief. O Edgar, Edgar, Edgar, my only love!). The people crowd round the catafalque, while twelve friars bless the assembly and the corpse, and Frank mounts some steps to stand near the catafalque and deliver the required eulogy. As he begins, the hooded monk walks among the people reminding them that the dead hero had, after all, set his paternal home on fire and taken to a life of debauchery. Frank attempts to ignore him and to continue with words more conventionally suited to the occasion, but the monk persists, and the crowd forces Frank to allow him his say. As Edgar was dying, asserts the monk, he asked that his sins be revealed publicly, as a penance for him and an example to others. The monk singles out some onlookers from Edgar's village, and they confirm that he had set fire to his house, wounded Frank, and fled with the courtesan Tigrana.

Encouraged in his recital of crimes, the monk accuses Edgar of having murdered a number of travellers in the forest near the castle where he lived his impious life with Tigrana. The crowd now approaches the catafalque menacingly, but Fidelia steps forward to defend both the dead body and the memory of the living man. Although he made one or two small mistakes, his heart was pure, she asserts. The assembled soldiers and citizens are moved by her words. Frank dismisses the soldiers, while Fidelia approaches the bier and strews flowers and laurel leaves over the body. The monk kneels, ostensibly in prayer, close to the catafalque on one side, and Frank keeps guard on the other side.

As Gualtiero leads Fidelia away from the bier, the monk and Frank approach each other and are seen to be speaking. Tigrana now enters and kneels in prayer by the catafalque, while the monk and Frank tell each other that her show of piety is a lie, her tears hypocritical. They approach her, and bribe her with jewels to speak out against Edgar.

Tigrana tries to hold out against temptation, but eventually she weakens and agrees to speak. The soldiers and people are reassembled to hear the monk repeat his accusations against Edgar which are now supported by Tigrana who, after an initial display of reluctance, agrees that Edgar was planning to betray his country for gold. The soldiers now storm the catafalque to lay hands on the corpse, but are disconcerted to find only an empty suit of armour. 'Vuota è l'armatura!' (The armour is empty) they cry, as the monk throws off his priestly garb, revealing himself as Edgar, and exclaiming 'Si, poichè vive Edgar' (Yes, because Edgar is alive). Edgar now turns on Tigrana, denouncing her as leprous filth, and embraces Fidelia, announcing that he has been reborn. Tigrana stabs Fidelia who falls dead on the spot, and Edgar throws himself in tears on the body of Fidelia as Tigrana is led off, presumably to immediate execution, by the soldiers.

As with other plays by the French poet, novelist and dramatist, Alfred de Musset (1810–1857) the title of his verse play La Coupe et les lèvres (The Cup and the Lips) refers to a well-known proverb.[1] Described by its author as a 'poème dramatique', the play on which Fontana based his Edgar libretto was intended for the study rather than the stage. Musset was only twenty-two when he wrote La Coupe et les lèvres, in July and August, 1832, and had not then had his celebrated but short-lived affair with the novelist George Sand. He was to find his métier in delicate, lightly romantic comedies with a touch of irony, rather than in the sub-Byronic melodrama of such dramatic poems as La Coupe et les lèvres which was frostily received by his literary friends when he read it to them in December, 1832.

Underneath its melodramatic trappings, Musset's play is concerned with the spiritual quest of its Byronic, quasi-autobiographical hero, Frank, who leaves his village in the Tyrol to embark upon a life of adventure, lured on by a wild temptress, Monna Belcolore. Eventually, sadder, wiser and full of self-disgust, Frank returns to the Tyrol and to his pure, innocent first love, Déidamia. They are about to be married when – there's many a slip 'twixt cup and lip – Déidamia is stabbed to death by the jealous Monna. The plot, such as it is, exhibits parallels with Carmen, which would have appealed to Puccini, while the characterization of Frank is not dissimilar to that of many another Byronic and Schillerian hero. Conrad in The Corsair and Karl Moor in Die Räuber, both of whom were turned into Verdi tenors, come to mind. Byron's Conrad and Schiller's Karl Moor were both given to making long speeches justifying their crimes on the grounds of their disillusionment

---

[1] The usual French form of the proverb given in English as 'There's many a slip 'twixt cup and lip' is 'Il y a loin de la coupe aux lèvres'; the text which Musset placed at the beginning of his play was 'Entre la coupe et les lèvres, il reste encore de la place pour un malheur.'

with traditional moral values. Frank, at the beginning of *La Coupe et les lèvres*, gives voice to his malaise in these terms:

> Votre communauté me soulève la bile,
> Je n'en suis pas encore à mendier mon pain.
> Mordieu! voilà de l'or, messieurs, j'ai de quoi vivre.
> S'il plaît à l'ennemi des hommes de me suivre,
> Il peut s'attendre encore à faire du chemin.
> Il faut être bâtard pour coudre sa misère
> Aux misères d'autrui. Suis-je un esclave ou non?
> Le pacte social n'est pas de ma façon:
> Je ne l'ai pas signé dans le sein de ma mère.
> Si les autres ont peu, pourquoi n'aurais-je rien?
> Vous qui parlez de Dieu, vous blasphémez le mien.
> Tout nous vient de l'orgueil, même la patience.
> L'orgueil, c'est la vertu, l'honneur et le génie;
> C'est ce qui reste encore d'un peu beau dans la vie,
> La probité du pauvre et la grandeur des rois.
> Je voudrais bien savoir, nous tous tant que nous sommes,
> Et moi tout le premier, à quoi nous sommes bons?
> Voyez-vous ce ciel pâle, au-delà de ces monts?
> Là, du soir au matin, fument autour des hommes
> Ces vastes alambics qu'on nomme les cités.
> Intrigues, passions, périls et voluptés,
> Toute la vie est là, – tout en sort, tout y rentre.
> Tout se disperse ailleurs, et là tout se concentre.
> L'homme y presse ses jours pour en boire le vin,
> Comme le vigneron presse et tord son raisin.[1]

The chorus of hunters to whom Frank addresses these words replies very sensibly in a speech which begins bluntly: 'Frank, une ambition terrible te dévore' (Frank, a dreadful ambition is devouring you). But it is not until four acts later that Frank comes to realize the force of their argument. Puccini's dreadful librettist fastened on the least valuable aspect of the play, the bare bones of its plot, which he then simplified

[1] Your society fills me with anger. I do not yet have to beg for my bread. My God! I have money, sirs, I can live. If the enemy of mankind wishes to dog my footsteps, he has some way to go yet before he reaches his goal. One has to be a mongrel to link one's misery with that of others. Am I a slave or not? The social contract is not to my taste: I did not sign it at my mother's breast. Just because others have little, why should I have nothing? You who speak of God blaspheme against my Deity. Everything comes to us from pride; even patience. Pride is virtue, honour, genius; it is all that is left in life with any beauty about it. The honesty of the poor and the grandeur of kings. I'd like to know what good lies in any of us. In myself, first of all. Do you see the pale sky over the mountains? Over there, from morning till night, vast stills known as cities fume and bubble around the men who live there. Intrigues, passions, perils, lust – all life is there. Everything comes out of it, and everything goes back in. Everything disperses while everything is concentrated. Man spends his days there, pressing his time to drink its wine, just as the wine grower presses and squeezes his grapes.

and subjected to meaningless and confusing alterations before spewing it forth again in limp Italian verse.

No one has thought to wonder why, in changing the locale from the Tyrol, Fontana chose Flanders in the precise year 1302. The answer to the question (which I concede may not be worth asking) surely is that it was at Courtrai in Flanders in 1302 that what the history books call the Battle of the Spurs took place. Philip IV of France had antagonized the Count of Flanders by attempting to penetrate his territory, and the Count turned to Edward I of England for support. In 1300, the Flemish nobility betrayed him and he lost both Flanders and his own liberty. However, French rule soon alienated the Flemish burghers and led in 1302 to a massacre of the French and to the battle of Courtrai, in which the burghers defeated an army comprising the flower of the French nobility. In Puccini's *Edgar*, the hero of the opera redeems himself by fighting bravely at Courtrai: as we have seen the final act of the opera is set outside a fortress close to Courtrai (which is the modern town of Kortrijk, in the province of Western Flanders in the north-west of Belgium).

Fontana, again for no clearly discernible reason, altered the names of the characters. Musset's hero Frank[1] is now called Edgar, and the name of Frank is given to another character in the opera. The two women in the hero's life, Déidamia (familiarly called Mamette) and Monna Belcolore, now have new names indicative of their contrasting natures, Fidelia and Tigrana.

In fairness to Fontana, it must be admitted that his Italian verse, though execrable, is not noticeably worse than Musset's French. Here, for comparison, are the final moments of the play and the opera. First, the play:

FRANK: Ah! massacre et tison d'enfer! C'est Belcolor!
              Restez ici, Mamette, il faut que je lui parle.

                                       (*Il saute par la fenêtre.*)
DÉIDAMIA: Mon Dieu! que va-t-il faire, et qu'est-il arrivé?
               Le voilà qui revient. Eh bien! l'as-tu trouvé?
FRANK (*à la fenêtre, en dehors*):
               Non, mais par le tonnerre, il faudra qu'il y vienne.
               Je crois que c'est un spectre, et vous aviez raison.
               Attendez-moi. Je fais le tour de la maison.[2]

---

[1] Frank is his family name. His full name, as he informs Monna Belcolore, is Charles Frank.

[2] FRANK: Ah, massacre and torments of hell! It's Belcolor. Stay here, Mamette. I must speak to her. [*He jumps out of the window.*]
      DÉIDAMIA: My God, what will he do, and what has happened? Here he is coming back. So, have you found him?
     FRANK [*at the window outside*]: No, but by heaven, he must come here. I think it is a ghost and that you are right. Wait for me while I look around the house.

DÉIDAMIA (*courant à la fenêtre*):
>Charles, ne t'en va pas! S'il s'enfuit dans la plaine,
>Laisse-le s'envoler, ce spectre de malheur.
>>(*Belcolore parait de l'autre côté de la fenêtre et s'enfuit aussitôt.*)
>Au secours! au secours! on m'a frappée au coeur.
>>(*Déidamia tombe et sort en se trainant.*)

LES MONTAGNARDS (*accourant au dehors*):
>Frank! que se passe-t-il? On nous appelle, on crie.
>Qui donc es là par terre étendi dans son sang?
>Juste Dieu! c'est Mamette! Ah! son âme est partie.
>Un stylet italien est entré dans son flanc.
>Au meutre! Frank, au meutre!

FRANK (*rentrant dans la cabane, avec Déidamia morte dans ses bras*):
>>O toi, ma bien-aimée!
>Sur mon premier baiser ton âme s'est fermée.
>Pendant plus de quinze ans tu l'avais attendu,
>Mamette, et tu t'en vas sans me l'avoir rendu.[1]

The ending of the opera is essentially similar, though the detail differs:

EDGAR:
>O lebbra, sozzura del mondo,
>O fronte di bronzo,
>Di bronzo e di fango,
>Tortura e gingillo giocondo . . .
>Va, fuggi, o t'infrango!
>>(*Edgar fa per afferrare Tigrana che gli sfugge e si rifugia presso i soldati.*)

TIGRANA (*gridando ai soldati*):
>Oh . . . il vil! Mi difendete![2]

[1] DEIDAMIA [*running to the window*]: Charles, don't go! If it flies off into the plain, this evil spectre, let it fly.
[*Belcolore appears on the other side of the window, and immediately dashes off.*] Help! Help! I am struck to the heart. [*Déidamia falls to the ground, and drags herself away.*]
THE MOUNTAINEERS [*rushing in*]: Frank, what's going on? We heard calls, and people crying out for us. Who is that, spread out on the ground in her own blood? My God, it's Mamette! Ah, her soul has departed. An Italian stiletto has pierced her side. Let us find the murderer, Frank! Let us catch him!
FRANK [*coming back into the cabin, with the dead body of Déidamia in his arms*]: Oh you, my beloved! On receiving my first kiss, your soul expired. The kiss for which you have waited for more than fifteen years, Mamette, and you have passed away without giving it back to me.

[2] EDGAR O leper, filth of the world,
O brazen visage,
Brazen and vile,
Tortured and useless plaything . . .
Go, flee or I shall crush you!
[*Edgar tries to seize Tigrana who flees from him and seeks refuge among the soldiers.*]
TIGRANA [*calling to the soldiers*]:
Oh . . . the wretch! Defend me!

I SOLDATI (*scacciando Tigrana*):
Va! T'allontana, abietta cortigiana!
EDGAR (*ai soldati umiliati*):
Maledizione a voi!
Redento io son!
(*abbracciando Fidelia*)
Io ritorno alla vita!
O gloria, o voluttà,
Bieche illusion, addio per sempre,
Per sempre addio!
(*Edgar s'avvia avvinto a Fidelia, mentre la folla si ritrae. Tigrana, con moti felini, quasi strisciando, si avvicina inosservata e violentemente colpisce con un pugnale Fidelia, che cade fulminata. Edgar e Frank si slanciano su Tigrana, la quale cerca sfuggire perdendosi tra la folla, ma essa è afferrata da alcuni soldati, mentre tutti, inorriditi, gridano:*)
CORO, I SOLDATI:
Orror! Orror!
EDGAR: A morte!
CORO, I SOLDATI:
A morte! A morte! Orror!
(*Edgar si abbandona sul corpo di Fidelia, singhiozzando; Frank abbraccia e sorregge Gualtiero. Alcuni soldati trascinano via Tigrana, mentre alcune giovanette fanno cerchio pietoso intorno al corpo di Fidelia, ed i frati ed il popolo si inginocchiano pregando.*)[1]

[1] SOLDIERS [*repulsing Tigrana*]:
Go! Away with you, worthless courtesan!
EDGAR [*to the humiliated soldiers*]:
A curse upon you!
I am redeemed!
[*embracing Fidelia*]
I have returned to life!
O glory, o ecstasy!
Evil illusion, farewell forever,
Forever farewell!
[*Edgar starts to leave with Fidelia, and the crowd makes way for them. With feline movements, almost creeping, Tigrana approaches them, unseen, and with a dagger violently stabs Fidelia who falls suddenly. Edgar and Frank throw themselves on Tigrana who tries to escape by losing herself in the crowd, but who is seized by a few soldiers as everyone, horrified, cries:*]
CHORUS, SOLDIERS:
Horror! Horror!
EDGAR: Kill her!
CHORUS, SOLDIERS:
Kill her! Kill her! Horror!
[*Edgar throws himself on Fidelia's body, sobbing; Frank embraces and supports Gualtiero. Some of the soldiers leave with Tigrana while a few young girls form a grieving circle around Fidelia's body, and the monks and the people kneel in prayer.*]

III

All of Verdi's operas, from *Oberto* in 1840 to *Falstaff* in 1893, are written in numbers. That is to say, they consist of arias, duets, trios, quartets, larger ensembles and choruses, each of which can be distinguished from the surrounding music and considered separately. In his later works, Verdi continued to think in terms of these units, though he also increasingly bore in mind the shape of scenes and of entire acts. If *Otello* seems less of a 'number opera' than *Nabucco*, it is not because the 'numbers' are missing from *Otello*, for they are not: Iago's Creed, Otello's 'Ora e per sempre, addio', the Otello–Iago duet which ends Act II, Desdemona's Willow Song are as much 'numbers' as are Abigaille's aria and cabaletta in Act I of *Nabucco*, or Zaccaria's 'Tu sul labbro' or Nabucco's 'Dio di Giuda'. The difference is that the music needed to advance the opera from one number to the next has increased in stature and importance, that recitative has been given more melodic interest, and has become, in many cases, something half-way between recitative and aria, a kind of continuing arioso, out of which the numbers emerge and back into which they sink. The continuous melody of Wagner is not all that continuous, or not all that melodic, depending on how you listen to it. Act I of *Die Walküre* is about as far as one can get in the nineteenth century from the old recitative and aria structure. It is what Wagner thought of as continuous melody, yet it is comparatively easy to stick in one's thumb and pull out the plums of Sieglinde's 'Der Männer sippe' and 'Du bist der Lenz', and Siegmund's 'Winterstürme'.

This apparent diversion is a preamble to the statement that, although after *Le villi* Puccini's scores are not set out in separate numbers, his operas nevertheless continue in the traditional style whose development owes so much to Verdi. Puccini, too, moves further away from formal recitative towards endless melody. But some melodies are more endless than others, as the late Samuel Goldwyn might have said, and even in Puccini's final opera, *Turandot*, the utterances of Liù and Calaf are thought by most listeners to be distinguishable as separate arias at such moments as 'Signore, ascolta', 'Tu che di gel sei cinta' and 'Nessun dorma!'.

Edgar begins without orchestral overture or prelude, the Prelude which the composer provided for the Madrid performances having been discarded during the final revisions of 1905.[1] After an introductory 24 bars based on a terse little phrase which is repeated and persists in the accompaniment of the opening chorus, the church bell is heard and, in the distance, the chorus sung by the villagers, simple unison phrases until the final bars. Fidelia sings the first stanza of her aria off-stage: 'O fior

[1] It was a short piece of 108 bars, lasting about four minutes, describing the approach of dawn, with a bell effect produced by leaps of a fifth in the base which gave way to the notes of a real bell as the curtain rose on the scene of the village square, with the angelus being pealed by the church bells.

del giorno' is a charming pastoral melody which, heard now, cannot fail to bring to mind the later 'flower' music for Cio-Cio-San and Suzuki in *Madama Butterfly*. After her exchange with Edgar in recitative, Fidelia then sings a second aria, which really bears the relation of a cabaletta to 'O fior del giorno': it is fascinating to find, in early Puccini, this faint remaining trace of the old aria–transitional passage–cabaletta which Verdi had gradually disposed of, and which had all but disappeared by the time of *Aida*. 'Già il mandorlo vicino' is in the same tempo as 'O fior del giorno', a steady *andante*, though its rhythms flow less smoothly. Both arias possess that curiously feminine delicacy of feeling which makes Puccini's writing for the solo soprano voice often so much more persuasive and convincing than his tenor heroics.

At the end of her aria, Fidelia's 'Addio' and Edgar's 'Fermati' (Wait) as she runs off are heard over an ominous chord in the orchestra which momentarily warns that the course of their true love will not run smooth. The chromatic passage of excited anticipatory music which leads to the entry of the chorus does nothing to dispel this impression, though the chorus, no more than a repetition of the opening phrases of Fidelia's greeting to the dawn, is in itself innocuous. That the chorus at this point should sing, not a variant of its earlier music but a snatch of the aria which 'belongs to' Fidelia, is an early instance of Puccini's apparent lack of interest in the niceties of dramatic characterization in music. Whether it is dramatically appropriate for the chorus to echo Fidelia's music was not a question which would have occurred to him. It was a good tune when Fidelia sang it, so why should it not work equally well for the chorus? This, one imagines, is the way Puccini's musical mind worked.

In the opera as we now have it, what is left of Tigrana's role after Puccini's cuts, more extensive in her music than in that of the other characters, has a higher *tessitura* than when Puccini first conceived it for the four-act *Edgar*. Although still designated in the score as mezzo-soprano, the role is really more suitable for a dramatic soprano. Indeed the first singer of the role in its original version in 1889, the soprano Romilda Pantaleoni, not only created Desdemona in *Otello* for Verdi, in 1887, but in 1891 was the first Santuzza in Mascagni's *Cavalleria rusticana*. Tigrana's first appearance is heralded and accompanied by a portentous flurry in the orchestra, with *tremolando* strings and Tigrana's own 'motif' blared out by the brass; but, after the sound of the organ is heard from within the church, the song in which she reminds Edgar of the lustful feelings he once entertained towards her is oddly tame ('Tu voluttà di fuoco, ardenti baci sognavi un dì': There was a time when you dreamed of a fiery lust and ardent kisses). Even its punctuation by Edgar with cries of 'Taci, demonio, taci' fails to raise the dramatic or emotional temperature, for he sounds more weary than angry.

Tigrana's theme is thrust at us again during her recitative scene with

Frank, and at one point is actually sung by Frank as he reminds her that she was brought up by everyone in the village [Ex. 2]. Frank's *andante*

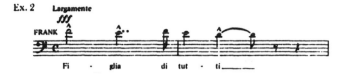

Ex. 2

aria, 'Questo amor, vergogna mia' (This love, which is shameful to me) lacks individuality but is effective in context, and even more effective is Tigrana's scene with the villagers: the pious chorus from within the church (for which Puccini used the beginning of the Kyrie from his Mass of 1880) followed by the spiky, livelier rhythms at the beginning of her song with the dembal. (Though described in the vocal score as a kind of lute, the dembal would appear really to be a gypsy tambourine.) Tigrana continues her mockery of the church congregation to a broad tune which does not sound at all mocking, and indeed will be heard at various times during the opera as a kind of theme expressing whatever the composer wants it to express at that particular moment. If Tigrana's sneers at religion are unconvincing, so too are the retaliatory cries of the religious, though the Verdian march-tune ('D'ogni sozzura simbolo') sung by the chorus is at least exhilarating.

The Act I finale really gets under way only with Edgar's return to the scene, and even then rarely rises to heights of distinction. The music which accompanies Edgar's re-entry into his house to set it on fire is not unlike the sound-track of a Universal or Columbia Pictures serial of the 1930s, which of course is where this kind of utility music was to end up. The big ensemble which then develops begins as an exercise in the manner of middle-period Verdi and ends sounding more like the *Gioconda* of Puccini's teacher, Ponchielli. The fight between Edgar and Frank takes place to more utility music, and the curtain falls on an emphatic orchestral restatement of the opening phrases of the ensemble.

At the beginning of Act II, the sinuous melody of an off-stage chorus, celebrating somewhat languidly the end of the night's orgies, is framed by brilliant orchestral flourishes, and followed by a change to darker, more introspective moods as the orchestra gives out, 'molto espressivo', the theme of the ensemble from the Act I finale, by way of prelude to Edgar's recitative, 'Orgia, chimera dall' occhio vitreo' (Orgy, you empty-eyed chimera) and aria, 'O soave vision' (Oh sweet vision). The recitative soon broadens into arioso of melodic interest: there is less recitative in *Edgar* than in *Le villi*, for although the score of *Edgar* is based on separate numbers they emerge more smoothly and from more interesting surroundings than was the case with *Le villi*. Edgar's aria, 'O soave vision', is by far the most attractive music he is given to sing in the entire opera, an ardent, lyrical melody, reminiscent perhaps of Massenet in its sentimentality and its feminine endings, but also looking forward to the self-pitying outbursts of such typical Puccini heroes as Cavaradossi and Pinkerton.

If the duet scene between Edgar and Tigrana sounds warmer, more passionate in tone, despite the tenor's usual cries of 'Taci, demonio, taci', this is probably because Puccini makes use of music from the first, four-act version of his opera, music which in that version was sung not by the evil Tigrana but by the innocent Fidelia. Again, one notes that the composer's notions of dramatic characterization through music were either primitive or non-existent. Whether dramatically apt or not, the music of what one might call this love-hate duet [Ex. 3] has a seductive

Ex. 3

quality which derives more clearly from French opera (Massenet, Saint-Saëns) than from Italian, despite the typically Italian direction in the score, 'con grande slancio' (with a great outburst), at the finale of the duet, and the brassy orchestral peroration.

The finale of Act II which Puccini informed Sybil Seligman was 'the most horrible thing that has ever been written', consists largely of exclamations from Edgar, Tigrana and Frank, above a jaunty march tune in the orchestra, though the martial accompaniment abates for Tigrana's final attempt to plead with Edgar and for his response which, although Puccini asks the tenor to sing it haughtily ('altero'), is set to a rather tender and sympathetic phrase of music. Edgar, Frank and the chorus of soldiers enthusiastically burst into the tune already given out by the orchestra at the conclusion of the Edgar–Tigrana duet and now used to express patriotic sentiments, and the orchestra repeats it as the curtain falls, Fidelia having taken the opportunity to add her voice in unison with Edgar's to express sentiments of a different kind.

The orchestral prelude to Act III is solemn, even melancholy, and Puccini's scoring is confident but not overemphatic until its final bars, when he was unable to resist the temptation to work up an inappropriately noisy climax. The Requiem music of the funeral procession with which the act begins reveals the young composer at his most impressive. Boys' voices are added to the chorus which chants the Requiem, an effective and affecting movement whose main theme derives from the orchestral *Capriccio Sinfonico* which Puccini had composed six years earlier. (Toscanini was right to consider the beginning of *Edgar*'s Act III worthy to be played at Puccini's funeral in 1924, when the soprano Hina Spani sang the music of Fidelia, mourning not the hero of the opera but its composer.) Fidelia twice adds her voice briefly in lament to the choral Requiem, and the music moves from being a prayer for the repose of Edgar's soul to a call for vengeance on his and his country's enemies who have been responsible for his death in battle; it reaches a stirring fortissimo climax of patriotic fervour at the words 'Iddio la Fiandra schiava non vuol' (God does not want an enslaved Flanders).

The orchestra recalls a phrase which preceded Fidelia's Act I aria, 'O fior del giorno', as she begins her moving aria of farewell to Edgar, 'Addio, addio, mio dolce amor' (Farewell, farewell, my sweet love). When the soprano soars to a high B flat, the chorus add their voices to her lament and bring the aria to a radiant conclusion, the chorus sopranos and tenors joining the solo soprano on the final B flat. The orchestral brass blazes and then gives way to the chanting of the priors, followed by a few uninspired pages of workaday music in which the action is advanced a stage further.

This nondescript music culminates in a singularly unconvincing chorus in which the crowd propose throwing to the crows the corpse which a few moments earlier they had venerated ('Ai corvi il suo cadavere': To the crows with his corpse). But Puccini recovers with Fidelia's recitative and aria, 'Nel villagio d'Edgar son nata anch'io' (In Edgar's village I too was born). The recitative contains some unexpected florid phrases, which seem to weave a delicate tracery of grief, and the mood is sustained in the aria, which is both lyrical and ardent, and touching in the manner of some of the heroine's utterances in *Madama Butterfly*. Even Puccini, when he came to reject most of *Edgar*, thought that 'O fior del giorno' and this second aria of Fidelia's in Act III were good. For the beginning of the aria, Puccini adapted a theme from an *Adagietto* for orchestra which he had composed during his student days in 1883. The orchestral prelude of the aria restates its theme and continues its mood, until the final bars when again Puccini inappropriately and inartistically unleashes his brass, *fortissimo*.

A brief trio, *allegro con fuoco*, for Tigrana, Edgar and Frank, brutally swift, almost in the manner of early Verdi, leads to an unexpectedly elegant and ironic little aria from Edgar, whose utterance is usually more straightforward in tone ('Bella signora, il pianto sciupa gli occhi': Beautiful lady, your weeping will ruin your eyes) [Ex. 4]. The irony,

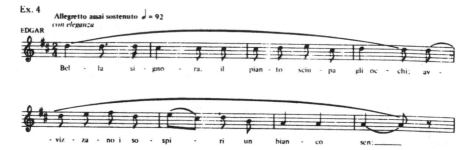

Ex. 4

worthy of the Verdi of *La forza del destino* or *Un ballo in maschera*, is in a vein which the mature Puccini was to develop in some of the music of Scarpia in *Tosca*, and of Ping, Pang and Pong in *Turandot*. The 'Bella signora' tune is heard again when Edgar, still disguised, and Frank combine in duet to bribe Tigrana, and when the orchestra momentarily takes it up.

The final pages of the opera contain little of musical interest, though it should not be beyond the bounds of possibility for a stage director to give some excitement, on a crude melodramatic level, to the scene in which the soldiers discover that the body is missing, and Edgar announces that he still lives! (In fact, he announces it three times.) Edgar's denunciation of Tigrana is as coarse musically as it is verbally: 'O lebbra, sozzura del mondo' (Oh leper, filth of the world), he begins, and when he has finished with her he sings a farewell to his illusions, rising to a final B natural. The death of Fidelia and the end of the opera follow within fifteen swift and undistinguished bars of music.

Neither of Puccini's first two operas can be counted a success, but views as to which is the better of the two have differed. *Le villi* was immature and eccentric. *Edgar* is closer to one's idea of the crude, conventional *verismo* opera, yet it contains pages which look forward to the mature Puccini alongside much that is completely without distinction. Many an opera has survived a poor libretto, but probably not when the composer has made little attempt to round out in music the flat and unconvincing characters of his librettist, and almost certainly not when the composer appears not even to have realized that there was any need to do so.

The operas of *verismo* were not necessarily realistic; indeed, they were as often as not sensational and melodramatic. The best of Puccini does not really belong to the genre, while the worst, by which one means *Le villi* and *Edgar*, rather curiously and not very confidently bridge a gap between the old romantic melodrama of earlier Italian opera and the new melodrama of the 'realistic' school. Puccini's principal failure in both works, and especially in *Edgar*, lay in his inability to show character in action. What can be said in his favour is that both operas were decently short. *Edgar* became shorter with each revision: its original, four-act version ran to 380 pages of vocal score, its second edition, in three acts, to 248 pages, and its final version to 202 pages. Act II is one of the shortest acts in any Puccini opera, taking no more than about eighteen minutes to perform. (Act II of *La Bohème* is even shorter.)

III

Manon Lescaut

an opera in four acts

Dramatis personæ:

Manon Lescaut	(soprano)
Lescaut, Sergeant of the King's Guard	(baritone)
Il Cavaliere Renato des Grieux, student	(tenor)
Geronte di Ravoir, Treasurer-General	(bass)
Edmondo, a student	(tenor)
Innkeeper	(bass)
A Dancing Master	(tenor)
A Musician	(mezzo-soprano)
A Lamplighter	(tenor)
A Naval Commander	(bass)
A Sergeant of Archers	(bass)
A Wigmaker	(mime)

LIBRETTO by Marco Praga, Domenico Oliva, Luigi Illica and Giuseppe Giacosa, based on *L'Histoire du Chevalier des Grieux et de Manon Lescaut* by Abbé Prévost

TIME: The second half of the eighteenth century

PLACE: Amiens, Paris, Le Havre, Louisiana

FIRST PERFORMED at the Teatro Regio, Turin, 1 February, 1893, with Cesira Ferrani (Manon), Giuseppe Cremonini (Des Grieux), Achille Moro (Lescaut), Alessandro Polonini (Geronte), conducted by Alessandro Pomé

Manon Lescaut

THE GENERAL RECEPTION accorded *Edgar* was hardly of a kind to encourage Puccini into thinking that his career was moving forward. He now had Elvira and two children to support, and an accumulation of debts to repay, and for a time he considered joining his brother Michele in South America. 'The theatres here are stingy,' he wrote to Michele, 'and because of the critics the public becomes more and more difficult. God help me! I am ready, absolutely ready to come, if you write. I shall come and we'll manage *somehow*. But I shall need money for the voyage, I warn you!'[1] His brother's reply dissuaded Puccini from emigrating, for Michele was struggling against poverty and illness in Argentina, and was hoping to save enough to return to Italy.

Puccini now turned his thoughts towards his next operatic project, various suggestions for subjects having been made to him. Giulio Ricordi commissioned from the playwright Giuseppe Giacosa a scenario on a Russian subject which Puccini rejected. 'I am tortured by doubt regarding Giacosa's libretto,' Puccini wrote to Ricordi.[2]

I fear that the subject is not suitable for me; I am afraid that I shall not succeed in writing the kind of music it should have. I wonder if you could find a way of suggesting to Giacosa, without hurting him, that he should leave it alone for the present? . . . We should look for, and certainly find, something more poetic, more pleasing, and less gloomy, and with a little more nobility of conception. That Russia of his frightens me and, to tell the truth, does not convince me!

Puccini also rejected a proposal that he write an opera based on one of Shakespeare's histories, for he had been reading an eighteenth-century French novel, *The Story of the Chevalier des Grieux and of Manon Lescaut* (popularly referred to as *Manon Lescaut*), by the Abbé Prévost, and had decided that this was the opera he wanted to compose. 'Manon', he told Ricordi, 'is a heroine I believe in and therefore she cannot fail to win the hearts of the public.' A *non sequitur*, one notes, and notes too that Puccini was no longer prepared to set whatever libretto was put in front of him and in whatever condition. The gestation period of the *Manon Lescaut*

---

[1] Letter of 30 April, 1889, quoted in Carner, op. cit.
[2] Letter of 19 July, 1889. Ibid.

libretto was long and difficult, as were those of most future Puccini operas.

Despite an assertion to the contrary by his first biographer, Fraccaroli,[1] there can be no doubt that Puccini was perfectly well aware of Massenet's opera, *Manon*, which had been given its successful première at the Opéra Comique in Paris five years earlier (in 1884, the year in which Puccini's first opera, *Le villi*, was produced). Though Massenet's opera was not produced in Italy until 1893, Puccini had at least examined a vocal score of it; to one of several people who had a hand in the libretto of his *Manon Lescaut* (titled thus to distinguish it from Massenet's *Manon*), he wrote that 'Massenet feels it as a Frenchman, with the powder and the minuets. I shall feel it as an Italian, with desperate passion.'[2]

Informing Ricordi that no 'idiotic librettist' could be allowed to ruin this opera and that he, the composer, would therefore write the libretto, Puccini set to work on the Abbé Prévost's *Manon*, but was obliged to accept his publisher's view that a professional librettist should be engaged. Initially the choice fell on Ruggiero Leoncavallo, who was only a few months older than Puccini; the composer of at least two operas which had yet to be performed, he was also a pupil of the poet Carducci and the author of his own libretti. (He had not yet composed *Pagliacci*, the opera with which he was to make his name.) Ricordi had been sufficiently impressed by Leoncavallo's libretto for his first opera, *Chatterton*, to commission him to adapt *Manon Lescaut*. Puccini, however, was dissatisfied with Leoncavallo's ideas regarding the treatment of the subject, and the young composer-librettist was therefore removed from the project.

At this point, Marco Praga, a well-known playwright with no experience as a librettist, joined the team. Praga many years later wrote an account of his involvement in the proceedings:

It was either the spring or the autumn – I do not now remember which – of 1890. One evening soon after the production of my play *La Moglie ideale*, I had dropped in, as usual, to Savini's for a game, when Puccini entered and asked to speak to me. We went out together and took a turn in the Galleria. Suddenly, without any warning, he said, 'You must write me a libretto.' I confess that although the unexpected proposal took my breath away, the friendship and admiration which I felt for Puccini made my resistance rather weak. I had never written a libretto; I had never even thought of writing one. 'That doesn't matter,' said Puccini, 'especially as you don't even need to be concerned about the choice of a subject: it is *Manon Lescaut*. You have a sure theatrical instinct; you know how to construct. If you refuse to write the poem' – for although I am the son of a poet, I had made it plain at the outset that I would not write the verses – 'you may choose your own collaborator.'

[1] In *La vita di Giacomo Puccini*, op. cit.
[2] Giuseppe Adami, *Puccini* (Milan, 1935).

'For that matter,' I replied, 'I can find the poet at once.' Indeed, Domenico Oliva, who had just then published a much-admired collection of poems and who was a very dear friend of mine, seemed to me to be best suited for the work, and I proposed him on the spot to Puccini, who agreed.[1] Before leaving us, he recommended me to read Prévost's novel again, leaving Massenet's libretto of *Manon* strictly alone, so that I might not be influenced in my conception, and to dash down my plot as quickly as possible, always keeping in mind his intention of composing an *opéra comique* in the classical sense of the term.

A few days later I had a second conversation with the composer and explained to him briefly how I should divide the acts: (1) The meeting of Des Grieux and Manon; (2) the wretched house of the two lovers, with the interested protection of Lescaut, his treacherous trick, his blustering immorality, his cynical counsels; (3) Manon amid the luxury which Geronte provides, the intervention of Des Grieux, the attempted theft, their flight, surprise, and arrest; and lastly (4) the desert and the death of Manon. Puccini was delighted. I wrote the plot. I submitted it to Puccini and Giulio Ricordi, who approved it. Domenico Oliva, to whom I had spoken at the beginning, and who had enthusiastically agreed to collaborate, lost no time in writing the verses, and the libretto was soon complete. In the summer I went with Puccini and Oliva to Cernobbio, where the Ricordi family was spending the summer, and we read the poem. Paolo Tosti was present at the reading. The success of it was complete. Tosti said that he had never read a more beautiful or more effective libretto. It was just the *opéra comique* of which Puccini had dreamed.

Back in Milan we concluded our agreement and Puccini departed with his, or rather with our, manuscript. Things could not have been better. But such a pleasant state of affairs was of short duration. A few months after, the composer was no longer satisfied with the plot or with the division of the acts. He could no longer feel that it was an *opéra comique*. He wished to eliminate the second act, substituting the third for it, and for the third finding a striking and dramatic situation. As a dramatist I did not approve of the change. Neither did I from my own point of view feel like changing the structure of the libretto. I declined the task, and handed over the whole matter to Domenico Oliva with complete liberty to change it as he thought fit. Oliva adopted Puccini's ideas and completely recast the work. The second act disappeared. The Havre act took shape, with the roll-call of the courtesans and their embarkation. But things went no more smoothly now than before. Every moment Puccini desired alterations and transformations. Oliva ended by wearying of the whole affair, and came to me to tell me that he could not go on with the work and that he too was now withdrawing his collaboration. It was then that Giacosa, acting for Ricordi, approached Luigi Illica,[2] who consented to take up and continue the work.

---

[1] Oliva, at the time drama critic of a Rome newspaper, was the author of a play, *Robespierre*.

[2] Luigi Illica (1857–1919) was already at work on the libretto of Catalani's *La Wally*. In addition to the operas of Puccini on which he was to collaborate, he was the sole librettist of Giordano's *Andrea Chénier* (1896).

From that moment I heard no more about the libretto of *Manon* and its vicissitudes.[1]

In the autumn of 1890, after six months had been spent on the libretto and with Oliva remaining as his collaborator, Puccini wrote to Ricordi with specific criticisms of Oliva's work:

> I have thought it advisable to send you Oliva's manuscript, that you may read it and get an exact idea of the defects and contortions which it contains. There are some good things in it, but the quartet, to take one example, is hideous. I do not understand why Oliva has departed here from the original scenario, which was so clear. The first scene, between Geronte and Lescaut, is good, as also is the second with Manon, except for some shortening necessary when Lescaut goes to fetch the old man, who is hiding. I think those asides are too long. Then if you look at the manuscript you will find some notes of mine, when Lescaut is talking with Des Grieux. The idea is perfectly clear: 'My dear fellow, there are so many ways of making money when one is intelligent: cards, beautiful women, more or less young, etc. etc.' Instead, as you will see from the libretto, all that is made vague, long, and tortuous. Then look at my notes. I do not like that disappearance of Renato and Lescaut to prepare a meal, because it makes Renato play an odious part. However does he come to the point of leaving Manon at the mercy of the old man? Do you remember how we fought with Leoncavallo to avoid that?
>
> And now for the quartet, although there are many other weak points. How charming, logical and interesting was the quartet in the first sketch! That *mythological* entry of Geronte, then Lescaut's *war in Poland* to distract Des Grieux! That storm between Geronte and Manon! Then it was better that they should sit down at the table as was decided. Where has it disappeared to, the little scene which fitted in so well, of the four drinking each other's health? In short, the whole scene of the quartet at table, which was rapid and full of interest, is replaced by another version of extraordinary length and rhetorical wordiness, to the detriment of the clearness and rapidity with which the play should unfold itself. After the exit of Geronte, it is good. But the fact is that I am not in the least satisfied, and I believe that you will share my dissatisfaction. The departure from the scenario has been an improvement in some respects, but in many others it has been greatly for the worse.
>
> I shall write to Oliva that the manuscript, with some criticisms of mine, is in your hands. I beg and beseech you to see him and explain the contents of this letter and say anything else that you think apposite on your own account.[2]

When Oliva decided he had had enough of Puccini, Ricordi sought the advice of Giuseppe Giacosa, the playwright whose Russian idea Puccini had rejected. Giacosa was not interested in actively becoming one of the cooks preparing the broth but suggested that another young playwright, Luigi Illica, should be approached. In due course, Illica agreed to reshape the libretto, though his task was made especially

[1] Adami, op. cit.   [2] Adami, op. cit.

difficult by the fact that Puccini had already begun to write music for a number of scenes whose words, presumably, could therefore not be altered. By the spring of 1891, Giacosa had been persuaded to help Illica and both playwrights were busily writing and rewriting scenes while Puccini worked on the music.

Ricordi continued to act as midwife as well as publisher, and even seems to have contributed some verses to the libretto. 'I am afraid of that whole act,' he wrote to Puccini in July of 1892, referring to Act II. 'But I do not always want to be the one who grumbles. Instead, dreaming about *Manon*, regard the four masterpieces which I send you as worthy of a Salvatore Rosa.'[1] In August, Ricordi was urging his composer to finish the opera quickly and not to be led astray by 'musical philosophy or the libretto'. In September, Puccini's publisher professed himself delighted to hear that the end was in sight, and added: 'I went to Verdi's for one day on business. That man [Verdi was then seventy-nine years of age] is a marvel. I know it and yet I cannot get over it, with the years. It will give you pleasure to know that both Verdi and his wife have interested themselves in you, asked me news about *Manon*, if you will have good performers etc. etc. They wish you success.'[2]

Finally, after three years of preparation, *Manon Lescaut* was completed in October, 1892. Six people had shared in the authorship of the libretto – Leoncavallo, Praga, Oliva, Giacosa, Illica and Ricordi – but not one of them was willing to acknowledge the fact. When the score was published, the opera was described as a 'lyric drama in four acts' by Giacomo Puccini, and there was no mention either of the librettists or of the Abbé Prévost.

Ricordi did not want to risk another Puccini failure at La Scala, and perhaps, too, he did not want the young composer's new opera to face the direct competition of Verdi's swansong, *Falstaff*, whose première was to take place at La Scala on 9 February, 1893. He arranged that *Manon Lescaut* should have its first performance a few days earlier, on 1 February, not in Milan but in Turin, at the Teatro Regio. Puccini went to Turin in January to supervise rehearsals, and from there wrote to Elvira: '. . . Let them say what they want – this time I have a feeling that I have done a successful piece of work. Here everybody is mad about it. Nevertheless the execution will be wretched, because the voices can hardly be heard. Goodbye. I'm hurrying to the rehearsal. It is 11.30. Your Topizio.'[3]

Despite Puccini's fears about the performance, the first night was a decided success. The applause began after the tenor's aria, 'Tra voi, belle', in Act I, when Puccini had to appear on stage to acknowledge cries of 'Bravo, bravissimo', and it mounted throughout the evening until, at the end, composer and cast took thirty curtain calls.

[1] Marek, op. cit.   [2] Ibid.   [3] Ibid.

Nor were the critics any less enthusiastic. Giuseppe Depanis, in the *Gazzetta Piemontese*, wrote of his

> satisfaction in recording that critics and the public were of one mind in paying tribute to and in acclaiming a robust opera of a young Italian maestro, one who has done honour to his name and to his country. Art has no boundaries, to be sure. None the less, national pride is legitimate: Last night was a good night for art and for Italy.

J. B. Nappi in the *Perseveranza* wrote in similar terms ('In my not brief career as journalist, it has rarely happened to me to be present at so important an evening as last night's . . .'), and Giovanni Pozza in the Milan *Corriere della sera* said:

> Between *Edgar* and this *Manon*, Puccini has vaulted an abyss. *Edgar* can be said to have been a necessary preparation, all redundancies, all flashes and indications; *Manon* is the work of the genius conscious of his own power, master of his art, a creator and perfector of it. *Manon* can be ranked among the classical operas. Puccini's genius is truly Italian. His song is the song of our paganism, of our artistic sensualism. It caresses us and becomes part of us.

With *Manon Lescaut*, Puccini's fame was assured. The opera was immediately staged throughout Italy, and before the end of the year had been seen abroad in Buenos Aires, Rio de Janeiro, St Petersburg, Madrid and Hamburg. Productions followed, in 1894, in Lisbon, Budapest, Prague, London, Montevideo, Philadelphia and Mexico. New York first saw *Manon Lescaut* in 1898, Vienna in 1908 and Paris in 1910. The King of Italy decorated Puccini with the Order of La Croce di Cavaliere, and the composer was offered several important teaching posts, among them that of professor of composition at the Milan Conservatorium, which the amount of royalties he was receiving from productions of the opera enabled him graciously to refuse.

For the 1894 London production of *Manon Lescaut* at Covent Garden, the conductor was Armando Seppilli, and the cast included Olga Olghina (Manon), Umberto Beduschi (Des Grieux) and Antonio Pini-Corsi (Lescaut). Bernard Shaw, who was then the music critic of *The World*, thought the Russian soprano Olghina 'just a little too ladylike' for Manon, but praised the tenor, Beduschi, and said of the opera that

> in *Manon Lescaut* the domain of Italian opera is enlarged by an annexation of German territory. The first act, which is as gay and effective and romantic as the opening of any version of *Manon* need be, is also unmistakably symphonic in its treatment. There is genuine symphonic modification, development, and occasionally combination of the thematic material, all in a dramatic way, but also in a musically homogeneous way, so that the act is really a single movement with episodes, instead of being a succession of

separate numbers, linked together, to conform to the modern fashion, by substituting interrupted cadences for full closes and parading a Leitmotif occasionally.

. . . Puccini, at least, shews no signs of atrophy of the melodic faculty: he breaks out into catching melodies quite in the vein of Verdi: for example, 'Tra voi, belle', in the first act of *Manon*, has all the charm of the tunes beloved by the old operatic guard.

On that and other accounts, Puccini looks to me more like the heir of Verdi than any of his rivals. He has arranged his own libretto from Prévost d'Exiles' novel; and though the miserable end of poor Manon has compelled him to fall back on a rather conventional operatic death scene in which the prima donna at Covent Garden failed to make anyone believe, his third act, with the roll-call of the female convicts and the embarkation, is admirably contrived and carried out: he has served himself in this as well as Scribe ever served Meyerbeer, or Boito Verdi.[1]

Puccini had not 'arranged his own libretto', though in the absence of any mention of a librettist it is not surprising that Shaw should have assumed he had done so. *Manon Lescaut* made its composer's name famous throughout the operatic world, and is still quite frequently performed, although it is not among the most popular of Puccini's operas. It is certainly the earliest of his works to have survived in the general operatic repertory.

II

Antoine-Francois Prévost d'Exiles, known as the Abbé Prévost, is known today principally as the author of *Manon Lescaut*, a novel still widely read in French and to a lesser extent in English translation. Born in 1697, Prévost in his youth vacillated between a career in the army and in the Church. After he took holy orders as a Benedictine, his taste for worldly pleasure led him into difficulties and at the age of thirty-one he found himself fleeing first to Holland and then to London to escape ecclesiastical reprisals and arrest. Prévost wrote a seven-volume novel, *Mémoires et aventures d'un homme de qualité* (1728–31), the last volume of which contains his best-known story, *L'Histoire du Chevalier des Grieux et de Manon Lescaut*. The popular abridgement of the title to *Manon Lescaut* obscures the fact that Des Grieux, the narrator of the story, or short novel, is as important a character as the lady generally thought of as its sole eponymous protagonist. From 1733 to 1740, Prévost published a magazine, *Le Pour et Contre*, which served to make English literature and English ideas better known to the French public. His other works include the romantic novels, *Le Philosophe anglais ou l'Histoire de Monsieur Cleveland* and *Le Doyen de Killerine*. Prévost died suddenly one afternoon in 1763; returning from a visit to some Benedictine colleagues, he was walking through the forest of Chantilly when he collapsed and fell by the

[1] *The World*, 23 May, 1894.

roadside. About twenty years after his death, the story circulated that when he fell he had merely suffered an apoplectic seizure, and that what killed him was the knife of a surgeon performing an autopsy while Prévost was in a coma. This rumour is now generally discounted.

Prévost's novel tells the story of the Chevalier des Grieux, a brilliant and talented youth of seventeen, a student of philosophy with the brightest of futures, and his encounter with Manon Lescaut, a girl a year younger than he, who is being sent by her family to enter a convent. Manon inspires in Des Grieux such love that he almost ruins his life in his efforts to satisfy her whims and expensive tastes. For her sake, and in spite of the fact that she is frequently unfaithful to him, he steals, lies, cheats, borrows money, is imprisoned, voluntarily accompanies her into exile, and gravely wounds the nephew of the Governor of Louisana in a duel. Manon dies of exhaustion in his arms in the desert where they have fled to escape the consequences of the duel.

Manon Lescaut was first adapted for the stage in France in 1765. The prolific librettist Scribe used it as the basis for a ballet with music by Halévy in 1830, and its first operatic treatment was by Auber, whose *Manon Lescaut*, with libretto by Scribe, was produced in Paris in 1856.[1] The most popular and most successful operatic adaptation of Prévost is Massenet's *Manon*, first performed in Paris in 1884. (The differences between Massenet's and Puccini's operas in their treatment of the original are summarized later in this chapter.)

Prévost's *Manon Lescaut* is a narration within a narration, a 'double flashback', to use a cinematic term. The anonymous 'homme de qualité', the Marquis de ——, postulated by Prévost as the author of the seven-volume *Mémoires et aventures d'un homme de qualité qui s'est retiré du monde* (Memoirs and adventures of a man of quality who has retired from the world), begins his account thus:

Je suis obligé de faire remonter mon lecteur au temps de ma vie où je rencontrai pour la première fois le chevalier des Grieux: ce fut environ six mois avant mon départ pour l'Espagne. Quoique je sortisse rarement de ma solitude, la complaisance que j'avais pour ma fille m'engageait quelquefois à divers petits voyages, que j'abrégeais autant qu'il m'était possible.

Je revenais un jour de Rouen, où elle m'avait prié d'aller solliciter une affaire au parlement de Normandie, pour la succession de quelques terres auxquelles je lui avais laissé des prétentions du côté de mon grand-père maternel. Ayant repris mon chemin par Évreux, où je couchai la première nuit, j'arrivai le lendemain pour dîner à Passy, qui en est éloigné de cinq ou six lieues. Je fus surpris, en entrant dans ce bourg, d'y voir tous les habitants en alarme; ils se précipitaient de leurs maisons pour courir en foule à la porte d'une mauvaise hôtellerie devant laquelle étaient deux chariots couverts. Les

---

[1] According to Mosco Carner, op. cit., Alfred Bunn's libretto for Balfe's *The Maid of Artois* (1836) drew upon Prévost.

chevaux, qui étaient encore attelés et qui paraissaient fumants de fatigue et de chaleur, marquaient que ces deux voitures ne faisaient qu'arriver.[1]

The Marquis has arrived at the moment when a dozen *filles de joie*, among them Manon, are being transported to Le Havre and thence to America. He is intrigued by the grief-stricken young man ('a person of birth and breeding') who has followed the young ladies and their guards from Paris, and he gets into conversation with this young man, Des Grieux, and learns part of his story. Two years later, he encounters Des Grieux again, and hears the rest of the story from him. 'This, then, is his story,' writes the Marquis, 'into which I shall intrude no word that is not his, until it be ended.' In fact, the Marquis intrudes no word even then, for *Manon Lescaut* ends as Des Grieux concludes his narrative: his faithful friend Tiberge (omitted from Massenet's and Puccini's operas) has helped him to return from America to France, and Des Grieux is now about to return to the bosom of his family.

Des Grieux's narrative begins, 'J'avais dix-sept ans, et j'achevais mes études de philosophie à Amiens, où mes parents, qui sont d'une des meilleures maisons de P . . . , m'avaient envoyé' (I was seventeen years of age, and was finishing my studies in philosophy at Amiens, where my parents, who come of one of the best families in P . . . , had sent me). The girl in the coach from Arras with whom Des Grieux fell in love at first sight, was even younger: 'Quoiqu'elle fût encore moins âgée que moi, elle recut mes politesses sans paraître embarrassée' (Although she was even younger than I, she received my polite compliments without appearing to be embarrassed). The extreme youth of the lovers is often obscured in productions of *Manon* and *Manon Lescaut*, for few prima donnas or leading tenors are able convincingly to portray teenagers.

Prévost's novel, a smoothly written, compact account of a romantic's obsession with a charming but amoral creature who is intensely practical and clear-headedly unromantic, founders on the novelist's decision to make Des Grieux a seventeen-year-old. Des Grieux and Manon are no Romeo and Juliet: for the novel to carry conviction, Des Grieux would have to be an older man, someone closer to the age of Prévost when he wrote *Manon Lescaut*. In an attempt to disguise the fact that his novel was

[1] I must ask my reader to hark back to that period of my life when I was to meet the Chevalier des Grieux for the first time: it was about six months before my departure for Spain. Although I rarely emerged from my solitude, my tenderness for my daughter engaged me at times in various trifling journeys which I cut as short as I could.

I was returning one day from Rouen, whither I had gone at her entreaty to plead a suit before the Parliament of Normandy regarding the succession to certain estates to which she had a claim through my maternal grandfather. Having returned through Evreux, where I stayed overnight, the next day I arrived in time to dine at Passy which is five or six leagues distant. To my surprise, on entering the town I found the inhabitants in a state of commotion, flocking from their houses to crowd around the door of a cheap hotel before which stood two covered wagons. The horses, still harnessed and steaming with heat and exhaustion, were evidence that the vehicles had only just arrived.

crypto-autobiographical, Prévost made the psychological mistake of turning Des Grieux into someone half the age he ought to be.

In an attempt to forget the faithless Manon, Des Grieux, in Prévost's novel, enters the Seminary at Saint-Sulpice. His account of his fall from grace again is written with the anguished, frustrated self-knowledge of a mature man, not the wounded sensibility of a boy:

I had passed almost a year in Paris without trying to learn anything of Manon's affairs. It had cost me a good deal at first to do myself this violence, but the ever-present counsels of Tiberge and my own reflections had won me the victory. The last months had flowed by in such tranquillity that I believed myself on the point of forgetting to eternity that charming and faithless creature. The time arrived for my public disputation in the School of Theology: I had asked several persons of distinction to honour me with their presence. My name was thus bruited about in every quarter of Paris. It even reached the ears of my false one. She could not be sure of it, disguised as I was now as an Abbé; but some flicker of curiosity or perhaps some remorse at having betrayed me (I have never been able to disentangle which sentiment it was) roused her interest in a name so like my own; she came to the Sorbonne with several other ladies. She was present at my declamation, and doubtless had small difficulty in recognizing me. I was completely unaware of her presence. There are in these places, as you know, special galleries for ladies, where they are hidden from view behind a lattice. I returned to Saint-Sulpice, covered with glory and laden with compliments. It was six o'clock in the evening. A moment after my return, they came to tell me that a lady was asking to see me. I went at once to the parlour. Oh God, what an apparition! There I found Manon. It was she, but lovelier, more dazzling than I had ever seen her. She was now in her eighteenth year. Her charms passed all description: an air so delicate, so sweet, so winsome, love's very self. Her whole face seemed to me one enchantment.

I stood dazed at the sight of her and, unable to guess the meaning of her visit, I waited with downcast eyes and trembling, till she should explain herself. Her own embarrassment was for some time equal to mine but, seeing that my silence persisted, she put her hand over her eyes to hide her tears. Timidly she told me that she knew her faithlessness deserved my hate, but that if I had really ever had any tenderness for her, there had been a good deal of hardness on my side in letting two years go by without ever trying to find out what had become of her, and far more now in seeing the state she was in in my presence, and never saying a word to her. The upheaval in my soul as I listened was beyond expression. She sat down, I remained standing, half turned away, not daring to look at her directly. Several times I began to reply, and had not the power to finish. At last, with an effort, I uttered one anguished cry, 'False Manon! Ah, false, false!' Again she said, weeping hot tears, that she did not mean to justify her falseness. 'What do you mean, then?' I cried. 'I mean to die', said she, if you do not give me your heart again, for I cannot live without it.' 'Then ask my life, false love,' I answered, with tears that I tried vainly to·restrain, 'ask my life, it is all that is left me to give you, for my heart has never ceased to be yours.' Scarcely had I uttered the last words when she rose in an ecstasy and came to clasp me in her arms. She overwhelmed me with a thousand passionate caresses. She called me by all the names that love can find for its most eager tendernesses. As yet I made but languid response. What a transition, in very truth, from the peace which had surrounded me to the stormy emotions which I now felt awakening! I was aghast. I was shivering as when one finds oneself at night in a desolate countryside: one feels oneself transported into a new order of things: one is seized by a secret terror that only abates after one has long considered one's surroundings.

This is Massenet's Act III, scene ii, the reception room of the seminary of Saint-Sulpice, with Des Grieux's 'Ah, fuyez, douce image' and Manon's 'N'est-ce plus ma main que cette main presse?'. It has no equivalent in Puccini's opera. The inevitable compression of Prévost's plot in order to keep their respective operas to a reasonable length leads both Massenet (*Manon*) and Puccini (*Manon Lescaut*) to depart in certain respects from the original. For example, in Prévost's novel, when Des Grieux first encounters Manon as she arrives in the coach at Amiens, she is escorted only by an elderly family servant. Massenet's librettists at this point introduce the guardsman Lescaut, Manon's cousin, who meets her coach as it arrives; in Puccini's opera Lescaut becomes Manon's brother and arrives in the coach with her. In Prévost's novel, Manon has a brother in the Life Guards, 'a brutal fellow and with no sense of honour'; but he does not make his appearance until Manon and Des Grieux are living together in Paris for the second time, after the Saint-Sulpice episode.

The principal scenes in the novel, from which a librettist could choose those he needed, are: (i) the meeting of Des Grieux and Manon at Amiens and their elopement; (ii) their apartment in Paris, Des Grieux's first suspicion of Manon's infidelity and (iii) his abduction by his father's lackeys; (iv) Des Grieux in his family home, unhappy and confused; (v) Saint-Sulpice; (vi) life at Chaillot where Des Grieux and Manon have taken a small house; (vii) Lescaut, Manon and Des Grieux living by their wits, gambling at the Hôtel de Transylvanie; (viii) Manon leaves Des Grieux a second time for a richer lover; (ix) the revenge of the rich lover, and the arrest of Manon; (x) Des Grieux confined at Saint-Lazare; (xi) his attempt to effect Manon's escape, which leads to the death of her brother; (xii) Manon betrays Des Grieux yet again, with 'M. de G . . . M . . .'; (xiii) the events leading to Manon's arrest; (xiv) Le Havre, whence Manon is to be deported to America; (xv) on the ship to America; (xvi) the episode of Synnelet, nephew of the Governor of Louisiana; (xvii) the lovers' flight, and Manon's death.

Clearly, no more than five or six of these episodes could be included in an opera of normal length. Massenet's librettists, Henri Meilhac and Philippe Gille, made their selection, and Puccini's initial advice to his collaborators was to avoid, as far as possible, those scenes made famous in Massenet's successful opera. Some overlap was, of course, unavoidable

if the plot of *Manon Lescaut* was to be at all comprehensible; but the effort
to minimize the inevitable points of similarity made the task of Puccini
and his librettists much more difficult than it would otherwise have been,
and left them with an unsatisfactory and ill-balanced libretto whose
principal defect is that, after showing the first meeting of Manon and
Des Grieux at Amiens, it proceeds in the very next scene to reveal Manon
living with her rich lover, Geronte, having already left Des Grieux – a
scene which ends with Manon's arrest. Puccini's final act, a long-drawn-
out duet ending with Manon's death in the desert outside New Orleans,
is disappointingly anti-climactic. By departing from Prévost, and having
Manon die on the road to Le Havre while Des Grieux is attempting her
rescue, Massenet's librettists produced a much more satisfactory finale.
Puccini's Act III is based on a relatively unimportant episode in Prévost,
and his final act is confusing unless one fills in the background by
reading Prévost.

Here, in tabular form, are the scenes from Prévost's original (in the
numbering given above) used in *Manon* and in *Manon Lescaut*:

Scene no.	Manon (Massenet)	Manon Lescaut (Puccini)
(i)	Act I	Act I
(ii)	Act II	
	Act III, sc. i (Promenade of the Cours-la-Reine in Paris, during a festival)	
(v)	Act III, sc. ii	
(vii)/(xiii)	Act IV	
(xii)/(xiii)		Act II
(xiv)	Act V	Act III
(xvii)		Act IV

In both Massenet's and Puccini's operas, the final curtain falls on a
grief-stricken Des Grieux as Manon dies in his arms. In Prévost's novel,
Des Grieux's faithful friend Tiberge follows him to America, to find him
truly repentant and in a state of grace. The novel ends thus, in Des
Grieux's narrative:

I could not sufficiently show my gratitude for so constant and so generous a
friend. I brought him to my house. I made him master of all I had. I told him
all that had befallen me since my departure from France; and to give him a
joy beyond his expectation, I told him that the seeds of goodness which he
had once sown in my heart were beginning at last to bring forth fruits that
might content him. He declared that such tidings recompensed him fully for
all the fatigues of his voyage.

We spent two months together at New Orleans, awaiting the arrival of the
ships from France, and, putting at last to sea, we landed a fortnight ago at

Havre-de Grâce. I wrote to my family on my arrival. I have learned, from my elder brother's reply, the sad news of the death of my father. The wind being favourable for Calais, I embarked at once, with the intention of coming to this town to the house of a gentleman of my own kin, where my brother writes that he will await my arrival.

Puccini's opera is in four acts, the first of which is set in Amiens. The time is the second half of the eighteenth century. The curtain rises on a large square near the Paris gate. It is evening. On the right is a wide street, and on the left an inn with a portico under which are a few tables. A small external stairway leads to the first floor of the inn. Students, citizens and soldiers are strolling about, or standing in groups, conversing. A few people sit at the tables, drinking and playing cards. A number of students led by Edmondo greet a fellow student, Des Grieux, who unwillingly and ironically joins in their banter with a group of girls.

The coach from Arras arrives and stops outside the inn. Among the passengers who alight are Lescaut, a Sergeant of the King's Guards, his teenage sister Manon, and a fellow passenger, an elderly gentleman, Geronte di Ravoir, Treasurer-General. When the two men enter the inn to arrange overnight accommodation, Des Grieux approaches Manon, overwhelmed by her beauty, and discovers that she is being sent by her family to a convent, and will be leaving at dawn on the final stage of her journey. After Manon is called by her brother to enter the inn, Des Grieux sings of his love for her but walks off when the students taunt him.

Geronte di Ravoir and Lescaut emerge from the inn in conversation, and Lescaut admits that he is sorry he has to escort his sister to a convent, but like a good soldier he is obeying orders. Geronte invites Lescaut and Manon to sup with him, and goes off to give instructions to the inn-keeper, while Lescaut becomes involved in a game of cards with the students. Geronte reappears and, seeing Lescaut engrossed in his game, calls the innkeeper and instructs him to have a coach and horses ready in an hour, for he intends to abduct Manon and carry her off to Paris. His words have been overheard by the student Edmondo who jokingly passes the information on to Des Grieux. Realizing how upset Des Grieux is, and how greatly he loves Manon, Edmondo agrees to help him foil Geronte's scheme.

While the students encourage Lescaut to drink more than he should, Des Grieux warns Manon of the plot and persuades her to elope with him instead. Edmondo appears, to announce that a carriage is waiting for them behind the inn, and Des Grieux and Manon rush off. When Geronte emerges, he is told that the young lady has left with a student. He urges Lescaut to follow them, but that cynical and practical young man replies that it is useless. His sister will be well on the way to Paris. It will be far better to follow at a leisurely pace: Manon loves pleasure, and a student's purse will soon be empty. Then Geronte will find her perfectly willing to leave a poor student for a rich Treasurer-General. Lescaut leads Geronte into the inn to supper as the curtain falls.

Act II takes place in Paris, in an extremely elegant salon in the house of Geronte di Ravoir. There are two doors at the back, and on the right are sumptuous draperies concealing an alcove. On the left by the window is a lavishly appointed dressing-table, and the room also contains armchairs, a settee and a table. Manon, wearing a white dressing gown, is seated at her dressing table while a hairdresser and two assistants put the finishing touches to her coiffure. Her brother enters: it is he who has been largely responsible for Manon leaving the impecunious Des Grieux for the rich Treasurer-General Geronte di Ravoir. Lescaut compliments his sister on her beauty, but finds Manon in pensive mood and unable to rid her mind of Des Grieux. She asks her brother for news of him, and Lescaut replies that he has been introducing the Chevalier to the joys of gambling, and that by winning a large sum at cards Des Grieux hopes to attract Manon back to him.

Manon now attempts a change of mood, and is helped by the entrance of a group of singers carrying sheets of music. The singers perform a madrigal composed by Geronte; they are followed by a dancing master and a quartet of musicians who enter with Geronte and a number of guests who watch while Manon is given a dancing lesson, and applaud her when she sings a solo cantata. Meanwhile, Lescaut has slipped away to find Des Grieux, sensing that his sister is bored with Geronte and his way of life.

When Geronte and company leave to join the fashionable promenade in the streets, Manon promises to join them shortly. But Des Grieux now arrives, and his reproaches soon give way to ardent expressions of love which Manon reciprocates. They are locked in an embrace on the sofa when Geronte suddenly returns. Manon taunts him, and he leaves in a cold fury. Manon is delighted to be free of Geronte, but when Lescaut presses her to leave 'questo tetto del vecchio maledetto' (this wretched old man's roof) her agreement is tinged with a certain regret at having to part with such luxury.

As Des Grieux reproaches her for her worldliness, Lescaut returns, breathless, to warn the lovers to flee, for Geronte has denounced Manon to the police as an immoral woman, and even now a detachment of guards and archers ('guardie e arcier') is on its way to arrest her. It is because Manon insists first on gathering up her jewels, emptying all the drawers of the various trinkets they contain, that their departure is fatally delayed. 'Just bring your heart with you,' Des Grieux begs, 'for I want only to salvage your love' ('Con te portar dei solo il cor. Io vo' salvar solo il tuo amor').

But it is too late. The police arrive with Geronte, and Des Grieux draws his sword but is persuaded by Lescaut not to use it. 'If you too are arrested,' Lescaut points out, 'who will be able to save Manon?' Some of the stolen jewellery drops from the folds of Manon's cloak as she is dragged away by the guards. Geronte bursts into sardonic laughter, and Des Grieux is restrained by Lescaut as he attempts to follow Manon.

An orchestral prelude, described in the score as an Intermezzo, is played before Act III. Printed above it is the following quotation, supposedly from the Italian translation of Prévost's novel (*Storia di Manon Lescaut e del cavaliere Des Grieux*), though it does not actually correspond to any passage in the original French:

> DES GRIEUX: . . . Gli è che io l'amo! La mia passione è così forte che io me sento la più sfortunata creatura che vive. Quello che non ho io tentato a Parigi per ottenere la sua libertà?! . . . Ho implorato i potenti! . . . Ho picchiato e supplicato a tutte le porte! . . . Persino alla violenza ho ricorso! . . . Tutto fu inutile. Una sol via mi rimaneva: seguirla! Ed io la seguo! Dovunque ella vada! . . . Fosse pure in capo al mondo! . . .[1]

Act III takes place at Le Havre, in a square near the harbour. In the background the harbour, with a warship at anchor, can be glimpsed. On one corner of the square is a barracks with a barred window, and an entrance guarded by a sentry. On the opposite corner, by a narrow street, is a house with an oil lamp flickering on a post outside. It is shortly before dawn. Des Grieux and Lescaut are standing opposite the barracks. Manon and a number of other women sentenced to be deported to America are under guard in the barracks: Lescaut has bribed one of the guards to allow Manon to speak with them, and he and Des Grieux intend to attempt her rescue.

When the guard is changed, Lescaut speaks to the new sentry who moves away to allow Des Grieux and Manon to converse through the barred window. Their talk is interrupted momentarily by a lamplighter who sings a popular song as he extinguishes the lamp in the square. Des Grieux informs Manon of the plan for her escape, but suddenly a shot is heard and Lescaut reappears to declare that his plan has failed. An alarm is sounded, and citizens begin to appear in the square asking one another what has happened.

The commander of the warship arrives with a detachment of marines, and the girls emerge as their names are read from a list. They cross the square in the direction of the ship to the accompaniment of ribald comments from the citizens. As Manon is dragged from his arms, Des Grieux pleads with the captain of the ship to take him on board in any

[1] DES GRIEUX: . . . How I love her! My passion is so strong that I feel myself to be the most unfortunate creature living. What have I not attempted in Paris to obtain her liberty? I have implored the powerful! . . . I have knocked and petitioned at all doors! . . . I have even had recourse to violence! . . . Everything was useless. Only one way remains to me: to follow her! And I will follow her! Wherever she goes! . . . Even to the ends of the earth! . . .

capacity, even as a cabin boy, so that he will not have to part from Manon. The Captain takes pity on him. 'Ah, so you want to populate America, young man? Well then, come on, cabin boy,' he replies. Des Grieux kisses the Captain's hand in gratitude and runs to Manon. Lescaut, who has been watching, shakes his head and walks away as the curtain quickly falls.

Act IV is set in America; more specifically, in what the libretto calls an immense landscape on the borders of New Orleans. The country is bare and undulating, the horizon vast, the sky cloudy. It is nightfall. Manon and Des Grieux come slowly into view, destitute and dressed in rags. Manon, pale and exhausted, is supported by Des Grieux. She can go no further, and begs to be allowed to rest while Des Grieux scans the horizon for a glimpse of shelter or water.

Left alone, Manon gives way to her despair. In the aria she sings, she reveals, obscurely, that, although America had at first seemed a peaceful country, 'my fatal beauty aroused new anger – they wanted to tear me from him' ('Ah, mia beltà funesta ire novelle accende – strappar da lui mi si volea'): this is all that is left in the opera of the episode in Prévost's novel in which Des Grieux kills the Governor's nephew who has fallen prey to Manon's charms.

Des Grieux returns as Manon is about to faint. He tries to revive and comfort her, but eventually realizes that she is dying. With her last breath, Manon swears to Des Grieux that she loves him. When Des Grieux in desperation cries that he will follow her by killing himself, she forbids him to do so. She dies, and Des Grieux, crazed with grief, falls senseless over her body.

III

The score of *Manon Lescaut* went through the usual number of Puccinian revisions: a copy of the 1915 full orchestral score in the possession of Ricordi & Company contains corrections in Puccini's hand, made as late as 1923. Most of the composer's revisions, however, were made by 1909.

Puccini was in his early thirties when he composed *Manon Lescaut*: he already had two operas behind him, operas written in his twenties when he was finding his way, charting his course between the Scylla and Charybdis of Wagner and Verdi. It took him longer to create his third opera than it had *Le villi* or *Edgar*, but from the opening bars of *Manon Lescaut* it is clear to us that Puccini was no longer an apprentice composer. The lessons to be gained from the two nineteenth-century giants of opera had been learned and thoroughly assimilated, and Puccini had not failed to take note of what was most useful to him in French opera as well. The Puccinian style is fully formed in *Manon Lescaut*, the final traces of the old clear-cut division between recitative and aria have been obliterated, and the influence of late Verdi and Wagner no longer seems in any way superimposed upon the younger composer: he has built upon the past to create the present. In later operas his melodic gift was to ripen, but his method and his style remained intrinsically what they were in *Manon Lescaut*. The composer of this opera is the composer of *Turandot*, and most of the choral and orchestral writing in this, Puccini's first mature opera, would not sound out of place in *Turandot*, his final work and, some would say, his masterpiece.

Puccini had never felt the need for a formal overture, and now he dispenses even with a short prelude, bringing up the curtain on Act I of *Manon Lescaut* during the cheerful vivacious orchestral preamble which sets the scene. Edmondo and his fellow students are in carefree mood, and so Puccini's music, a warm, bustling *allegro brillante*, sounds lighthearted, giving no hint that the drama to be unfolded is more than somewhat lachrymose. It has been said that Puccini's operas, or at least his first acts, are symphonic in design, based on the classical first-movement sonata form. But there seems little point in asking an operatic audience to listen to a drama or comedy in the same way that they might listen to a piece of abstract symphonic musical thought. The composer of an opera goes where the drama leads him, though of course he must balance musical and dramatic considerations.

On the 29th bar of Puccini's high-spirited orchestral scene-setting, the curtain rises on Edmondo and the other students, sitting at tables, drinking and playing cards. Edmondo begins a madrigal, in his lyric tenor, singing in a style which Puccini asks for: 'tra il comico ed il sentimentale' (between the comic and the sentimental). He is soon interrupted by the other students, and embarks upon a second madrigal, inspired by the arrival of a group of working girls. 'Giovinezza è nostro nome' (Our name is youth), Edmondo sings, followed by the students (sopranos and tenors), and the music veers momentarily towards the sentimental. There is in Puccini's writing for the voices something of that feverish gaiety, with its underlying suggestion of sadness, which is a mood well known in adolescence. More tenors, and basses join the ensemble of students and working girls in the last few bars before the entrance of Des Grieux (tenor).

'Tra voi, belle, brune e bionde' (Among you, beautiful ones, dark or blonde) is Des Grieux's bantering response to being teased by the students. A gently mocking serenade, it is elegant and lightly ironic, with no hint of the passionate tone which will enter Des Grieux's utterance from his first sight of Manon a few moments later. Its interruption of the general gaiety is brief, for the crowd now continues with its merrymaking, and the chorus builds up to a return of the opening tempo of the act, making use of material heard earlier in the orchestra. The arrival of the coach from Arras is heralded by the postillion's horn, or Puccini's equivalent which is a cornet in A, played off-stage, and the coach makes its appearance to a reprise of the opening bars of the opera.

The leitmotif, as used by Wagner, is not something to be looked for in Puccini. However, Puccini does associate appropriate musical phrases with certain characters or feelings, though one can never be sure that he will not make inappropriate use as well of such phrases or motives. In *Manon Lescaut* the device is used sparingly and appropriately. As Manon steps out of the coach, the strings in the orchestra are silent, while the woodwind offer a phrase which will come to be associated with Manon at other moments in the opera – a phrase which knowledge of the later operas leads one to describe as quintessentially Puccinian. Also Puccinian is the way in which, orchestrally, melody remains a constant major ingredient. The melody passes to the voices in arias and duets, but at other times it is there in the orchestra, and the voices fit in above it with their parlando or their arioso passages.

In a moment or two now, after Manon has entered the inn, Des Grieux will sing his second aria, 'Donna non vidi mai simile a questa' (I have never seen a woman like this one); but already, as he begins to speak to Manon, the strings give out what is to become the opening phrase of the aria. Manon tells Des Grieux her name – 'Manon Lescaut mi chiamo' – and the words and musical phrase will fit neatly into the aria when Des Grieux quotes them, his verbal reminiscence matching the musical repetition. One could almost say that Puccini's orchestra, in accompanying Des Grieux's flirtation with Manon, anticipates the blossoming of his love for her, and that he almost immediately confirms the orchestra's prescience when he sings his words to music which has expressed his feelings even before he was able to articulate them. (Incidentally, when he tells Manon who he is, Des Grieux offers a first name, Renato, which is not mentioned again, and which does not exist in Prévost. Everyone, including Manon, addresses the Chevalier as 'Des Grieux'.)

Now, to the violin phrase of Ex. 5, but transposed up from G to the

Ex. 5

Andante lento espressivo

key of B flat to display the tenor's upper notes, Des Grieux sings 'Donna non vidi mai', whose ardently romantic tone is in vivid contrast to the light-hearted flippancy of 'Tra voi, belle'. Though the musical material has partly been heard before, the aria is made to sound like a spontaneous outpouring of feeling by Puccini's method of placing the melodic continuity in the orchestra, leaving the vocal line an apparent freedom. In fact, the aria is shaped as expertly as the flight of Cupid's arrow.

Edmondo and the students, to the music heard at the beginning of the act, return to taunt Des Grieux. From here to the end of Act I, Puccini's fluent parlando style carries the action forward, with occasional lyrical interludes. The dialogue between Lescaut (baritone) and Geronte (bass) is carried on for the most part above the orchestra's agitated allegro, which momentarily subsides as Lescaut joins the students at cards. The lively tempo is abandoned as Edmondo warns Des Grieux of Geronte's plot to abduct Manon, and the orchestra gives us the opening strains of 'Donna non vidi mai' again, to herald the scene between Manon and Des Grieux. This broadens into a duet in which he declares his love for her, and Manon responds, their voices blending in unison [Ex. 6]. The

Ex. 6

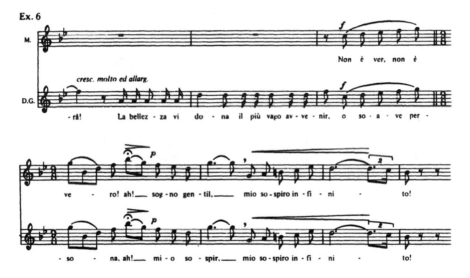

mood is shattered by an exclamation from Lescaut, and the rest of the dialogue between Manon and Des Grieux is carried on in a more practical parlando. As they leave, the orchestra thunders out a reprise of a theme heard earlier in their duet when it was played by a solo flute. Now it serves as climax and release, as the young lovers flee to Paris.

Lescaut's advice to Geronte is given in a charming arioso, which begins with the words, 'Vedo Manon con sue grazie leggiadre ha suscitato in voi un affetto di padre!' (I see that Manon with her attractive graces has aroused a father's affection in you!). Softly, the students join in to mock the two men, to the tune of Des Grieux's first aria, 'Tra voi, belle'. The students' derisive laughter and a final four bars of noise from the orchestra bring the act to an end.

Act II opens with dialogue between Manon and her hairdresser; phrases of musical small talk behind which the orchestra produces a musical background much more elegant than the livelier sounds of Act I. Lescaut's arioso, 'Sei splendida e lucante' (You are splendid and radiant), a graceful, languid piece in itself, serves the purpose of telling the audience where Manon is and how she got there. Her aria, 'In quelle trine morbide' (In those silken hangings), is an early attempt at the kind of soprano aria Puccini would perfect in his later operas. It begins tenderly [Ex. 7] with a new and affecting phrase of its own, but as it

Ex. 7

In quel - le trine morbi - de nell' al - co - va do - ra - ta

develops we hear a repetition of the melody sung by Lescaut in his arioso.

A short duet for Manon and her brother ends with her ecstatic rise to high C, and his laughter as he contemplates the picture he has painted of Des Grieux as gambler. There is a change of mood and of tempo as Manon completes her toilette, and a further change in the direction of eighteenth-century formality with the entrance of the musicians, for whom Puccini provides his brand of musical pastiche. The madrigal sung by a mezzo-soprano with a chorus of three sopranos and two contraltos turns out to be the Agnus Dei from the Mass Puccini had composed in 1880, the music adapting itself quite happily to the words of pastoral love. Manon's dancing lesson follows, in the course of which a string quartet on stage (its sound provided by the orchestral strings) plays two minuets, for which Puccini uses two of three minuets for string quartet which he had composed some years earlier.

'L'ora, o Tirsi, è vaga e bella' (The hour, o Thyrsis, is attractive and beautiful), the little cantata which Manon sings to Geronte's guests, has a sprightly character: the chorus of guests joins in and, at the conclusion, the strings of the orchestra play the tune in unison while Geronte and the guests make their departure. Almost immediately, to an upward surge of strings, Des Grieux enters, and a lengthy duet ensues, one in which Manon's passion is met at first by Des Grieux's reproaches but which eventually turns into a love duet. 'Tu, tu, amore? Tu?' (Is it you, you, my love? You?), Manon begins, with a passionate urgency. It is to her foolish plea, 'Io voglio il tuo perdono. Vedi? Son ricca' (I want your forgiveness. See? I am rich) that we hear for the first time a musical phrase [Ex. 8] which will occur significantly later in the opera. Des

Ex. 8

Io vo - glio il tuo per - do - no Ve - di? Son ric - ca!___

Grieux's responses remain aloof and bitter until, at Manon's great phrase arching up to C flat at 'pensavo [a un avvenir di luce]' (I thought [of a radiant future]), he begins to weaken.

It is from this point that the encounter turns into a love duet as Manon, now confident, continues her seduction of the helpless

Chevalier. A welter of yearning falling sevenths, reminiscent of the *Tristan und Isolde* love music, brings Des Grieux back into the arms of Manon, who is not above quoting his 'Donna non vidi mai' against him, causing Des Grieux to admit, to an altered form of a theme he sang in Act I, that he loves her ('Son vinto: io t'amo': I am conquered: I love you). Curiously, the climax of the duet, from the tenor's 'Nel occhio tuo profondo' (In the depths of your eyes) onwards, is less convincing than the earlier part, for the music takes on a quasi-martial aspect which leads one to suspect that Puccini may here be making use of music conceived to fit words of a different temper. Whether or not this is no, for a few bars one has the distinct impression that one is listening to two Verdi characters exulting at the moment of victory rather than two Puccinian lovers in passionate embrace. But the retreat from the climactic B flat, the detumescence so to speak, is convincing, and the aftermath of passion is delicately conveyed in the final pianissimo bars of the duet.

The mood is abruptly shattered by the arrival of Geronte. After he has gone again, threatening vengeance, a sombre note comes into the music as Des Grieux warns Manon that they must leave immediately. Her foolish reluctance to give up such luxury draws from him an angry arioso, 'Ah, Manon, mi tradisce il tuo folle pensier' (Ah, Manon, your foolish thoughts betray me), almost his only moment of insight and self-knowledge throughout the opera. Manon's remorse is perfunctorily expressed, and no doubt rightly so. From here, with the return of Lescaut, to the end of the act, the music moves as swiftly as the action, in a frantic trio. In a not dissimilar dramatic situation, Verdi did this kind of thing better (*Un ballo in maschera*: the exciting trio in Act II in which Renato and Amelia persuade Riccardo to flee), and one cannot help thinking that Puccini has Verdi's example at the back of his mind.

The Intermezzo which serves as a prelude to Act III makes use of a number of themes already heard in the opera. It is often described as 'Tristanesque'; certainly its first 12 bars, scored for strings alone, reveal Wagner's *Tristan und Isolde* prelude to be their source of inspiration, but the broad *andante* melody which follows immediately is typical of the 'big tunes' we associate with Puccini at his moments of deepest feeling. This particular tune derives from a phrase of remorse sung by Manon in the Act II duet to the words 'Un' altra volta, un' altra volta ancora' (Again, once again [forgive me]). The music becomes more intense, reaching a climax based on another phrase sung earlier by Manon, still somewhat Wagnerian in its chromaticism, before subsiding into a vein of less passionate regret. Into this Intermezzo we are to read all those events in the novel which we have not seen portrayed on the stage, events which have taken place between Acts II and III of Puccini's opera.

At the beginning of Act III, we encounter a mood of self-pitying despair which we shall find in a number of later Puccini operas, a mood which usually brought forth some of the composer's most effective and convincing music. This mood, despite Lescaut's assertion that Manon will be rescued, pervades the opening exchange of dialogue between Des Grieux and Lescaut, and only lightens to a certain extent with the duet for Manon and Des Grieux. To a sad reprise of the 'Donna non vidi mai' theme, the lovers greet each other tenderly, through prison bars. Their colloquy is twice interrupted by snatches of song by the Lamplighter (tenor), a song so different in mood both in its tune and its imaginative accompaniment, that the contrast emphasizes the misery of Manon and Des Grieux. The accompanying tune played by the violas while Des Grieux tries to reassure Manon ('Manon, disperato è il mio prego': Manon, my plea is desperate) is lifted by Puccini from *Crisantemi*, an elegy for string quartet which he had composed overnight in January, 1890, on the death of Duke Amadeo of Savoy.

The incongruously martial theme from the end of the Act II love duet blares forth from the orchestra at the conclusion of the scene for Manon and Des Grieux, and is interrupted by a rifle shot from off-stage and by Lescaut's report that the plans for Manon's rescue have gone awry. This takes place to the accompaniment of mere 'utility music'. Puccini regains his mastery with the next scene, in which the names of the women to be deported are called, and the women, one by one, cross the square while the townsfolk mutter their comments. This is one of the most effective scenes in the entire opera: as the tension builds up, the disjointed fragments are gathered into a full ensemble, with Manon, Des Grieux and Lescaut voicing their sentiments while the inevitable roll-call continues, and the people of Le Havre express moral outrage, contempt or amusement in *sotto voce* asides.

As the roll-call comes to an end, and the girls are marched on to the waiting ship, the lower strings and woodwind play in unison a phrase which, a few moments later, is sung, its mood transformed, by Des Grieux, to the opening words of his aria, 'Guardate, pazzo son' (See, I am mad) [Ex. 9]. After Des Grieux's violently powerful aria, the end of the act follows swiftly. A *fortissimo* reprise of the 'martial' theme from the end of the Act II love duet brings the curtain down.

Ex. 9

In the short final act, which takes less than twenty minutes to perform, the only two characters to appear are Manon and Des Grieux; the act is simply an extended duet which ends with the death of Manon. Puccini creates a mood of total despair immediately with the opening five bars of the act, played as the curtain rises. A chromatic phrase heard under the opening pages of dialogue comes from the *Crisantemi* quartet also quoted in the preceding act. Various themes from earlier in the opera briefly pass in review, until Manon sends Des Grieux off to search for water. Left alone, she sings the aria, 'Sola, perduta, abbandonata' (Alone, lost, abandoned). She is neither 'sola' nor 'abbandonata', for the man whom she has treated shabbily has remained true to her. But Manon is, understandably, sorry for herself. Her sorrows are no less heavy for being largely brought upon herself, and Puccini lavishes his sympathy upon her in the lachrymose aria, for displays of self-pity came easily to him. (Fearing that this act, though short, was monotonous, Puccini decided to delete the aria, and for a number of years it did not appear in printed scores. But the composer reinstated it for the thirtieth anniversary production of the opera at La Scala under Toscanini in 1923, and it has remained intact ever since.)

Among the various themes quoted as Manon approaches death, the most curious, and least appropriate in dramatic terms, is the echo of the Act II minuet, for one would have thought neither Manon nor her composer would want Des Grieux or the audience to be reminded at this solemn moment of her flippant, frivolous, amoral behaviour. But Puccini was never to become a great musical dramatist, and at this stage of his career he was still comparatively inexperienced, and apt to use whatever tune came into his head at any given moment. At least the curtain falls, not to another over-emphatic *fortissimo*, but to the phrase with which Act IV began.

Manon Lescaut is the first of Puccini's mature works. The step forward that he took between *Edgar* and *Manon Lescaut* is greater than that from *Manon Lescaut* to *La Bohème*. Already in *Manon Lescaut* we have heard the Puccinian harmonies, the romantic melodies, the strokes of theatrical (though not necessarily dramatic) effectiveness which we shall encounter in the more successful operas to follow. No one who responds to the familiar Puccini of *La Bohème* and *Madama Butterfly* is likely to be disappointed by *Manon Lescaut*, though it is only fair to add that no one who knows Massenet's *Manon* is likely to prefer Puccini's opera to the earlier work, which approaches more closely the manner and the matter of Prévost's novel.

IV

La Bohème

an opera in four acts

Dramatis personæ:

Marcello, a painter	(baritone)
Rodolfo, a poet	(tenor)
Colline, a philosopher	(bass)
Schaunard, a musician	(baritone)
Bénoit, landlord	(bass)
Mimi	(soprano)
Parpignol, a toy-seller	(tenor)
Alcindoro, a Councillor of State	(bass)
Musetta	(soprano)
Customs Officer	(bass)
Sergeant	(bass)

LIBRETTO by Giuseppe Giacosa and Luigi Illica, based on *Scènes de la vie de Bohème* by Henry Murger

TIME: about 1830

PLACE: The Latin Quarter of Paris

FIRST PERFORMED at the Teatro Regio, Turin, 1 February, 1896, with Cesira Ferrani (Mimi), Evan Gorga (Rodolfo), Camilla Pasini (Musetta), Tieste Wilmant (Marcello), Antonio Pini-Corsi (Schaunard), Michele Mazzara (Colline), conducted by Arturo Toscanini

La Bohème

I

WHILE HE WAS at work on *Manon Lescaut*, Puccini had informed his brother in South America that his next opera would be about the Buddha. He does not appear to have told this to anyone else; instead, after *Manon Lescaut* his immediate intention was to compose *La lupa* (The She-Wolf), based on a short story by Giovanni Verga, another of whose stories had formed the basis of Mascagni's *Cavalleria rusticana*. In the spring of 1894, Puccini visited Verga in Sicily in order to discuss details and to soak up the Sicilian atmosphere. While he was so far south, he took the opportunity to visit Malta. There the British authorities arrested him on suspicion of being a spy when he was seen taking photographs of the naval fortifications.

By the time he returned to Torre del Lago, Puccini was beginning to have second thoughts about Verga's story. 'Since my return from Sicily and my conversations with Verga,' he wrote to Giulio Ricordi, 'I confess that, rather than feeling inspired by *La lupa*, I am assailed by a thousand doubts which have made me decide to postpone the composition . . .' In the same letter, he says that, instead, he will plunge into *La Bohème* – about which, as we shall see, he had already been thinking – 'a corpor morto' (head over heels). In fact, on the return voyage from Sicily he had encountered the Countess Beaudine Gravina, Cosima Wagner's daughter by her first marriage to the conductor Hans von Bülow, and the Countess had expressed her revulsion at 'questo dramma di sensualità e di delitto a un episodio religioso' (this drama of sensuality and crime and with a religious procession in it). That decided Puccini against *La lupa*.

La Bohème, based on the picaresque novel, *Scènes de la vie de Bohème* by Henry Murger, is, as everyone knows, the opera which Puccini proceeded instead to compose. What no one can be certain of is how the idea first occurred to the composer. In March, 1893, shortly after his return from Turin and the première of *Manon Lescaut*, Puccini encountered in a café his fellow composer, Ruggiero Leoncavallo, who, the previous year, had achieved fame with his opera *Pagliacci*. When Puccini mentioned that he was working on an opera based on Murger's novel, to be called *La Bohème*, Leoncavallo angrily reminded the composer that he, Leoncavallo, was also at work on *La Bohème*. He had shown Puccini his libretto the previous winter, and had at that time even offered the libretto to him. He was now composing the opera, and claimed prior rights in the subject. The following day, a newspaper owned by Leoncavallo's publisher announced that Leoncavallo had been at work on *La Bohème* for some time, and the day after that the *Corriere della sera* printed a response from Puccini:

> The declaration made by Maestro Leoncavallo in *Il Secolo* yesterday must convince the public that I have acted in perfectly good faith. For it is clear that if Maestro Leoncavallo, with whom I have been linked for a long time by vivid feelings of friendship, had told me at the outset what he unexpectedly told me the other evening, I would not have thought of *La Bohème* by Murger. But now, for reasons easy to see, I am no longer willing to oblige him as I would a friend and fellow musician.
>
> For the rest, what does it matter to Maestro Leoncavallo? Let him compose, and I shall compose, and the public will judge. Success in art need not mean that one brings the same ideas to the same subject. I will only stress that for two months, that is since the first production of *Manon Lescaut* in Turin, I have been working seriously on this plan and have made no secret of it to anybody.

The tone of this is a trifle disingenuous: Puccini was highly competitive, and is quite likely to have decided to compose his *Bohème* on hearing that a rival composer was at work on the subject. No legal rights were involved, and both composers in fact raced ahead with their respective versions. The race was won by Puccini, whose opera reached the stage in Turin in February, 1896. Though Leoncavallo's *La Bohème*, produced in Venice in May of the following year, was more popular at its première than Puccini's, its success did not prove lasting.

The librettists chosen by Puccini and Ricordi for Puccini's *La Bohème* were Giuseppe Giacosa and Luigi Illica, two of the cooks who had helped to prepare the *Manon Lescaut* broth: the pair were to be responsible for the libretti of Puccini's three most popular operas, *La Bohème, Tosca* and *Madama Butterfly*. Giacosa (1847–1906), the more important of the two collaborators, was a playwright, poet and author of short stories. Several of his plays had been produced with great success, among them *Tristi Amori* (Sad Loves) in which Eleanora Duse played the leading role, *Il Trionfo d'Amore* (The Triumph of Love), and *La Dame de Challant* (The Lady of Challant), interpreted by Duse's great rival Sarah Bernhardt. Giacosa was also the editor of an influential Italian literary magazine, *La Lettura*. Illica (1857–1919) was a prolific librettist, whose original plays were less important or interesting than those of Giacosa. What Illica brought to the partnership was a certain theatrical flair, to balance Giacosa's less firmly based imaginative quality.

The *Bohème* libretto was begun while Puccini was still vacillating between *La Bohème* and *La lupa*. Illica first produced a scenario drawn from Murger's novel, and sent it to Giacosa whose task it was to turn it into verse dialogue. Illica's scenario was in five scenes, one of which (a party given for the Bohemians by Musette [Musetta] while her furniture is being removed due to her non-payment of the rent) was deleted some months later, leaving the four scenes which correspond to the four acts of *La Bohème* as we know it.

Giacosa soon became dissatisfied with his own contribution to the libretto, and complained to Ricordi that what he was doing was 'not artistic work, but minute pedantry and most wearisome'. By the autumn of 1893, he had decided to withdraw. 'For a week now', he told Ricordi,

> I have been stuck in the scene with the ear-boxing [Musetta and Marcello in Act III]. I must have rewritten it a hundred times, but I have not managed to write a single verse that pleases me . . . If Puccini were not in such a hurry . . . then perhaps I could make myself find the strength again . . . Since I despair of finishing the work in the short time allowed me . . . I take the heroic decision and withdraw from a task which, I am sure, Illica will be able to bring to its happy conclusion alone.[1]

Ricordi refused to accept Giacosa's resignation, and the task of hammering out a libretto was continued. By the following spring, Puccini had decided to drop *La lupa* and concentrate on *La Bohème*, but it was now Illica's turn to complain, and to attempt to withdraw from the project, on the grounds that his work was not sufficiently appreciated and that he felt himself 'used, cast aside, taken up again, and once more shoved away like a dog'. Again, Ricordi managed to keep the enterprise afloat, although Puccini was less inclined to placate Illica. 'If he says now that I have sent him packing', the composer wrote to his publisher,

> whose fault is it? All I wanted was that the work should be what it ought to be: logical, terse and well balanced. But at the moment it is none of these things. Must I blindly accept Illica's gospel? . . . Illica should calm down and then we shall get on with the work. But I too want to have my say, as the necessity arises, and I am not prepared to do anybody's bidding . . .[2]

Most of *La Bohème* was composed at Torre del Lago where Puccini had made a number of friends both among the village people and the small group of painters who worked in the vicinity. During the composition of the opera, the friends formed the Bohème Club, which met in an old hut to eat, drink and play cards. Puccini was the Club's honorary president, and its constitution contained these articles:

> Article 1. The members of Club la Bohème, true interpreters of the spirit in which it was founded, pledge themselves to be well and to eat better.
> Article 2. Grouches, pedants, weak stomachs, fools, grumblers and other

---

[1] Carner, op. cit.   [2] Ibid.

wretches of this kind will not be admitted but will be chased away by the members.

Article 3. The president functions as conciliator in disputes, but pledges himself to hinder the treasurer in the collection of members' subscriptions.

Article 4. The treasurer is empowered to abscond with the funds.

Article 5. The illumination of the club-room shall be by means of a paraffin lamp. Should there be a shortage of paraffin, the *moccoli* of the members will be used. [A pun: *moccoli* means both candle-ends and swear-words.]

Article 6. It is forbidden to play cards honestly.

Article 7. Silence is prohibited.

Article 8. Wisdom is not permitted, except in special cases.[1]

Throughout 1895, Puccini worked on the opera, constantly requiring minor changes to be made to the libretto. As late as November, the words for the quartet of Bohemians in the last act were still not right, but finally, one night in December, Puccini finished scoring the last act, and nearly three years of work was brought to an end. The composer years later told his biographer, Fraccaroli, that, when he had finished the opera with the scene of Mimi's death, 'I had to get up and, standing in the middle of my study, alone in the silence of the night, I began to weep like a child. It was as though I had seen my own child die.'[2]

By this time, it had been agreed that, as with *Manon Lescaut*, the première of the opera would be at the Teatro Regio, Turin, although Puccini would have preferred Naples or Rome; the date fixed was 1 February, 1896. A reasonable cast was assembled, headed by the soprano Cesira Ferrani, who had been the first Manon in the same theatre three years earlier. Puccini's suggestions for conductor had included the excellent Leopoldo Mugnone, who had conducted the première of Mascagni's *Cavalleria rusticana* in 1890, and the famous Arthur Nikisch. However, Ricordi chose the new young musical director of the Teatro Regio, who was rapidly making his name both as musician and as despot, the twenty-eight-year-old Arturo Toscanini.

Early in January, rehearsals began in Turin under Puccini's supervision. The composer thought his Mimi good, his Musetta even better, and found Toscanini 'highly intelligent and a very sweet and nice man'. He was worried about the performers of Rodolfo and Marcello. The tenor 'hasn't got such a bad voice, but I doubt whether he will last', while 'the baritone is full of good will, but a terrible actor . . . moreover his voice is coarse, and Marcello is such a gentle man'.[3] Toscanini and the orchestra were 'extraordinary'.

The success of *La Bohème* on its first night was undoubted, without being overwhelming. The wild enthusiasm with which *Manon Lescaut* had been greeted, three years earlier to the day, in the same theatre, was

[1] A. Fraccaroli: *La vita di Giacomo Puccini*, Milan, 1925.

[2] Quoted in Carner, op. cit.

[3] The quotations are from Puccini's letters to his wife, Elvira.

lacking. In Act I, Rodolfo's aria, 'Che gelida manina', was warmly applauded, and at the end of the act Puccini took three curtain calls, but it was not until the end of the opera that the audience really made its approval known. And, in the press within the next few days, the critics were in general rather cool.

Carlo Bersezio in *La Stampa* thought that Puccini had composed his music hurriedly and with very little labour of selection and polishing, and even found Mimi's death scene deficient in musical form and colour. '*La Bohème*,' he concluded, 'even as it leaves little impression on the minds of the audience, will leave no great trace upon the history of our lyric theatre, and it will be well if the composer returns to the straight road of art, persuading himself that this has been a brief deviation.'

'We ask ourselves', wrote the critic of the *Gazzetta del popolo*,

what has pushed Puccini along this deplorable road of *Bohème*. The question is a severe one, and we do not pose it without feeling a pang, we who have applauded and are still applauding *Manon*, which revealed a composer who knew how to marry orchestral mastery with an Italian feeling. Maestro, you are young and strong. You have talent, culture and imagination such as few possess. Today you have made the public applaud where and when you wanted. For this once, let us say no more about it, but in the future return to the great and difficult battles of art.

'Let us await better things from the strong endowment of this composer, when he will find a subject less exigent,' said the *Corriere della sera*.

The critic of *Fanfulla*, a Turin newspaper, swam against the tide:

I am not so fortunate as to be able to agree with my distinguished colleagues of the Turin press who have pronounced a sentence on the new Puccini opera very different from the judgement of the public. Both the critics and the public have undergone for more than a month the difficult experience of Wagnerian music,[1] and they needed all their strength in order to liberate themselves from this experience. But the public . . . was able to detach itself from Scandinavian impressions to enter into the spirit of the Parisian *Bohème* . . . and to breathe (let us say frankly) an air more agreeable to Italian lungs. The gentlemen of the press, however, completely suffused by symbols which surround them like the magic ring of fire of Valhalla, have not been able to take leave of Wotan, Siegfried, Brünnhilde, and have preferred to immerse themselves, in the company of various mythological divinities, in a vague whirlpool. They remained at the Twilight of the Gods, and they did not see and did not understand that an everyday and prosaic dawn, such a one as preludes a sad winter's day, such a one as takes place in the third act of *La Bohème*, can also lead a composer to transporting emotion. They did not

[1] Some weeks earlier in Turin, Toscanini had given the first performances in Italy of *Götterdämmerung*.

know how to leave the world of German transcendentalism in order to hear music which expresses sweet sentiments of the soul and which speaks in exquisite melodies of eternal human passions.

Between the two contestants, I will side with the public.

The public's enthusiasm for *La Bohème* increased from performance to performance, and when the opera was performed some months later in Palermo, the excitement was tremendous, the Sicilians being less under the sway of Wagner than their northern Italian cousins. Since then, *La Bohème* has been well able to fend for itself. Within three years, it had been performed in Buenos Aires, Alexandria, Moscow, Lisbon, Manchester, Berlin, Rio de Janeiro, Mexico, London, Vienna, Los Angeles, The Hague, Prague, Barcelona, Athens, New York, Paris, on Malta, in Valparaiso, Warsaw, Zagreb, Smyrna, Helsinki, St. Petersburg and Algiers – in that order. Today, there can surely be no opera house where *La Bohème* does not feature regularly in the repertoire, for it has become one of the world's most popular operas. Even the fastidious who wince at the Puccini of *Tosca* and *Butterfly* tend to feel some affection for Mimi, Rodolfo and the other Bohemians.

II

The opera is set in the Latin Quarter of Paris, around 1830. Act I takes place on Christmas Eve in the garret shared by Rodolfo, a playwright, and his friend Marcello, a painter. Their two other friends who make up the quartet of Bohemians are Colline, a philosopher, and Schaunard, a musician. Colline and Schaunard do not, as far as one can tell, actually reside in the same garret studio as Rodolfo and Marcello: they merely spend most of their time there.

When the curtain rises on the shabbily furnished attic room, with its enormous but grimy skylight window partly covered with snow, its two couches pushed against the walls, and its pathetic stove failing to give out heat, Marcello (baritone) and Rodolfo (tenor) are attempting to work. It is early evening. Marcello is having difficulty with his painting of the passage of the Israelites through the Red Sea, while Rodolfo's attempt to concentrate on a magazine article he is writing has been temporarily defeated by the cold. The two men are about to use their only remaining chair for fuel for the stove when Rodolfo suddenly has a better idea. The manuscript of his fiery drama will provide heat, he exclaims, as he consigns Act I of it to the furnace. Their philosopher friend Colline (bass) now enters, flinging on to the table a bundle of books which he has been unable to dispose of, as the pawnshops are closed on Christmas Eve. Act II of Rodolfo's play goes the way of Act I, but it fails to generate much heat, so the remaining three acts are dispatched simultaneously to the accompaniment of lighthearted banter from the Bohemians. But the fire soon gets low again. 'What a flimsy, useless drama,' Colline complains, and he and Marcello shout 'Abasso l'autor!' (Down with the author).

Their horseplay is interrupted by the arrival of the musician Schaunard (baritone), preceded by two messenger boys laden with food, wine, and a bundle of firewood. Scattering money on the floor, Schaunard explains that he had been engaged by an eccentric Englishman, Lord someone-or-other, to play for him to cover the sounds of a noisy parrot expiring in an adjacent apartment. He had played for three days, then bribed the maid to feed parsley to the parrot which obligingly choked upon it and died.

His friends are about to fall upon the food when Schaunard stops them. The food is to be stored for future use, for Christmas Eve is no time to stay at home. First, a drink, and then off to the warm and inviting cafés of the Latin Quarter. At this moment, the landlord, Benoit (bass), arrives to demand the last quarter's rent which is overdue. Benoit is plied with drink, encouraged to admit that he was seen recently in a café with a girl half his age, and then denounced as a lecher and thrown out of the garret. The friends now decide to go off to the Café Momus. Rodolfo says he will follow shortly, for he must first finish his article. Marcello, Colline and Schaunard make their way noisily down to the street, and Rodolfo sits at the table to write.

After a few moments in which the words refuse to come, he decides to give up. There is a knock at the door, and Rodolfo opens it to discover a young woman, Mimi (soprano). Her candle has gone out on the dark staircase, and she begs a light. Rodolfo invites her in, and, when Mimi coughs as she enters, he asks if she is ill. She swoons, and he catches her and seats her in the chair. A glass of wine helps to revive her, Rodolfo relights her candle, and she is about to go when she discovers she has dropped her key. Her candle blows out again in the draught, and Rodolfo takes the opportunity surreptitiously to blow out his own candle. By the light of the moon which shines through the skylight, they search for Mimi's key. As they do so, Rodolfo tells Mimi who he is, how he lives, and how attractive he finds her. In return, she tells him her name and describes her own life: she does embroidery for a living, she is a neighbour of his, and she lives alone.

The voices of his three friends are heard from the courtyard, calling on Rodolfo to hurry. He calls back to them that they should go on to the Café Momus and save two places. Turning around, he sees Mimi framed in the moonlight. They sing a duet in which they confess their love for each other, and then slowly make their way downstairs.

Act II takes place a few minutes later, outside the Café Momus, under whose awnings are a number of tables, most of them occupied. A crowd mills about in the street, street vendors ply their wares, an air of festivity prevails. Schaunard is haggling with a tinker over the price of a pipe and a horn, Colline negotiates the purchase of a cloak from a second-hand shop, Marcello strolls about in the crowd, and Mimi and Rodolfo enter a milliner's shop. When they emerge, Mimi is wearing a new bonnet which Rodolfo has bought her. She is introduced to his friends, and they all sit at one of the café tables and order supper. Children cluster around Parpignol, the toy-seller, as he makes his way through the crowd.

Musetta (soprano) now appears with an elderly admirer, Alcindoro (bass), a pompous Councillor of State. Catching sight of her ex-lover, Marcello, Musetta chooses a table next to the party of Bohemians, and does all she can to attract Marcello's attention without arousing Alcindoro's suspicions. Marcello tries to ignore her, but he is still as much in love with Musetta as she is with him. Claiming that her shoe is hurting her, Musetta sends Alcindoro off with it to find a cobbler. During his absence, she and Marcello embrace passionately, and Alcindoro returns to find that Musetta has departed with Mimi and the four men, leaving him to pay the bill for all of them.

Act III takes place several weeks later. It is dawn on a cold February morning, at a toll gate at the Barrière d'Enfer, the gate leading out of Paris, by the rue d'Enfer, in the direction of Orléans. To the left of the gate is a tavern, the Port of Marseilles, whose inn sign is Marcello's Red Sea painting. A few customs guards are seated before a brazier. There is snow on the ground. From the tavern can be heard occasional sounds of music and laughter.

A customs officer opens the gate to admit a group of street sweepers, followed by peasants with their carts. Mimi enters, and asks one of the customs officers to direct her to the tavern where a painter is working. She is directed to the Port of Marseilles, where Marcello has been at work transforming his painting into the inn sign, and painting a number of pictures for the walls. Marcello is called for, and emerges from the inn, where he and Musetta have been living for the past month, he painting and she giving singing lessons.

Mimi tells Marcello that she and Rodolfo have quarrelled because of his insane jealousy, and that they cannot continue to live together. She asks Marcello to help and advise them. Marcello tells her that Rodolfo is, at that moment, inside the inn. Mimi, coughing heavily, retreats to a copse of trees to hide as Rodolfo comes out of the inn. She overhears Rodolfo telling Marcello that he wants to separate from her. He accuses Mimi of flirting with other men, but he is also aware that her constant fits of coughing are a sign of consumption, and that she cannot have long to live.

The two men are made aware, by the sound of sobbing and coughing, that Mimi is near by and has heard their conversation. Rodolfo attempts to comfort her, but finally he and Mimi agree to part when the spring comes. Meanwhile, Marcello and Musetta have been carrying on one of their vituperative arguments, and both couples say farewell to each other, Marcello and Musetta angrily, Rodolfo and Mimi regretfully.

The last act takes place in the garret shared by Rodolfo and Marcello. Both are trying to work, though each is thinking of his lost love. Rodolfo has encountered Musetta driving a fine carriage, and Marcello says he has seen Mimi, also in a rich carriage, dressed like a queen. Schaunard and Colline enter with food and drink, and all four attempt to forget their poverty and their unsatisfactory love affairs by indulging in their usual high-spirited horseplay. At the height of their frivolity, Musetta suddenly enters with the news that Mimi has left the Viscount who was keeping her, is dangerously ill, and is waiting outside the door. She fears she is dying and wants to spend her last hours with Rodolfo.

Mimi, in a state of collapse, is brought in and placed on the couch. Her hands are cold, and she asks for a muff. Musetta gives her earrings to Marcello to sell, to get money to buy medicine, Colline donates his old cloak, and Musetta leaves to collect her muff. Left alone with Mimi, Rodolfo comforts her, and they recall the happier days of their love. Musetta returns with the muff, and the others with medicine, but while Rodolfo is placing Musetta's cloak over the window to keep the sun out, Schaunard notices that Mimi has already died. Reading the truth from the silence and the faces of his friends, Rodolfo rushes to Mimi and falls in tears over her body.

Henry Murger,[1] author of *Scènes de la vie de Bohème* (Scenes from Bohemian Life) from which the libretto of *La Bohème* derives, was born in Paris in 1822, the son of a man who exercised the joint calling of tailor and door keeper. Murger's literary career was launched when, at the age of nineteen, he began to write and publish essays in the literary journals. For a time he edited fashion magazines, the *Moniteur de la mode* and *Castor*, an organ of the hat trade. In 1844, Murger joined the staff of a magazine called *Le Corsaire*, in which he began to publish in instalments his *Scènes de la vie de Bohème*, the *Pickwick Papers* of French Romanticism. The *Scènes* were lightly disguised autobiography, and the amusing and ironic picture they presented of life among the artists and writers was something new in the literature of the time. When, in 1851, the *Scènes* were published in book form, as a picaresque novel, the edition quickly sold 70,000 copies.

At this time, Murger was living in an attic in the Latin Quarter, in circumstances resembling those of Rodolphe in his novel. When he was

---

[1] One encounters various forms of the author's name. His works were published in French as by Henry Murger. His name was originally Henri Murger, but at the suggestion of an editor he adopted the English spelling, Henry. Later, Murger added an umlaut to his surname (Mürger), thinking that this would facilitate the correct pronunciation of his name abroad. Presumably, it encouraged the Germans to mispronounce it.

visited by Théodore Barrière, a young playwright who wished to adapt *Scènes de la vie de Bohème* for the stage, Murger was forced to receive his visitor in bed, for he had loaned his only pair of trousers to a friend to wear to be interviewed for a job. *La vie de Bohème*, the play based on Murger's book, was in due course staged in Paris, and met with so phenomenal a success that Murger was able to move from the Latin Quarter and its cheap lodgings, and live the life of a successful man of letters. He died after a sudden illness in 1861, at the early age of thirty-nine.

Murger's principal characters are all based on real people, Rodolphe (Rodolfo in the opera) being Murger himself. In the *Scènes* he is described as 'un jeune homme dont la figure se perdrait au fond d'un énorme buisson de barbe multicolore. Comme une antithèse à cette abondance de *poil mentonnier*, une calvitie précose avait dégarni son front, qui ressemblait à un genou' (a young man whose face was hidden by a dense thicket of beard of several distinct shades. By way of a balance to this wealth of hair on his chin, a precocious baldness had despoiled his forehead, which was as bald as a knee).

The painter, Marcel (Marcello) is a composite of the writer Champfleury, with whom Murger once shared lodgings, and two painters, Lazare and Tabar. It was Tabar who began a large painting, *The Passage of the Red Sea*, which ended up as *Niobe and her children slain by the arrows of Apollo and Diana*, when Tabar found the cost of models and costumes prohibitive. Colline, the philosopher, was based on Jean Wallon, a student of theology whose ecclesiastically styled coat was invariably stuffed with books at the four cardinal points, each pocket being given the name of a different public library. A subsidiary model for the character of Colline was one Trapadoux who was given to wearing a tall hat and a long green coat, which earned him the nickname of 'the Green Giant'. Schaunard is Alexandre Schanne who gave up painting for music, and composed (as does Schaunard in the novel) a symphony 'on the influence of blue in art'. Murger lightly disguised his name as Schannard, which a printer's error turned into Schaunard.

Mimi is a composite character whose chief model was a girl named Lucile – 'Mi chiamano Mimi, ma il mio nome è Lucia' (they call me Mimi, but my name is Lucia), Puccini's heroine sings in Act I. Lucile was apparently a pale, sickly creature, and even more amoral than as described by Murger. Murger's Mimi is twenty-two, small, delicate and arch in manner, with clear blue eyes which wear, at certain moments of weariness or ill-humour, 'un caractère de brutalité presque fauve, où un physiologiste aurait peut-être reconnu l'indice d'un profond égoïsme ou d'une grande insensibilité' (an expression of almost savage brutality, in which a physiologist would perhaps have recognized the indication of profound egotism or great insensibility). Murger leaves his readers in no doubt that Mimi had the instincts of a mercenary little tart and that her attachment to Rodolphe was intermittent and lukewarm.

The original of Musette was Mariette, a model very popular with the painters and sculptors of Montparnasse. She was a woman very careful with her money; after amassing, from modelling and related pursuits, a sum large enough to retire on, she resolved to live with her sister in Algiers, embarked at Marseilles, and was drowned when the boat sank somewhere in the Mediterranean. Murger's Musette was 'une jolie fille de vingt ans, qui, peu de temps après son arrivée à Paris, était devenue ce que deviennent les jolies filles quand elles ont la taille fine, beaucoup de coquetterie, un peu d'ambition et guère d'orthographe' (a pretty girl of twenty who shortly after her arrival in Paris had become what many pretty girls become when they have a neat figure, plenty of coquettishness, a dash of ambition and hardly any education).

The Café Momus, frequented by the Bohemians, was a real establishment of that name. Schanne (Schaunard) left a description of it in the memoirs which he published in 1887, a few months before his death:

The Café Momus was located at No. 15 in the silent and gloomy Rue des Prêtres Saint-Germain-l'Auxerrois. The house still stands but now shelters other industries. Murger and his friends preferred the upstairs room where smoking was allowed. There they were to some extent private and free from intrusion, the master of the establishment seeing to this . . . The almost daily frequenters of the Café Momus were, besides Murger and his group of intimates, Champfleury, already known to the reading public, André Thomas the romance writer, Monselet, fresh-looking and plump as an abbé of the last century, Jean Journet the chemist of Carcassonne . . . the strange but captivating Baudelaire, author of the *Fleurs du mal* . . . Gérard de Nerval, who related to us his travels in the East prior to writing them . . .[1]

Murger's Preface to the first edition of *Scènes de la vie de Bohème* is a fascinating description of the Bohemian life. Its final paragraphs are reproduced here:

The Bohemians know everything and go everywhere, according as they have patent leather pumps or burst boots. They are to be met one day leaning against the mantel-shelf in a fashionable drawing room, and the next seated in the arbour of some suburban dancing place. They cannot take ten steps on the Boulevard without meeting a friend, and thirty, no matter where, without encountering a creditor.

Bohemians speak amongst themselves a special language borrowed from the conversation of the studios, the jargon of behind the scenes, and the discussions of the editor's room. All the eclecticisms of style are met with in this unheard-of idiom, in which apocalyptic phrases jostle cock-and-bull stories, in which the rusticity of a popular saying is wedded to extravagant periods

[1] Alexandre Schanne, *Souvenirs de Schaunard* (Paris, 1887).

from the same mould in which Cyrano de Bergerac cast his tirades; in which the paradox, that spoilt child of modern literature, treats reason as the pantaloon is treated in a pantomime; in which irony has the intensity of the strongest acids and the skill of those marksmen who can hit the bull's-eye blindfold; a slang intelligent, though unintelligible to those who have not its key, and the audacity of which surpasses that of the freest tongues. This Bohemian vocabulary is the hell of rhetoric and the paradise of neologism.

Such is in brief that Bohemian life, badly known to the puritans of society, decried by the puritans of art, insulted by all the timorous and jealous mediocrities who cannot find enough of outcries, lies, and calumnies to drown the voices and the names of those who arrive through the vestibule to renown by harnessing audacity to their talent.

A life of patience, of courage, in which one cannot fight unless clad in a strong armour of indifference impervious to the attacks of fools and the envious, in which one must not, if one would not stumble on the road, quit for a single moment that pride in oneself which serves as a leaning staff; a charming and a terrible life, which has its conquerors and its martyrs, and on which one should not enter save in resigning oneself in advance to submit to the pitiless law *væ victis*.

Puccini's opera is based both on Murger's novel and on the five-act play adapted from it, the composer and his librettists having decided to concentrate on the Rodolphe–Mimi relationship (as did Barrière in shaping a play from the rambling, plotless novel), retaining Marcel and Musette as subsidiary characters and reducing the other Bohemians, Schaunard and Colline, to the status of mere providers of background. Giacosa and Illica, as they stated in a preface to their libretto, took pains to ensure that the essential spirit of Murger's novel was retained, and what the four acts of *La Bohème* lack in dramatic thrust they make up for in period atmosphere and naïve charm. The libretto contrives to be faithful to Murger in spirit even when it has to compress and alter details from the novel, as for instance in the opera's cleverly constructed final act containing Mimi's death scene (so much more moving because less drawn out and less melodramatic than that of Manon in Puccini's previous opera). The act is based on the following excerpt from *Scènes de la vie de Bohème* (note, on p. 97, Marcel's sensible comments on Manon and the Chevalier des Grieux):

It was the 24th of December, and that evening the Latin Quarter bore a special aspect. Since four o'clock in the afternoon the pawnbroking establishments and the shops of the second-hand clothes dealers and booksellers had been encumbered by a noisy crowd, who, later in the evening, took the ham and beef shops, cook shops, and grocers by assault. The shopmen, even if they had had a hundred arms, like Briareus, would not have sufficed to serve the customers who struggled with one another for provisions. At the baker's they formed a string as in times of dearth. The wine-shop keepers got rid of the produce of three vintages, and a clever statistician would have found it difficult to reckon up the number of knuckles of ham and of sausages which were sold at the famous shop of Borel, in the Rue Dauphine. In this one evening Daddy Cretaine, nicknamed Petit-Pain, exhausted eighteen editions of his cakes. All night long sounds of rejoicing broke out from the lodging houses, the windows of which were brilliantly lit up, and an atmosphere of revelry filled the district.

The old festival of Christmas Eve was being celebrated.

That evening, towards ten o'clock, Marcel and Rodolphe were proceeding homeward somewhat sadly. Passing up the Rue Dauphine they noticed a great crowd in the shop of a provision dealer, and halted a moment before the window. Tantalized by the sight of the toothsome gastronomic products, the two Bohemians resembled, during this contemplation, that person in a Spanish romance who caused hams to shrink only by looking at them.

'That is called a truffled turkey,' said Marcel, pointing to a splendid bird, showing through its rosy and transparent skin the Perigordian tubercles with which it was stuffed. 'I have seen impious folk eat it without first going down on their knees before it,' added the painter, casting upon the turkey looks capable of roasting it.

'And what do you think of that modest leg of salt marsh mutton?' asked Rodolphe. 'What fine colouring! One might think it was just unhooked from that butcher's shop in one of Jordaen's pictures. Such a leg of mutton is the favourite dish of the gods, and of my grandmother, Madame Chandelier.'

'Look at those fish!' resumed Marcel, pointing to some trout; 'they are the most expert swimmers of the aquatic race. Those little creatures, without any appearance of pretension, could, however, make a fortune by the exhibition of their skill; fancy, they can swim up a perpendicular waterfall as easily as we should accept an invitation to supper. I have almost had a chance of tasting them.'

'And down there – those large golden fruit, the foliage of which resembles a trophy of savage sabre blades! They are called pineapples, and are the pippins of the tropics.'

'That is a matter of indifference to me,' said Marcel. 'So far as fruits are concerned, I prefer that piece of beef, that ham, or that simple gammon of bacon, cuirassed with jelly as transparent as amber.'

'You are right,' replied Rodolphe; 'ham is the friend of man, when he has one. However, I would not repulse that pheasant.'

'I should think not; it is the dish of crowned heads.'

And as, continuing on their way, they met joyful processions proceeding homewards, to do honour to Momus, Bacchus, Comus, and all the other divinities with names ending in '-us', they asked themselves who was the Gamacho whose wedding was being celebrated with such a profusion of victuals.

Marcel was the first who recollected the date and its festival.

'It is Christmas Eve,' said he.

'Do you remember last year's?' inquired Rodolphe.

'Yes,' replied Marcel; 'at Momus's. It was Barbemuche who stood treat. I should never have thought that a delicate girl like Phémie could have held so much sausage.'

'What a pity that Momus has cut off our credit,' said Rodolphe.

'Alas,' said Marcel; 'calendars succeed but do not resemble one another.'

'Would you not like to keep Christmas Eve?' asked Rodolphe.

'With whom and with what?' inquired the painter.

'With me.'

'And the coin?'

'Wait a moment,' said Rodolphe; 'I will go into this café, where I know some people who play high. I will borrow a few sesterces from some favourite of fortune, and I will get something to wash down a sardine or a pig's trotter.'

'Go,' said Marcel; 'I am as hungry as a dog. I will wait for you here.'

Rodolphe went into the café where he knew several people. A gentleman who had just won three hundred francs at cards, made a regular treat of lending the poet a forty sous piece, which he handed over with that ill-humour caused by the fever of play. At another time and elsewhere than at a card table, he would very likely have been good for forty francs.

'Well?' inquired Marcel, on seeing Rodolphe return.

'Here are the takings,' said the poet, showing the money.

'A bite and a sup,' said Marcel.

With this small sum they were however able to obtain bread, wine, cold meat, tobacco, fire, and light.

They returned to the lodging-house in which each had a separate room. Marcel's which also served him as a studio, being the larger, was chosen as the banqueting hall, and the two friends set about the preparations for their feast there.

But to the little table at which they were seated, beside a fireplace in which the damp logs burned away without flame or heat, came a melancholy guest, the phantom of the vanished past.

They remained for an hour at least, silent, and thoughtful, both no doubt preoccupied by the same idea and striving to hide it. It was Marcel who first broke silence.

'Come,' said he to Rodolphe; 'this is not what we promised ourselves.'

'What do you mean?' said Rodolphe.

'Oh!' replied Marcel. 'Do not try to pretend with me now. You are thinking of that which should be forgotten and I too, by jove, I do not deny it.'

'Well?'

'Well, it must be for the last time. To the devil with recollections that make wine taste sour and render us miserable when everybody else are amusing themselves,' exclaimed Marcel, alluding to the joyful shouts coming from the rooms adjoining theirs. 'Come, let us think of something else, and let this be the last time.'

'That is what we always say and yet – ,' said Rodolphe, falling anew into a reverie.

'And yet we are continually going back to it,' resumed Marcel. 'That is because instead of frankly seeking to forget, we make the most trivial things a pretext to recall remembrances, which is due above all to the fact that we persist in living amidst the same surroundings in which the beings who have so long been our torment lived. We are less the slaves of passion than of habit. It is this captivity that must be escaped from, or we shall wear ourselves out in a ridiculous and shameful slavery. Well, the past is past, we must break the ties that still bind us to it. The hour has come to go forward without looking backward; we have had our share of youth, carelessness, and paradox. All these are very fine – a very pretty novel could be written on them; but this comedy of amorous follies, this loss of time, of days wasted with the prodigality of people who believe they have an eternity to spend – all this must have an end. It is no longer possible for us to continue to live much longer on the outskirts of society – on the outskirts of life almost – under penalty of justifying the contempt felt for us, and of despising ourselves. For, after all, is it a life we lead? And are not the independence, the freedom of manners, of which we boast so loudly, very mediocre advantages? True liberty consists in being able to dispense with the aid of others, and to exist by oneself, and have we got to that? No, the first scoundrel, whose name we would not bear for five minutes, avenges himself for our jests, and becomes our lord and master the day on which we borrow of him five francs, which he lends us after having made us dispense the worth of a hundred and fifty in ruses or in humiliations. For my part, I have had enough of it. Poetry does not alone exist in disorderly living, touch-and-go happiness, loves that last as long as a bedroom candle, more or less eccentric revolts against those prejudices which will eternally rule the world, for it is easier to upset a dynasty than a custom, however ridiculous it may be. It is not enough to wear a summer coat in December to have talent; one can be a real poet or artist while going about well shod and eating three meals a day. Whatever one may say, and whatever one may do, if one wants to attain anything one must always take the commonplace way. This speech may astonish you, friend Rodolphe; you will say that I am breaking my idols, you will call me corrupted; and yet what I tell you is the expression of my sincere wishes. Despite myself, a slow and salutary metamorphosis has taken place within me; reason has entered my mind – burglariously, if you like, and perhaps against my will, but it has got in at last – and has proved to me that I was on a wrong track, and that it would be at once ridiculous and dangerous to persevere in it. Indeed, what will happen if we continue this monotonous and idle vagabondage? We shall get to thirty, unknown, isolated, disgusted with all things and with ourselves, full of envy towards all those whom we see reach their goal, whatever it may be, and obliged, in order to live, to have recourse to shameful parasitism. Do not imagine that this is a fancy picture I have conjured up especially to frighten you. The future does not systematically appear to me all black, but neither does it all rose-coloured; I see it clearly as it is. Up till now the life we have led has been forced upon us – we had the excuse of necessity. Now we are no longer to be excused, and if we do not re-enter the world, it will be voluntarily, for the obstacles against which we have had to struggle no longer exist.'

'I say,' said Rodolphe, 'what are you driving at? Why and wherefore this lecture?'

'You thoroughly understand me,' replied Marcel, in the same serious tones. 'Just now I saw you, like myself, assailed by recollections that made you regret the past. You were thinking of Mimi as I was thinking of Musette. Like me, you would have liked to have had your mistress beside you. Well, I tell you that we ought neither of us to think of these creatures; that we were not created and sent into the world solely to sacrifice our existence to these commonplace Manon Lescauts, and that the Chevalier Des Grieux, who is so fine, so true, and so poetical, is only saved from being ridiculous by his youth and the illusions he cherishes. At twenty he can follow his mistress to America without ceasing to be interesting, but at twenty-five he would have shown Manon the door, and would have been right. It is all very well to talk; we are old, my dear fellow; we have lived too fast, our hearts are cracked, and no longer ring truly; one cannot be in love with a Musette or a Mimi for three years with impunity. For me it is all over, and I wish to be thoroughly divorced from her remembrance. I am now going to commit to the flames some trifles that she has left me during her various stays, and which oblige me to think of her when I come across them.'

And Marcel, who had risen, went and took from a drawer a little cardboard box in which were the souvenirs of Musette – a faded bouquet, a sash, a bit of ribbon, and some letters.

'Come,' said he to the poet, 'follow my example, Rodolphe.'

'Very well, then,' said the latter, making an effort; 'you are right. I too will make an end of it with that girl with the white hands.'

And, rising suddenly, he went and fetched a small packet containing souvenirs of Mimi of much the same kind as those of which Marcel was silently making an inventory.

'This comes in handy,' murmured the painter. 'This trumpery will help us to rekindle the fire which is going out.'

Indeed,' said Rodolphe, 'it is cold enough here to hatch polar bears.'

'Come,' said Marcel, 'let us burn in a duet. There goes Musette's prose; it burns like punch. She was very fond of punch. Come, Rodolphe, attention!'

And for some minutes they alternately emptied into the fire, which blazed clear and noisily, the reliquaries of their past love.

'Poor Musette!' murmured Marcel to himself, looking at the last object remaining in his hands.

It was a little faded bouquet of wildflowers.

'Poor Musette, she was very pretty though, and she loved me dearly, is it not so, little bouquet? Her heart told you so the day she wore you at her waist. Poor little bouquet, you seem to be pleading for mercy; well, yes; but on one condition; it is that you will never speak to me of her any more, never! Never!'

And profiting by a moment when he thought himself unnoticed by Rodolphe, he slipped the bouquet into his breast pocket.

'So much the worse, it is stronger than I am. I am cheating,' thought the painter.

And as he cast a furtive glance towards Rodolphe, he saw the poet, who had come to the end of his auto-da-fé, putting quietly into his own pocket, after having tenderly kissed it, a little nightcap that had belonged to Mimi.

'Come,' muttered Marcel, 'he is as great a coward as I am.'

At the very moment that Rodolphe was about to return to his room to go to bed, there were two little taps at Marcel's door.

'Who the deuce can it be at this time of night?' said the painter, going to open it.

A cry of astonishment burst from him when he had done so.

It was Mimi.

As the room was very dark Rodolphe did not at first recognize his mistress, and only distinguishing a woman, he thought that it was some passing conquest of his friend's, and out of discretion prepared to withdraw.

'I am disturbing you,' said Mimi, who had remained on the threshold.

At her voice Rodolphe dropped on his chair as though thunderstruck.

'Good evening,' said Mimi, coming up to him and shaking him by the hand which he allowed her to take mechanically.

'What the deuce brings you here and at this time of night?' asked Marcel.

'I was very cold,' said Mimi, shivering; 'I saw the light in your room as I was passing along the street, and although it was very late I came up.'

She was still shivering, her voice had a crystalline sonority that pierced Rodolphe's heart like a funeral knell, and filled it with a mournful alarm. He looked at her more attentively. It was no longer Mimi, but her ghost.

Marcel made her sit down beside the fire.

Mimi smiled at the sight of the flame dancing merrily on the hearth.

'It is very nice,' said she, holding out her hands blue with cold. 'By the way, Monsieur Marcel, you do not know why I have called on you?'

'No; indeed.'

'Well,' said Mimi, 'I simply came to ask you whether you could get them to let me a room here. I have just been turned out of my lodgings because I owe a month's rent and I do not know where to go.'

'The deuce!' said Marcel, shaking his head. 'We are not in very good odour with our landlord and our recommendation would be a most unfortunate one, my poor girl.'

'What is to be done then?' said Mimi. 'The fact is I have nowhere to go to.'

'Ah!' said Marcel. 'You are no longer a viscountess, then?'

'Good heavens, no! Not at all.'

'But since when?'

'Two months ago, already.'

'Have you been playing tricks on the viscount, then?'

'No,' said she, glancing aside at Rodolphe, who had taken his place in the darkest corner of the room. 'The viscount kicked up a row with me on account of some verses that were written about me. We quarrelled, and I sent him about his business; he is a nice skin-flint, I can tell you.'

'But,' said Marcel, 'he had rigged you out very finely, judging by what I saw the day I met you.'

'Well,' said Mimi, 'would you believe it, that he took everything away from me when I left him, and I have since heard that he raffled all my clothes at a wretched table d'hôte where he used to take me to dine. He is wealthy enough, though, and yet with all his fortune he is as miserly as a clay fire-ball and as stupid as an owl. He would not allow me to drink wine without water, and made me fast on Fridays. Would you believe it, he wanted me to wear black stockings, because they did not want washing so often as white ones. You have no idea of it, he worried me nicely I can tell you. I can well say that I did my share of purgatory with him.'

'And does he know of your present situation?' asked Marcel.

'I have not seen him since and I do not want to,' replied Mimi. 'It makes me sick when I think of him; I would rather die of hunger than ask him for a sou.'

'But,' said Marcel, 'since you left him you have not been living alone.'

'Yes, I assure you, Monsieur Marcel,' exclaimed Mimi quickly; 'I have been working to earn my living, only as artificial flower making was not a very flourishing business I took up another. I sit to painters. If you have any jobs to give me,' she added, gaily.

And having noticed a movement on the part of Rodolphe, whom she did not take her eyes off whilst talking to his friend, Mimi went on:

'Ah! but I only sit for the head and hands. I have plenty to do, and I am owed money by two or three, I shall have some in a couple of days, it is only for that interval that I want to find a lodging. When I get the money I shall go back to my own. Ah!' said she, looking at the table, which was still laden with the preparation for the modest feast which the two friends had scarcely touched. 'You were going to have supper?'

'No,' said Marcel, 'we are not hungry.'

'You are very lucky,' said Mimi, simply.

At this remark Rodolphe felt a horrible pang in his heart. He made a sign to Marcel, which the latter understood.

'By the way,' said the artist, 'since you are here, Mimi, you must take pot-luck with us. We were going to keep Christmas Eve, and then – why – we began to think of other things.'

'Then I have come at the right moment,' said Mimi, casting an almost famished glance at the food on the table. 'I have had no dinner,' she whispered to the artist, so as not to be heard by Rodolphe, who was gnawing his handkerchief to keep him from bursting into sobs.

'Draw up, Rodophe,' said Marcel to his friend. 'We will all three have supper together.'

'No,' said the poet, remaining in his corner.

'Are you angry, Rodolphe, that I have come here?' asked Mimi gently. 'Where could I go to?'

'No, Mimi,' replied Rodolphe. 'Only I am grieved to see you like this.'

'It is all my own fault, Rodolphe, I do not complain, what is done, is done, so think no more about it than I do. Cannot you still be my friend, because you have been something else? You can, can you not? Well then, do not frown on me, and come and sit down at the table with us.'

She rose to take him by the hand, but was so weak that she could not take a step, and sank back into her chair.

'The heat has dazed me,' she said. 'I cannot stand.'

'Come,' said Marcel to Rodolphe, 'come and join us.'

The poet drew up to the table, and began to eat with them. Mimi was very lively.

'My dear girl, it is impossible for us to get you a room in the house.'

'I must go away then,' said she, trying to rise.

'No, no,' said Marcel. 'I have another way of arranging things, you can stay in my room, and I will go and sleep with Rodolphe.'

'It will put you out very much, I am afraid,' said Mimi, 'but it will not be for long, only a couple of days.'

'It will not put us out at all in that case,' replied Marcel. 'So it is understood, you are at home here, and we are going to Rodolphe's room. Good night, Mimi, sleep well.'

'Thanks,' said she, holding out her hand to Marcel and Rodolphe, who moved away together.

'Do you want to lock yourself in?' asked Marcel as he got to the door.

'Why?' said Mimi, looking at Rodolphe, 'I am not afraid.'

When the two friends were alone in Rodolphe's room, which was on the same floor, Marcel abruptly said to his friend:

'Well, what are you going to do now?'

'I do not know,' stammered Rodolphe.

'Come, do not shilly-shally, go and join Mimi! If you do, I prophesy that tomorrow you will be living together again.'

'If it were Musette who had returned, what would you do?' inquired Rodolphe of his friend.

'If it were Musette that was in the next room,' replied Marcel, 'well, frankly, I believe that I should not have been in this one for a quarter of an hour past.'

'Well,' said Rodolphe, 'I will be more courageous than you, I shall stay here.'

'We shall see that,' said Marcel, who had already got into bed. 'Are you coming to bed?'

'Certainly,' replied Rodolphe.

But in the middle of the night, Marcel, waking up, perceived that Rodolphe had left him.

In the morning, he went and tapped discreetly at the door of the room in which Mimi was.

'Come in,' said she, and on seeing him, she made a sign to him to speak low in order not to wake Rodolphe who was asleep. He was seated in an armchair, which he had drawn up to the side of the bed, his head resting on the pillow beside that of Mimi.

'It is like that that you passed the night?' said Marcel in great astonishment.

'Yes,' replied the girl.

Rodolphe woke up all at once, and after kissing Mimi, held out his hand to Marcel, who seemed greatly puzzled.

'I am going to find some money for breakfast,' said he to the painter. 'You will keep Mimi company.'

'Well,' asked Marcel of the girl when they were alone together, 'what took place last night?'

'Very sad things,' said Mimi. 'Rodolphe still loves me.'

'I know that very well.'

'Yes, you wanted to separate him from me. I am not angry about it, Marcel, you were quite right, I have done no good to the poor fellow.'

'And you,' asked Marcel, 'do you still love him?'

'Do I love him?' said she, clasping her hands. 'It is that that tortures me. I am greatly changed, my friend, and it needed but little time for that.'

'Well, now he loves you, you love him and you cannot do without one another, come together again and try and remain.'

'It is impossible,' said Mimi.

'Why?' inquired Marcel. 'Certainly it would be more sensible for you to separate, but as for your not meeting again, you would have to be a thousand leagues from one another.'

'In a little while I shall be further off than that.'

'What do you mean?'

'Do not speak of it to Rodolphe, it would cause him too much pain, but I am going away for ever.'

'But whither?'

'Look here, Marcel,' said Mimi, sobbing, 'look.'

And lifting up the sheet of the bed a little she showed the artist her shoulders, neck and arms.

'Good heavens!' exclaimed Marcel mournfully. 'Poor girl.'

'Is it not true, my friend, that I do not deceive myself and that I am soon going to die?'

'But how did you get into such a state in so short a time?'

'Ah!' replied Mimi. 'With the life I have been leading for the past two months it is not astonishing; nights spent in tears, days passed in posing in studios without any fire, poor living, grief, and then you do not know all, I tried to poison myself with Eau de Javelle. I was saved but not for long as you see. Besides I have never been very strong, in short it is my fault, if I had remained quietly with Rodolphe I should not be like this. Poor fellow, here I am again upon his hands, but it will not be for long, the last dress he will give me will be all white, Marcel, and I shall be buried in it. Ah! if you knew how I suffer because I am going to die. Rodolphe knows that I am ill, he remained for over an hour without speaking last night when he saw my arms and shoulders so thin. He no longer recognized his Mimi. Alas! my very looking-glass does not know me. Ah! all the same I was pretty and he did love me. Oh, God!' she exclaimed, burying her face in Marcel's hands. 'I am going to leave you and Rodolphe too, oh, God!' and sobs choked her voice.

'Come, Mimi,' said Marcel. 'Never despair, you will get well, you only want care and rest.'

'Ah! no,' said Mimi. 'It is all over, I feel it. I have no longer any strength, and when I came here last night it took me over an hour to get up the stairs. If I had found a woman here I should have gone down again by way of the window. However, he was free since we were no longer together, but you see, Marcel, I was sure he loved me still. It was on account of that,' she said, bursting in to tears, 'it is on account of that that I do not want to die at once, but it is all over with me. He must be very good, poor fellow, to take me back after all the pain I have given him. Ah! God is not just since he does not leave me only the time to make Rodolphe forget the grief I caused him. He does not know the state in which I am. I would not have him lie beside me, for I feel as if the earthworms were already devouring my body. We passed the night in weeping and talking of old times. Ah! how sad it is, my friend, to see behind one the happiness one has formerly passed by without noticing it. I feel as if I had fire in my chest, and when I move my limbs it seems as if they were going to snap. Hand me my dress, I want to cut the cards to see whether Rodolphe will bring in any money. I should like to have a good breakfast with you, like we used to; that would not hurt me. God cannot make me worse than I am. See,' she added, showing Marcel the pack of cards she had cut. 'Spades. It is the colour of death. Clubs,' she added more gaily. 'Yes, we shall have some money.'

Marcel did not know what to say in presence of the lucid delirium of this poor creature, who already felt, as she said, the worms of the grave.

In an hour's time Rodolphe was back. He was accompanied by Schaunard and Gustave Colline. The musician wore a summer jacket. He had sold his winter suit to lend money to Rodolphe on learning that Mimi was ill. Colline on his side had gone and sold some books. If he could have got anyone to buy one of his arms or legs he would have agreed to the bargain rather than part with his cherished volumes. But Schaunard had pointed out to him that nothing could be done with his arms or his legs.

Mimi strove to recover her gaiety to greet her old friends.

'I am no longer naughty,' said she to them, 'and Rodolphe has forgiven me. If he will keep me with him I will wear wooden shoes and a mob cap, it is the same with me. Silk is certainly not good for my health,' she added with a frightful smile.

At Marcel's suggestion, Rodolphe had sent for one of his friends who had just passed as a doctor. It was the same who had formerly attended Francine. When he came they left him alone with Mimi.

Rodolphe, informed by Marcel, was already aware of the danger run by his mistress. When the doctor had spoken to Mimi, he said to Rodolphe,

'You cannot keep her here. Save for a miracle she is doomed. You must send her to the hospital. I will give you a letter for La Pitié. I know one of the house surgeons there; she will be well looked after. If she lasts till the spring we may perhaps pull her through, but if she stays here she will be dead in a week.'

'I shall never dare propose it to her,' said Rodolphe.

'I spoke to her about it,' replied the doctor, 'and she agreed. Tomorrow I will send you the order of admission to La Pitié.'

'My dear,' said Mimi to Rodolphe, 'the doctor is right; you cannot nurse me here. At the hospital they may perhaps cure me, you must send me there. Ah! you see I do so long to live now, that I would be willing to end my days with one hand in a raging fire and the other in yours. Besides, you will come and see me. You must not grieve, I shall be well taken care of: the doctor told me so. You get chicken at the hospital and they have fires there. Whilst I am taking care of myself there, you will work to earn money, and when I am cured I will come back and live with you. I have plenty of hope now. I shall come back as pretty as I used to be. I was very ill in the days before I knew you, and I was cured. Yet I was not happy in those days, I might just as well have died. Now that I have found you again and that we can be happy, they will cure me again, for I shall fight hard against my illness. I will drink all the nasty things they give me, and if death seizes on me it will be by force. Give me the looking-glass: it seems to me that I have a little colour in my cheeks. Yes,' said she, looking at herself in the glass, 'my colour is coming back, and my hands, see, they are still pretty; kiss me once more, it will not be the last time, my poor darling,' she added, clasping Rodolphe round the neck, and burying his face in her loosened tresses.

Before leaving for the hospital, she wanted her friends the Bohemians to stay and pass the evening with her.

'Make me laugh,' said she. 'Cheerfulness is health to me. It is that wet blanket of a viscount who made me ill. Fancy, he wanted to make me learn orthography; what the deuce should I have done with it? And his friends, what a set! A regular poultry yard, of which the viscount was the peacock. He marked his linen himself. If ever he marries I am sure that it will be he who will suckle the children.'

Nothing could be more heart breaking than the almost posthumous gaiety of poor Mimi. All the Bohemians made painful efforts to hide their tears and continue the conversation in the jesting tone started by the unfortunate girl, for whom fate was so swiftly spinning the linen of her last garment.

The next morning Rodolphe received the order of admission to the hospital. Mimi could not walk, she had to be carried down to the cab. During the journey she suffered horribly from the jolts of the vehicle. Amidst all her sufferings the last thing that dies in woman, coquetry, still survived; two or three times she had the cab stopped before the drapers' shops to look at the display in the windows.

On entering the ward indicated in the letter of admission Mimi felt a terrible pang at her heart, something within her told her that it was between these bare and leprous walls that her life was to end. She exerted the whole of the will left to her to hide the mournful impression that had chilled her.

When she was put to bed she gave Rodolphe a final kiss and bid him good-bye, bidding him come and see her the next Sunday which was a visitors' day.

'It does not smell very nice here,' said she to him. 'Bring me some flowers, some violets, there are still some about.'

'Yes,' said Rodolphe. 'Good-bye till Sunday.'

And he drew together the curtains of her bed. On hearing the departing steps of her lover, Mimi was suddenly seized with an almost delirious attack of fever. She suddenly opened the curtains, and leaning half out of bed, cried in a voice broken with tears:

'Rodolphe, take me home, I want to go away.'

The sister of charity hastened to her and tried to calm her.

'Oh!' said Mimi. 'I am going to die here.'

On Sunday morning, the day he was to go and see Mimi, Rodolphe remembered that he had promised her some violets. With poetic and loving superstition he went on foot in horrible weather to look for the flowers his sweetheart had asked him for, in the woods of Aulnay and Fontenay, where he had so often been with her. The country, so lively and joyful in the sunshine of the bright days of June and July, he found chill and dreary. For two hours he beat about the snow-covered thickets, lifting the bushes with a stick, and ended by finding a few tiny blossoms, and as it happened, in a part of the wood bordering the Le Plessis pool, which had been their favourite spot when they came into the country.

Passing through the village of Chatillon to get back to Paris, Rodolphe met in the square before the church a baptismal procession, in which he recognized one of his friends who was the godfather, with a singer from the opera.

'What the deuce are you doing here?' asked the friend, very much surprised to see Rodolphe in those parts.

The poet told him what had happened.

The young fellow, who had known Mimi, was greatly saddened at this story, and feeling in his pocket took out a bag of christening sweetmeats and handed it to Rodolphe.

'Poor Mimi, give her this from me and tell her I will come and see her.'

'Come quickly, then, if you would come in time,' said Rodolphe, as he left him.

When Rodolphe got to the hospital, Mimi, who could not move, threw her arms about him in a look.

'Ah! there are my flowers,' said she, with the smile of satisfied desire.

Rodolphe related his pilgrimage into that part of the country that had been the paradise of their loves.

'Dear flowers,' said the poor girl, kissing the violets. The sweetmeats greatly pleased her too. 'I am not quite forgotten, then. The young fellows are good. Ah! I love all your friends,' said she to Rodolphe.

This interview was almost merry. Schaunard and Colline had rejoined Rodolphe. The nurses had almost to turn them out, for they had overstayed visiting time.

'Good-bye,' said Mimi. 'Thursday without fail, and come early.'

The following day on coming home at night, Rodolphe received a letter from a medical student, a dresser at the hospital, to whose care he had recommended the invalid. The letter only contained these words:

'My dear friend, I have very bad news for you. No. 8 is dead. This morning on going through the ward I found her bed vacant.'

Rodolphe dropped on to a chair and did not shed a tear. When Marcel came in later he found his friend in the same stupefied attitude. With a gesture the poet showed him the letter.

'Poor girl!' said Marcel.

'It is strange,' said Rodolphe, putting his hand to his heart; 'I feel nothing here. Was my love killed on learning that Mimi was to die?'

'Who knows?' murmured the painter.

Mimi's death caused great mourning amongst the Bohemians.

A week later Rodolphe met in the street the dresser who had informed him of his mistress's death.

'Ah! my dear Rodolphe,' said he, hastening up to the poet. 'Forgive me the pain I caused you by my heedlessness.'

'What do you mean?' asked Rodolphe in astonishment.

'What,' replied the dresser, 'You do not know? You have not seen her again!'

'Seen whom?' exclaimed Rodolphe.

'Her, Mimi.'

'What?' said the poet, turning deadly pale.

'I made a mistake. When I wrote you that terrible news I was the victim of an error. This is how it was: I had been away from the hospital for a couple of days. When I returned, on going the rounds with the surgeons, I found Mimi's bed empty. I asked the sister of charity what had become of the patient, and she told me that she had died during the night. This is what had happened. During my absence Mimi had been moved to another ward. In No. 8 bed, which she left, they put another woman who died the same day. That will explain the mistake into which I fell. The day after that on which I wrote to you, I found Mimi in the next ward. Your absence had put her in a terrible state; she gave me a letter for you and I took it on to your place at once.'

'Good God!' said Rodolphe. 'Since I thought Mimi dead I have not dared go home. I have been sleeping here and there at friends' places. Mimi alive! Good heavens! what must she think of my absence? Poor girl! poor girl! how is she? When did you see her last?'

'The day before yesterday. She was neither better nor worse, but very uneasy; she fancies you must be ill.'

'Let us go to La Pitié at once,' said Rodolphe, 'that I may see her.'

'Stop here for a moment,' said the dresser, when they reached the entrance to the hospital. 'I will go and ask the house surgeon for permission for you to enter.'

Rodolphe waited in the hall for a quarter of an hour. When the dresser returned he took him by the hand and said these words:

'My friend, suppose that the letter I wrote to you a week ago was true?'

'What!' exclaimed Rodolphe, leaning against a pillar. 'Mimi – '

'This morning at four o'clock.'

'Take me to the ampitheatre,' said Rodolphe, 'that I may see her.'

'She is no longer there,' said the dresser. And pointing out to the poet a large van which was in the courtyard drawn up before a building above which was inscribed *Amphithéâtre*, he added, 'She is there.'

It was indeed the vehicle in which the corpses that are unclaimed are taken to their pauper's grave.

'Good-bye,' said Rodolphe to the dresser.

'Would you like me to come with you a bit?' suggested the latter.

'No,' said Rodolphe, turning away. 'I need to be alone.'[1]

That is not the end of Murger's *Scènes de la vie de Bohème*. There is a further chapter in which, a year after Mimi's death, the four young men emerge from Bohemia into the arms of the artistic establishment. Marcel achieves success when two of his paintings are hung in an important annual exhibition of pictures and one of them is bought by a rich Englishman who had been one of Musette's lovers. Rodolphe has a book published to critical acclaim, Schaunard composes an album of songs which are taken up by the leading singers of the day, while Colline inherits money and marries well. Musette gives herself a week of freedom in which she says farewell to 'la vie de Bohème' and sleeps with Marcel for the last time before marrying a postmaster, the guardian of her previous lover. In the closing lines of the novel, Marcel complains to Rodolphe, 'We are done for, old fellow. We are dead and buried. Youth is fleeting! Where are you going to dine this evening?'

'If you like,' said Rodolphe, 'we will go and dine for twelve sous at our old restaurant in the Rue du Four, where they have plates of village crockery, and where we used to feel so hungry when we had done dinner.'

'No,' replied Marcel, 'I am quite willing to look back at the past, but it must be through the medium of a bottle of good wine and sitting in a comfortable armchair. What would you, I am corrupted. I only care for what is good!'

[1] From the anonymous translation of Murger's novel, published in London (1888) as *The Bohemians of the Latin Quarter*.

III

Puccini's *La Bohème* begins without preamble or prelude. The curtain goes up as the orchestra gives out a theme [Ex. 10] which will be

Ex. 10

associated throughout the opera with the Bohemians at work or play, and which Puccini has taken from his 1883 *Capriccio Sinfonico*, altered slightly and transposed down a major fourth. The dialogue between Marcello (baritone) and Rodolfo (tenor) is carried on in fragments of melody which will be repeated and developed at various points. When Rodolfo sings of the smoke arising from the Paris roof tops ('Nei cieli bigi'), it is to a tune [Ex. 11] which we shall hear again from him in the

Ex. 11

course of his aria 'Che gelida manina'. This tune, too, is one which Puccini had composed before he began work on *La Bohème*: it survives from his sketches for the abortive *La lupa*. A variation of it, a few bars after its first appearance, takes the tenor up to an optional high B flat. The music to which the first act of Rodolfo's drama is consigned to the flames wittily describes the process, and a wisp of the Bohemians' theme accompanies the entrance of Colline (bass).

The warmth of the orchestral strings simulates a sudden outburst of flame as the second act of Rodolfo's play is thrust into the oven, but it is only momentary. 'La brevità, gran pregio' (Brevity is the soul of wit), the playwright comments philosophically, and the third act is quickly sacrificed. But when the flame dies down to a flicker, and the music to a very faint *ppppp*, Marcello and Colline shout 'Abasso l'autor' (Down with the author), and Rodolfo is saved only by the arrival of Schaunard (baritone) with food and drink, and his own thematic phrase to which Schaunard remarks that for them the Bank of France has ruined itself ('La banca di Francia per voi si sbilancia'). A scherzo-like quartet develops as Schaunard tells the tale of the English lord and the noisy parrot, at one point imitating the Englishman's pinched, upper-class English accent, though this passes so quickly that the audience is usually unaware of it. Schaunard has his brief lyrical moment as he describes Christmas in the Latin Quarter, and the friends are settling down to drink when a knock at the door announces their landlord, Benoit (bass).

The orchestra closely follows the mock-terror of the Bohemians and their sly method of avoiding the payment of rent by pressing wine on the landlord and teasing him into confessing his amorous exploits. Their ironic toast to Benoit's health is uttered to a unison phrase [Ex. 12]

Ex. 12

which plays an important part in the scene, and Marcello flatters the old man to an insinuating little tune which would not sound out of place issuing from the mouth of Verdi's Iago [Ex. 13]. Eventually the landlord

Ex. 13

is got rid of, and the other three leave for the Café Momus while Rodolfo, to the quiet string accompaniment of his 'Nei cieli bigi' tune [Ex. 11], announces that he will follow shortly.

Mimi's theme, which later becomes the opening phrase of her aria, 'Si, mi chiamano Mimi', accompanies her entrance. The mood of the act now changes: comical horseplay has gone out of the door with the other Bohemians, and love has walked in. From here to the close of the act, Puccini's lyrical genius operates at its highest level, in the sequence of tenor aria, soprano aria and duet in which Mimi and Rodolfo discover their love for each other. Murger's romanticism still had one foot in the world of reality, but Puccini's romanticism is total, and totally divorced from reality. It is pointless to complain that the composer is functioning at the aesthetic level of the cheap romantic novel, when he achieves his aim with such conviction.

Murger's lovers like the look of each other, and pop into bed at the end of the evening. So, presumably, do Puccini's, for in the duet Mimi implies that she is willing to when she teasingly replies 'Curioso' to Rodolfo's 'E al ritorno?' ('And when we get back?' 'Wait and see'); however, the musical language which the composer gives them is that of romantic, idealized love, not erotic passion. Even the short, conversational phrases with which the Mimi-Rodolfo scene begins reveal a tenderness far removed from the robust comedy of the first half of the act.

Rodolfo's aria, 'Che gelida manina' (literally 'Such a cold little hand'; known in English by the first phrase of the translation for singing, 'Your tiny hand is frozen'), grows naturally and conversationally out of this background of dialogue, its first nine notes murmured on the same pitch, before the lyrical melody of the first part of the aria takes wing [Ex. 14]. 'Che gelida manina' is really two arias linked by a passage of

Ex. 14

heightened recitative-arioso ('Chi son? Chi son? Sono un poeta': Who am I? I am a poet). After the recitative-like nine bars, tenor and orchestra between them transform Ex. 11 from the *allegro* guise in which Rodolfo first presented it at the opening of the opera to a fervent hymn to the happy poverty out of which his poetry emerges ('In povertà mia lieta': In my happy poverty). This leads to the broad romantic melody of the second aria, or second part of Rodolfo's two-part aria [Ex. 15], a

Ex. 15

full-blooded avowal of love at whose climax the tenor is offered a high C or an alternative phrase which takes him no higher than A flat [Ex. 16]. In performances of the opera, those tenors who cannot produce a

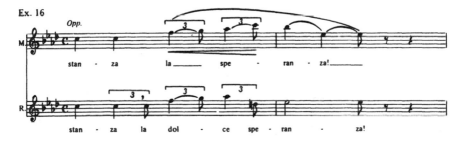

Ex. 16

high C do not gratefully seize on the composer's alternative phrase, as they should; instead, they attempt to disguise their lack of the high C by taking the higher option but singing the entire aria in a lower key.

Rodolfo's aria ends in the conversational tone out of which it sprang, with a question to Mimì. She answers it in her aria, 'Mi chiamano Mimì' (They call me Mimì). This, too, is in two parts, more strongly contrasted than the two sections of 'Che gelida manina': with the broadly phrased melody of the second section, 'Ma quando vien lo sgelo' (But when the thaw comes) [Ex. 17] we have arrived at the emotional climax of Act I.

Ex. 17

The aria ends with a delightfully natural descent from the poetry of melody to the prose of recitative, as Mimi emerges from her dream of spring, and brings Rodolfo back to the present with her, reminding him that she is simply his importunate neighbour.

The romantic atmosphere is only temporarily dispelled by the Bohemians' 'noises off', and then the magical love duet begins as Rodolfo turns to see Mimi framed in the moonlight, and exclaims 'O soave fanciulla, o dolce viso di mite circonfuso alba lunar' (Oh, lovely maiden, your sweet face bathed in the light of the rising moon). The duet is composed mainly of phrases already heard earlier in the act, and its construction is unusual in that it builds away from instead of up to a climax. That climax begun in unison by Mimi and Rodolfo, is an adaptation of Ex. 15 from Rodolfo's aria, 'Che gelida manina', and the duet proceeds, continuing to make use of the closing phrases of that aria, until it breaks up into flirtatious conversational small-talk, still based on phrases from 'Che gelida manina'. With the tenor's 'Dammi il braccio, o mia piccina' (Give me your arm, my dear), the lovers slowly begin to make their exit, the music now echoing the opening phrases of 'Che gelida manina', until their final notes are sung off-stage, the last chord, *pianissimo* and fading away in the distance, taking the soprano up to a high C to blend with the tenor's lower E – except of course when bull-necked tenors insist on joining the soprano on the higher note, ruining Puccini's delicate, poetic conclusion to the act.

The dramatic action of the opera is not advanced at all in Act II of *La Bohème*, which is a mere twenty minutes long and which contents itself with showing us the Bohemians at play at the Café Momus surrounded by the hustle and bustle of the city. Musically, there is nothing of the leisurely lyricism of the latter part of Act I, but the music makes up in pace and gaiety what it lacks in memorable melody. The trumpets blare forth a theme which in fact was briefly and quietly heard in Act I when Schaunard suggested going out to eat in the Latin Quarter. The curtain goes up on a scene of Christmas Eve festivity, and until the end of the act there will be no relaxation of pace except for Musetta's song. The opening chorus of street vendors, citizens and children occasionally quietens sufficiently for one to hear individual voices, Schaunard complaining that a horn he is about to buy is defective, and then, simultaneously, Colline bargaining for a coat, and Mimi and Rodolfo discussing the purchase of a bonnet. Wisps of phrases already heard, themes which will be heard again, occasionally apt details which Puccini has meticulously inserted although they can never be noticed in performance – it is of these that this loosely structured act is composed.

The call of Parpignol, the toy-seller (tenor) is heard in the distance as Rodolfo introduces Mimi to his friends, and they all sit at a table and order supper. In 'Dal mio cervel sbocciano i canti' (Songs flow from my brain), Rodolfo has a miniature solo of nine bars into which, though it takes the tenor no more than twenty seconds to sing, the composer has poured all the ecstasy of young love. Parpignol's curiously sad cry is heard again as the toy-seller appears, surrounded by children and their mothers, all of them adding to the general gaiety and noise, with the children providing the jauntiest tune and the mothers scolding quite mellifluously. A whining child has the last word, sung to the same musical phrase as Parpignol's cry.

When Parpignol and the children have moved on, Marcello asks Mimi what rare gift she has just been given by Rodolfo. Her reply, beginning 'Una cuffietta' (a bonnet), is another arietta, not unlike Rodolfo's 'Dal mio cervel' though several bars longer, which leads to a sequence in which the voices of the four men are heard consecutively, first Schaunard, then Colline, Marcel, then, ringing out above these darker male voices, Rodolfo's tenor. Mimi and the four men have just begun to raise their voices in a toast when a commotion off-stage announces the arrival of Marcello's ex-lover, Musetta (soprano), accompanied by her current protector, Alcindoro (bass).

It is not long before Musetta has drawn everyone's attention to herself by her extravagant behaviour. When she is satisfied that all eyes are upon her, and even the sweet murmuring of Rodolfo and Mimi to each other has been stilled, she launches into her waltz song, 'Quando me'n vo' soletta per la via' (As I walk alone through the streets), the only full-scale aria in Act II, and one of Puccini's most popular tunes [Ex. 18].

Ex. 18

Musetta begins this insouciant waltz alone, but soon her admirers past and present, Alcindoro and Marcello, add their comments, and just before the climax of the melody Musetta is joined by Mimi. A short ensemble develops. When Musetta gets rid of Alcindoro, Marcello begins a reprise of the 'Quando m'en vo'' tune in a sturdy *forte*, to the words 'Gioventù mia, tu non sei morta' (My youth, you are not dead). The other characters join in, and a splendid sextet ensues in which individual characterization is thrown to the winds and 'Quando m'en vo'' is enthusiastically belted out, after which Musetta and Marcello fall into each other's arms. Since Musetta's song captures to perfection the mood of carefree youth and gaiety of this act, it comes as something of a surprise to realize that Puccini had written the tune much earlier as a piano piece, and had then adapted it for use at a ceremony in Genoa for the launching of a battleship, before it came to rest as Musetta's waltz!

Off-stage drum rolls herald the approach of the military band sounding a retreat, and when the six side-drums and trumpets and four piccolos appear, surrounded by their hangers-on, citizens and children, with a tune which is apparently based on an authentic French march of the period, Puccini stirs fragments of themes already heard into the mixture to produce a rousing vocal and orchestral conclusion to the act.

After two *fortissimo* chords from the orchestra, Puccini's method of telling the audience to shut up and listen, Act III begins with a bleak evocation of winter, a winter of the landscape and of the spirit, staccato chords for flutes and harp suggesting the falling snow, the icy ground. Even the sounds of revelry from within the inn are dispirited, and the sad little theme of the flutes and harp persists throughout the beginning of the act, infecting the snatches of chorus from the customers and reducing the tempo of Musetta's rendition of her waltz to that of a gloomy *largo*. The monotonous phrases of the customs officers, peasants, lamplighters and merchants add to the general atmosphere of hopeless pessimism. In the midst of this, a repetition of the *fortissimo* chords to which the curtain was raised seems a miscalculation on the composer's part.

Mimi enters as her 'Mi chiamano Mimi' theme steals in on the strings: the theme breaks off suddenly with her violent fit of coughing. After bells of a near-by hospital have rung out to signify the start of a new day, Marcello emerges from the inn and, in his duet scene with Mimi, 'C'è Rodolfo?' (Is Rodolfo there?), her anguish is movingly portrayed. When Rodolfo enters, he and the orchestra between them produce a reminiscence from the happier past of Act I which is hardly appropriate to the situation; but then, to quote Ernest Newman, 'Puccini rarely pauses to ask himself whether the circumstances in which he now wants to revive an old tune have any relevance to the circumstances in which it first appeared.'[1] Rodolfo's long solo passage ('Mimi è una civetta': Mimi

---

[1] I have done Newman the kindness of attributing to him the words he clearly intended to write. What he actually wrote (in *More Opera Nights*, London, 1954) does not make sense: 'Puccini rarely pauses to ask himself whether the circumstances in which he now wants to revive an old tune have any relevance to the circumstances in which it is now to appear.'

is a flirt), which has not quite the status of an aria, is a passionate lament. At 'Mimi è tanto malata' (Mimi is so ill), it sinks to a hopeless monotone which, in context, is oddly moving. At 'Una terribil' tosse' (A terrible coughing) [Ex. 19], the music conjures up the relentless progres-

Ex. 19

sion of Mimi's illness, and its mood permeates the brief trio which leads to Mimi's aria, 'Donde lieta' (Back to that place), with its sentimental, nostalgic view of the end of an affair, and its message, 'Addio senza rancore' (Farewell without anger).

This mood is sustained throughout the ensuing duet for Mimi and Rodolfo in which the lovers' sentimental, quasi-masochistic musings on their relationship are lifted by the music on to a higher level of brooding melancholy, or of what Puccini thought of as a kind of desperate passion.[1]

The duet becomes a quartet when the quarrelling Musetta and Marcello join in, the tone of the two separate discussions contrasting effectively and, again, movingly. At the very end of the act, the ex-lovers walk off together much as they did at the first meeting at the end of Act I. This time, however, as the curtain comes down on Act III, Puccini shatters the sentimental mood and ends the act as he had begun it, with two sudden loud chords.

Act IV begins similarly to Act I with the Bohemians' theme [Ex. 10]. Rodolfo and Marcello exchange gossip about their ex-mistresses and at the same time attempt to work, but as the orchestra remembers Ex. 15, the big tune from 'Che gelida manina', they put aside pen and brush, and reminisce about their respective loves in the duet, 'O Mimi, tu più non torni' (O Mimi, you will never return) [Ex. 20], a dream of past happiness that is both tender and ardent. When Colline and Schaunard arrive, the boisterous high spirit of the Bohemians asserts itself: that the jollity seems a trifle forced this time is perhaps understandable, but this scene is musically the weakest in Puccini's score, and one is relieved when Musetta enters with the news that Mimi is seriously ill, and the composer is able to get back to the mood of despair he is so adept at

---

[1] 'Passione disperata' was the phrase Puccini had used in a letter to Marco Praga, during the composition of *Manon Lescaut*, when contrasting himself with Massenet's 'powder and minuets'.

Ex. 20

depicting. While he was writing the opera, Puccini had told Ricordi that the last act of *La Bohème* was being composed almost entirely of logical repetitions, and it is these reminiscences of past happiness which make the last part of the act so moving, the fleeting recollections of phrases from the music of Mimi and Rodolfo in Act I.

Colline's little song to his 'old coat', 'Vecchia zimarra', is dramatically a mistake and musically slight, but the final duet scene for Mimi and Rodolfo, 'Sono andati?' (Have they gone?), opens the flood-gates of remembered melody for the last time. As Mimi becomes weaker, the delicate orchestral accompaniment becomes fainter. Mimi tries a few bars of 'Che gelida manina' but has not strength enough to continue. A little later, she is reduced to murmuring phrases on one note, while the orchestra provides the melody of Rodolfo's Act I aria, pausing for one bar at the moment when Mimi dies. Her death is not immediately noticed by the other characters. When Rodolfo is made aware of it, his first words are not sung, but spoken, and then with a cry of 'Mimi' he flings himself on to her bed as the orchestra thunders forth the beginning of 'Sono andati?', followed, for no good dramatic reason, by the coda of Colline's song to his coat.

Thus ends an opera which some find too cloyingly sentimental to stomach, but which many more surrender to completely, and which certainly possesses more than its fair share of memorable melodies. Those who are uncertain whether it is proper to enjoy so unashamedly popular an opera may take comfort in the remark which Debussy is reported as having made to Manuel de Falla: 'If one did not keep a grip on oneself one would be swept away by the sheer verve of the music. I know of no one who has described the Paris of that time as well as Puccini in *La Bohème*.'[1]

[1] Jaime Pahissa, *Manuel de Falla* (London, 1954).

V

Tosca

an opera in three acts

Dramatis personæ:

Floria Tosca, a celebrated singer	(soprano)
Mario Cavaradossi, a painter	(tenor)
Baron Scarpia, Chief of Police	(baritone)
Cesare Angelotti, an escaped political prisoner	(bass)
A Sacristan	(bass)
Spoletta, a police agent	(tenor)
Sciarrone, a gendarme	(bass)
A Gaoler	(bass)
A Shepherd Boy	(boy soprano)

LIBRETTO by Giuseppe Giacosa and Luigi Illica, based on the play *La Tosca* by Victorien Sardou.

TIME: June, 1800
PLACE: Rome

FIRST PERFORMED at the Teatro Costanzi, Rome, 14 January, 1900, with Hariclea Darclée (Tosca), Emilio de Marchi (Cavaradossi), Eugenio Giraldoni (Scarpia), conducted by Leopoldo Mugnone.

Tosca

I

LA TOSCA, A play written by the French playwright Victorien Sardou for Sarah Bernhardt, was produced in Paris in November, 1887, and it was in May, 1889, two weeks after the première of *Edgar*, that Puccini first expressed his interest in it as a subject for an opera. He wrote to Ricordi to say that he was eager to start work on his next project: 'I am thinking of *Tosca*. I implore you to take the necessary steps in order to obtain Sardou's permission. If we had to abandon this idea, it would grieve me exceedingly. In this *Tosca* I see the opera which exactly suits me, one without excessive proportions, one which is a decorative spectacle, and one which gives opportunity for an abundance of music . . .'

The idea was not taken further at that time, and Puccini proceeded instead to compose his *Manon Lescaut*. However, Ricordi commissioned Illica to fashion a libretto from *La Tosca*, which he offered to another of the composers whom he published, one Alberto Franchetti, three of whose operas had been staged quite successfully. Franchetti signed a contract with Ricordi for an opera to be based on Sardou's play. When Puccini heard of this, although he was now at work on *La Bohème*, his strong vein of possessiveness asserted itself. He demanded that Ricordi somehow retrieve the subject from Franchetti. Ricordi, Puccini and the librettist Illica were all in agreement that, if Puccini were to compose the opera which in due course became *Tosca* (without the definite article of the French title), it would be a much finer work than anything Franchetti could possibly create, and they all proceeded to act, unethically, towards this end. Ricordi and Illica persuaded Franchetti that, having thought the matter over more carefully, they were wrong to advise him to compose *Tosca*. The subject, they now told him, was really most unsuitable for an opera, far too violent with its scenes of torture and brutality, and with a political background which modern opera audiences would find incomprehensible. Franchetti was convinced by their arguments, and relinquished his rights to the libretto, whereupon, the very next day, those rights were acquired by Puccini.

One or two commentators, including Vincent Seligman[1] and Richard Specht,[2] have asserted that the composer saw Sarah Bernhardt in *La Tosca*

---

[1] In *Puccini Among Friends*, op. cit.
[2] In *Giacomo Puccini* (Berlin, 1932).

at the Teatro Filodrammatico in Milan, in the spring of 1889. What is certain is that Puccini made a special journey to Florence in October, 1895, to see Bernhardt in the play in which she was still touring, but found her performance so mechanical and without feeling that he began to wonder if he had been mistaken about the play. He wrote to Ricordi, who assured him that, in Milan, Bernhardt had been magnificent as Tosca, and that she was ill during the Florence performances.

It is probable that Puccini's interest in *Tosca* had been rekindled on hearing that the eighty-one-year-old Verdi had been present when Illica read his libretto to Sardou at the playwright's home in Paris, and that the great composer had been very impressed by it. Verdi is said to have been so moved by Cavaradossi's farewell to life in the last act that he seized the manuscript from the librettist's hand and read the passage in a voice trembling with emotion.

Puccini having acquired Illica's libretto, Illica's *Bohème* collaborator Giuseppe Giacosa was now called in to help with the versification. Giacosa was at first reluctant, complaining that, with the exception of the torture scene, the play was virtually a series of duets either for Tosca and Cavaradossi or Tosca and Scarpia. He thought this justified in the play, since it was conceived as a vehicle to convey the virtuosity of Sarah Bernhardt to admiring audiences, but he was convinced that, in an opera, such a succession of duets would lead to monotony. (Giacosa cannot have remembered Verdi's *Rigoletto*, a highly successful and un-monotonous series of duets, and designed as such by its composer.)

Despite his misgivings, Giacosa worked on the libretto steadily, and was soon able to announce to Ricordi that the end was in sight, and to complain of Puccini's dilatoriness:

> I swear to you I am not wasting one hour. But permit me to add that Puccini wastes an infinite number of hours – whether in hunting or fishing, I don't know. I understand very well that a composer cannot start with his work until he has the entire libretto in his hands. But he has in his possession the entire libretto, and two acts of it are in their definitive form. For the third act he has not only a clear outline of the individual scenes but also the substance and drift of the dialogue well outlined . . . if he wants the dialogue rendered definitive before he starts to compose, he has only to say so; but once the dialogue is really definitive, don't let him come afterwards and propose new alterations at every turn.[1]

After the première of *La Bohème* in February 1896, Puccini did not plunge immediately into the composition of *Tosca*. He made a beginning in the summer, but his work during the following eighteen months or so was frequently interrupted by visits to Milan to supervise the Scala production of *La Bohème*, to England for that opera's British première

---

[1] Nardi, *Giacosa* (quoted in Carner, *Puccini*, op. cit.).

mounted by the Carl Rosa Company, and, in November, 1897, to Rome to listen to the sound of Roman church bells from the platform of the Castel Sant' Angelo. During 1898, Puccini worked on the composition and orchestration of *Tosca* at Torre del Lago, though he also made two journeys to Paris in connection with the first French production of *La Bohème* at the Opéra Comique. On the second of these visits, Illica joined Puccini in Paris and together they called on Sardou to discuss their handling of the last act of *Tosca*.

In the summer of 1898, Puccini and Elvira rented a villa in the hills above Lucca, and here the composer continued to work on *Tosca*. The following January, in Paris, he had further meetings with Sardou, after one of which he wrote to Ricordi:

This morning I spent an hour with Sardou, who told me of various things in the finale that he does not like. He wants that poor woman dead at all costs! . . . But I certainly cannot agree with him. He accepts her access of madness, but would like her to swoon and die like a fluttering bird . . . In sketching the panorama for me, Sardou wished the course of the Tiber to pass between St Peter's and the Castello!! I pointed out to him that *flumen* flows past on the other side, just under the Castello, and he, as calm as a fish, answered, 'Oh, that doesn't matter!' Curious fellow, all life and fire and full of historico-topo-panoramic inexactitudes![1]

Tosca was finally completed at the end of September, 1899, and the score of Act III sent off to Ricordi, the earlier acts having been sent as soon as each was ready. To Puccini's great dismay, his publisher wrote him a long letter expressing his disappointment with this final act. Ricordi thought the entire act 'a grave error of conception and craftsmanship' which would 'cancel out the splendid impression of Act I' as well as 'the overwhelming effect that Act II is bound to create, which is a true masterpiece of dramatic power and tragic expression'. In his opinion, the Tosca–Cavaradossi duet in Act III was so fragmentary as to reduce the characters 'to the stature of pygmies'. He complained, too, that one of Giacosa's 'most beautiful passages of lyrical poetry', 'O dolci mani', had been given only 'a scrappy and modest melody which, to make matters worse, comes from *Edgar*'. What, he asked, had happened to the Puccini of noble, warm and vigorous inspiration?

Puccini replied from Torre del Lago on 11 October:

My dear Signor Giulio,
    Your letter was an extraordinary surprise to me. I am still suffering from the impact of it. Nevertheless, I am quite convinced that if you read the act through again you will change your opinion! This is not vanity on my part. No, it is the conviction of having, to the best of my ability, given life to the drama which was before me. You know how scrupulous I am in interpreting

[1] Adami, op. cit.

the situation or the words, and how important it is, first of all, to achieve that. The detail of my having used a fragment of *Edgar* can be criticized by you and those few who are able to recognize it, and can be regarded as a labour-saving device if you like. As it stands, if one rids oneself of the idea that it belongs to another work, Act IV of *Edgar* which has in any case been abolished, it seems to me full of the poetry which emanates from the words. Oh, I am sure of this, and you will be convinced when you hear it in its proper place, which is in the theatre. As for its being fragmentary, that was deliberate. This cannot be a uniform and tranquil situation as is the case with other love duets. Tosca's thoughts continually return to the necessity that Mario's fall should be convincingly simulated, and that his behaviour should appear natural in front of the firing squad. As for the end of the duet (the so-called Latin Hymn of which I have not yet had the pleasure of seeing the poets' version), I too have my doubts about it, but I hope that it will go well in the theatre.

The duet in Act III has always been the great stumbling-block. The poets have not succeeded in producing anything good or, above all, anything with real feeling in it. (I am speaking of the end.) They are academic, academic all the time, and offer nothing but the usual amorous embroideries. I have had to contrive to get to the end without boring the audience too much, and without indulging in any academic stuff whatsoever.

Mugnone, to whom I have *sung* this act on several occasions, is so enthusiastic about it that he even prefers it to Act IV of *Bohème*. Various friends and members of my own household have formed an excellent impression of it. As far as my own experience goes, I am not displeased with it either.

I really cannot understand your unfavourable impression. Before I set to work to do it again (and would there be time?) I shall take a run up to Milan and we shall discuss it together, *just we two alone*, at the piano and with the music in front of us, and if your unfavourable impression persists we shall try, like good friends, to find, as Scarpia says, a way to save ourselves.

I repeat, it is not vanity on my part. It is just my defence of a work which is the product of my thought – and a great deal of thought.

I have always encountered in my dear 'papa Giulio' great delicacy of feeling, not to speak of affection which, you may be sure, is reciprocated in full measure. And I am grateful to you for the interest you take in me, and have always taken since that day when I had the good fortune first to encounter you. I disagree with you about this third act: it is the first time that we have had a difference of opinion. But I hope, and will go so far as to say I am sure, that you will change your view. We shall see!

Toscanini is coming today – and perhaps I shall come back with him tomorrow or the following day. I shall wire you.

I am still working at the Prelude [to Act III] which is giving me much trouble, but it is coming along.

I shall have a very short time to stay in Milan, as I must get back to work and have to go to Florence on Sunday.[1]

In the event, no changes were made to Act III. Ricordi arranged for the opera to be given its première, appropriately, in Rome, where its

[1] Ibid.

action takes place. His son, Tito, took charge of the production. The first performance at the Teatro Costanzi on 14 January, 1900, was an extraordinary occasion. Tito Ricordi had upset a number of Roman musicians and critics by refusing to allow visitors at rehearsals, and he had also given offence by bringing with him Federico von Hohenstein, La Scala's scenic artist, to design the sets. The atmosphere in the theatre on the first night was tense. Fifteen minutes before the curtain was due to rise, a police officer called on the conductor, Mugnone, in his dressing room, to advise him that it was possible that a bomb would be thrown during the performance, in which event he was immediately to strike up the national anthem.

An international audience had assembled. Royalty was represented by Queen Margherita, and the world of music by a number of Puccini's rivals including Franchetti, who had been tricked out of composing his own *Tosca*. A nervous Mugnone entered the orchestra pit and began the performance, but the opening bars were greeted so noisily, with shouts of 'Down with the curtain', that he broke off and rushed back-stage. The disturbance, however, had been caused not by terrorists but by latecomers, and when the opera began for the second time, it was heard through without further interruption. Several encores were demanded during the evening: both tenor arias, the soprano's 'Vissi d'arte', the Act I finale and the Act III duet. At the end, applause was respectful rather than enthusiastic, though after the encore of Cavaradossi's 'E lucevan le stelle' in Act III Puccini was called on to the stage five or six times. (So much for *verismo*!)

In general, the critics wrote unfavourably of *Tosca* after the first night, though most agreed that the lyrical passages were successful and that Puccini's orchestration was skilful and effective. Many found the sado-masochistic elements of physical and mental torture distressing and dis-tasteful, and the *Corriere d'Italia* thought it a pity that the composer 'should have attempted something the futility of which ought not to have escaped him'.

The cast of the Rome production performed the opera in Turin, but at La Scala, in March, only the Scarpia (Eugenio Giraldoni) remained, and the opera was conducted by Toscanini. The most successful and most enthusiastically acclaimed of the early Italian performances were those in Genoa in May, with Angelica Pandolfini (Tosca), Giuseppe Borgatti (Cavaradossi) and Mario Sammarco (Scarpia). The opera arrived in Great Britain more quickly than *La Bohème* had, its first Covent Garden performance following six months after the Rome première, in July, 1900. The principal singers in London were Milka Ternina (Tosca), Fernando de Lucia (Cavaradossi) and Antonio Scotti (Scarpia), and the work and its interpreters were received with great enthusiasm. Herman Klein wrote in the *Sunday Times*:

I had memories of Bernhardt in Sardou's play, and was fain to ask 'Is this a subject for an opera, much less a part for Ternina?' The greater was my surprise therefore when the answer came . . . the impression that Ternina made was simply thrilling, De Lucia was a first-rate Cavaradossi and a new baritone, Antonio Scotti, succeeded greatly as Scarpia where he had previously made little effect on his début as Don Giovanni.

Some London critics found the torture scene in Act II objectionable.

Puccini had travelled to London for the Covent Garden production. To his sister, Dide, he wrote:

> *Tosca* is being produced on the 12th [July]. Last night, *La Bohème* was given with great success at the same theatre, Covent Garden. I am going into the country tomorrow with Rothschild, who invited me last night. I am well, but I have had enough of London. It is cold here, quite like autumn. The rehearsals are going very well; with a rush, however, which savours of the American, and with no great attention to finish . . . London would be a better and more interesting place to stay in than Paris. It is the language difficulty which is so depressing. I don't understand a syllable of it. Well, I know the numerals (the first ten) and some addresses to which I can go in a cab!

Immediately before the Covent Garden dress rehearsal, Puccini wrote to Elvira:

> Tomorrow, Wednesday, general rehearsal . . . Friday a big party at Rothschild's. Patti is going to be there.
>
> We went to see the slums of London, which interested me very much. I am almost always invited out, tonight also. I went to dine with some friends at Maxime's, where there were plenty of *cocottes*. What elegance and what beauties! But afterwards we went home, quietly, quietly, like good boys . . . The theatre is completely sold out. I hope to have a great success because the artists are very good . . . better than at the Scala . . . In the tragic moments Ternina is extraordinary. In moments of love and lightness, she has little *charme*. The second act, however, she does wonderfully, except the 'Vissi d'arte', which she sings a little like a German . . . Scotti marvellous; bad voice, but talent, and of a grand stature in the part.

While he was in London, Puccini was taken to see an American play, *Madame Butterfly*; he understood hardly a word of it, yet was interested and moved by the plight of the Japanese geisha girl.

Seven months after its London production, *Tosca* arrived, in February, 1901, at the Metropolitan Opera, New York, with two of the London principals, Ternina and Scotti, and a new tenor, Giuseppe Cremonini. Again, the opera was popular with the public, though critical reaction was varied. Henry Krehbiel in the New York *Tribune* thought that much of it was like shreds and patches of many things with which the operatic stage has long been familiar . . . much comes out of Wagner's workshops, and like all else of the same origin in the score is impotent because there is no trace of Wagner's logical mind either in the choice of material or its development . . . the real melos of the piece from beginning to end is of that hot-blooded passionate type which came in with Mascagni and will not probably go out until composer as well as public have wearied of melodramas and returned either to lyric drama or opera.

Before the New York première, *Tosca* had already been staged in Buenos Aires, Rio de Janeiro, Constantinople, Madrid, Lisbon and Odessa, and within the next few years it was translated and performed in Rumanian, Polish, German, English, French, Czech, Hungarian, Swedish, Russian, Finnish, Slovenian, Danish, Lettish, Estonian, Croatian, Norwegian, Serbian, Lithuanian, Hebrew and Bulgarian. There can now hardly be an opera house in whose repertory *Tosca* does not have a permanent place.

II

The events of the opera take place in Rome on a day in June, 1800. (In Sardou's play, it is 17 June.) Act I is set in the church of Sant' Andrea della Valle, during the morning. On the right is the entrance to the Attavanti chapel, and on the left a platform has been erected in front of an unfinished painting which is covered with a cloth. As the curtain rises, a man dressed in prison garb, dishevelled, fatigued and in a state of fear, enters furtively, looking behind him. Muttering that his sister has hidden a key for him at the base of the statue of the Madonna, he goes to the statue, searches at its base, finds a key and uses it to open the gate of the Attavanti chapel which he enters.

The Sacristan now appears, carrying painters' brushes which he has been cleaning, and expressing surprise at not finding the artist, the Cavalier Cavaradossi, at work. He notices that Cavaradossi's basket of food is still intact. As the Angelus sounds, the Sacristan kneels to pray, and while he is at prayer Cavaradossi enters, mounts the platform and uncovers the painting, revealing it to be a portrait of Mary Magdalene, a Magdalene with big blue eyes and a wealth of golden hair. The Sacristan recognizes the model as a young woman who has been coming into the church for some days past to pray, and Cavaradossi confirms that, while she was absorbed in prayer, he used her face for his portrait.

Cavaradossi begins to work on the portrait, but pauses and, taking from his pocket a miniature portrait of his beloved, the singer Floria Tosca, he sings a reflective aria on contrasting types of beauty: Tosca, dark with black eyes, and the blue-eyed blonde of the portrait. Meanwhile, the Sacristan mutters pious remarks to himself, referring to Cavaradossi and, it seems, artists in general, as 'cani di volterriani'

(Voltairean dogs), atheists and enemies of the 'santissimo governo', the Vatican.

As soon as the Sacristan has left, the man in prison clothes who had hidden in the Attavanti chapel emerges from it. He is at first startled to see Cavaradossi, but then recognizes him and greets him as an old friend. After he has peered closely at the man, Cavaradossi in turn recognizes him and salutes him as 'Angelotti, the Consul of the destroyed Roman Republic'. Angelotti reveals that he has escaped from imprisonment in the Castel Sant' Angelo, and Cavaradossi offers his help. Hearing Tosca's voice calling his name, 'Mario', the painter hastily explains that a jealous woman is about to arrive, and pushes Angelotti back into the chapel, giving him the basket of provisions.

Tosca enters. She is in a suspicious mood, having heard voices from outside, and accuses Mario of entertaining a woman in the church. Cavaradossi manages to convince her that she was mistaken, and they plan to meet that evening, after her performance, and go together to his villa in the country. As Tosca is about to leave, she looks at Cavaradossi's painting, and complains that the face of the Magdalene is too beautiful. She has seen those blue eyes before, and after a moment's thought recognizes the face as that of the Marchesa Attavanti. Tosca's jealousy flares up again, but Cavaradossi eventually persuades her that it is without cause, and Tosca at last goes, her final instruction to Cavaradossi being to change the colour of the Magdalene's eyes to black, like hers.

Angelotti re-emerges from the chapel, and Cavaradossi says he has not mentioned him to Tosca because, although she is trustworthy, she tells everything to her confessor. Angelotti now reveals that the apparently pious young woman who has unwittingly acted as model for Cavaradossi was indeed the Marchesa Attavanti, Angelotti's sister, who had hidden women's clothes under the altar for him, in readiness for his escape. As soon as it is dark he will disguise himself and leave the church. The two men speak with loathing of Baron Scarpia, the chief of the Roman police and a hypocritical, sadistic bully, and Cavaradossi advises Angelotti to flee from Rome immediately. He gives Angelotti the key to his villa, and adds that, in an emergency, he can hide in a concealed chamber half-way down the well in the garden.

Suddenly, the report of a cannon is heard, the signal that a prisoner has escaped from Sant' Angelo, and Cavaradossi quickly decides to accompany Angelotti. They rush off through the chapel. The Sacristan, when he enters with what to him is the good news that Napoleon Bonaparte has been defeated in battle, is surprised not to find Cavaradossi still at work. Priests and choir boys now enter, and the Sacristan announces the news of Napoleon's defeat to them, but their noisy rejoicing is cut short by the entrance of Scarpia with his henchman Spoletta and several police agents. While the others make a

Above, left: The composer's father, Michele Puccini

Above, right: The composer's mother, Albina Puccini Magi

Left: Giacomo Puccini as a student

Water-colour sketch by Frederick von Hohenstein for Act II of
Le villi

Puccini and Ferdinando Fontana,
librettist of *Le villi* and *Edgar*

Puccini at the time of *Le villi*

Water-colour sketch by Giuseppe Palanti for Act II of *Edgar*

The original costume designs for Edgar and Tigrana in *Edgar*

Left to right: Verdi, Puccini, Boito, Mascagni, Leoncavallo and Giordano

Sketch by Ferruccio Pagni of the hut used for meetings of the *Club la Bohème*. The cabin is no longer standing, and the lake frontage has changed beyond recognition

Page from the autograph score of *La Bohème*, Act I

Cover of the earliest English vocal score of *Madam Butterfly*, published
by Ricordi (design by Leopoldo Metlicovitz)

Right: Enrico Caruso

Below: Caricature by Caruso of a rehearsal of *La fanciulla del west* at the Metropolitan Opera House, New York

Puccini at the time of *Turandot*

thorough search, Scarpia questions the terrified Sacristan, informing him that a prisoner of state has escaped and taken refuge in the church. In the Attavanti chapel Scarpia finds a fan with the crest of the Attavanti on it, and then notices the unfinished painting whose model he recognizes as the Marchesa. Told by the Sacristan that the artist is Mario Cavaradossi, Scarpia exclaims 'He! Tosca's lover, a man under suspicion and a Voltairean,' and when the Sacristan expresses his surprise that the painter's food basket has been found in the chapel, and empty, Scarpia realizes that Cavaradossi is an accomplice in Angelotti's escape.

Tosca now returns, and Scarpia murmurs to himself that, just as Iago used a handkerchief to drive a jealous lover to distraction, so he, Scarpia, will use a fan. He suggests to Tosca that, since the Marchesa Attavanti's fan was found in the painter's food basket, she and Cavaradossi had probably used the church for their amorous assignations. Tosca finds this only too easy to believe, and rushes out in a jealous rage, hoping to surprise Cavaradossi and the Marchesa at the painter's villa. Scarpia orders his men to follow her. As the church now begins to fill up with the faithful, and the *Te Deum* begins, Scarpia broods on his own lust for Tosca, and his scheme to win her and to have her lover executed. Suddenly emerging from his day-dream, he recollects where he is, and, crossing himself, joins in the chant of the *Te Deum* as the curtain falls.

Act II takes place that evening in Scarpia's apartment in the Palazzo Farnese. Scarpia is seated at a table, taking his supper, and wondering whether his men have yet captured Angelotti and Cavaradossi. He calls a gendarme, Sciarrone, and asks if Tosca has arrived at the reception which Maria Carolina, Queen of Naples, is giving in another part of the palace 'in honour of Mélas'.[1] Scarpia sends Sciarrone to wait for Tosca with a note summoning her to him, after her performance for the guests of the Queen of Naples. Sciarrone returns with Spoletta who reports that Tosca had been followed to Cavaradossi's villa. Angelotti could not be found there, but Cavaradossi himself has been apprehended since his taunting manner suggested that he probably knew where Angelotti was.

Cavaradossi is now brought in, and questioned in the presence of a judge and Roberti, the torturer and executioner. He denies all knowledge of Angelotti. Tosca's voice has been heard through an open window, singing in a cantata, and a few moments later she enters Scarpia's apartment breathlessly, and rushes to embrace Cavaradossi. In an undertone, Cavaradossi warns her to say nothing of what she has seen at his villa, and she indicates by a gesture that she understands. Cavaradossi is led off to an adjacent torture chamber, followed by Roberti and the judge, while Spoletta stands at the door to transmit Scarpia's instructions.

[1] Thus the libretto: 'in onore di Mélas.' Baron Michael Mélas was the Austrian general who had met Napoleon in battle at Marengo.

Scarpia now begins to interrogate Tosca. At first she is defiant, having realized that her jealousy of the Marchesa Attavanti was ill-founded, but Mario's cries of pain from the adjacent chamber cause her to weaken. Scarpia explains that Cavaradossi is bound hand and foot, with a ring of iron around his temples which is being tightened at each unsatisfactory answer. He orders Spoletta to open the door so that Tosca can hear her lover's screams more clearly. Tosca runs to the door, asking Mario for permission to speak, but he refuses. Finally, she can bear the sounds of his torture no more. She tells Scarpia of Angelotti's hiding place in the well in the garden of the villa.

An unconscious Cavaradossi is dragged back into Scarpia's study. As he comes to, Tosca assures him she has not spoken, at which Scarpia loudly announces Angelotti's hiding place to Spoletta and instructs him to return to the villa and arrest him. Mario curses Tosca for having betrayed him, and Sciarrone rushes in to announce bad news, a victory for Bonaparte at Marengo. Mario expresses his triumphant joy at this, and Scarpia has him dragged from the room, ordering that he be hanged as a traitor.

Left alone with Scarpia, Tosca begs him to save Cavaradossi. But, Scarpia points out, it is only she who can save him. At what price, asks Tosca, to which Scarpia replies that he would never dream of taking money from a woman. The price he has in mind is Tosca herself. Disgusted, Tosca runs to the door, thinking that she will appeal to the Queen, but stops when Scarpia points out that she is, of course, free to go, but by the time the Queen grants pardon to Cavaradossi she will be granting it to a corpse. Tosca realizes she is defeated, and sinks to her knees in prayer, seeking to ask why her life of piety and good works should be thus rewarded.

'You ask of me a life', Scarpia tells her, 'and in return I ask of you only an instant.' Spoletta now returns to report that Angelotti has killed himself rather than be taken, but that all is ready for the execution of Cavaradossi. Tosca is forced to agree to Scarpia's bargain, but asks that Mario be freed immediately. Scarpia explains that this cannot be. A mock execution before a firing squad will have to be arranged – 'as with Count Palmieri,' he instructs Spoletta, who, understanding perfectly what that implies, leaves to carry out Scarpia's orders.

Tosca, left alone with the police chief, demands from Scarpia a safe-conduct pass for herself and Cavaradossi. While Scarpia is writing this at his desk, Tosca's glance falls upon a sharp knife lying on the supper table. She picks it up and hides it behind her back. As Scarpia advances towards her exclaiming 'Tosca, finalmente mia' (Tosca, at last you're mine), she stabs him in the heart, crying as she does so 'Questo è il bacio di Tosca' (This is Tosca's kiss). As Scarpia collapses, writhing in agony, she taunts him, standing over him with the knife, ready to strike again if need be. It is only when Scarpia breathes his last that she pardons him, adding scornfully, 'E avanti a lui tremava tutta Roma!' (And before this man, all Rome trembled).

Tosca has to search for the safe-conduct pass, finding it eventually in the dead man's hand. Before she leaves, she places a candle at either side of Scarpia's head, and, taking a crucifix from the wall, lays it on his breast. Cautiously, she makes her exit as the curtain falls.

Act III takes place just before dawn the following morning, on the platform of the Castel Sant' Angelo. In the distance can be seen the Vatican and the Basilica of St Peter's. It is still dark. As dawn approaches the sounds of church bells tolling for matins can be heard, and the voice of a shepherd boy, singing. A gaoler with a lantern mounts the staircase from below, and sits drowsily at a table. Shortly afterwards, Cavaradossi is led up to the platform by guards, and handed over to the gaoler. Told he has an hour to live, Cavaradossi asks permission to write a note of farewell to the woman he loves. He gives his ring to the gaoler who, in return, promises to deliver the note. Cavaradossi begins to write, but is overwhelmed by memories of his happiness with Tosca and by the realization that now, when he values life so much because of her, he is about to die.

Tosca arrives, accompanied by Spoletta, and shows Cavaradossi the safe-conduct pass for them both, signed by Scarpia. She tells Cavaradossi of the bargain she was forced to make, and of how she killed Scarpia rather than submit to him. She impresses upon Cavaradossi that he must play his part well in the mock execution, and fall realistically when the shots ring out. He promises to do so, 'come la Tosca in teatro' (just like Tosca in the theatre), and, when the firing squad lines up, he is able to face them boldly. They fire and he falls, impressing Tosca by his performance. 'Ecco un artista' (What an artist), she exclaims. But when the firing squad has departed and she rushes to her beloved Mario to help him to his feet, she finds her hands covered in his blood. Scarpia had outwitted her, and Cavaradossi's execution was indeed 'just like Palmieri's'.

From below, Sciarrone and Spoletta can be heard approaching, with soldiers. Scarpia's body has been discovered, and Spoletta appears with a cry of 'Tosca, you shall pay dearly for his life.' 'With my own,' answers Tosca, as she runs to the ledge of the platform and, with a final cry of 'O Scarpia, avanti a Dio!' (O Scarpia, we shall meet before God), flings herself from the parapet to her death. Sciarrone and the soldiers rush to the parapet and look down, while Spoletta stands stunned and pale as the curtain quickly falls.

'Sardoodledom' was the term invented by George Bernard Shaw, writing theatre criticism in London in the 1890s, to describe the work of Victorien Sardou (1831–1908), the playwright who was for nearly forty years the most popular writer for the French theatre. Shaw, who was concerned to promote Ibsen when London theatre managements preferred to produce Sardou, wrote that

> Sardou's plan of playwriting is first to invent the action of his piece, and then to carefully keep it off the stage and have it announced merely by letters and telegrams . . . When the news is not brought by post, the characters are pressed into the service . . . as thus: 'Stanley French arrived in Bellagio this morning', 'Mr Harding will arrive in Bellagio tomorrow afternoon', 'Miss Harding lives in that villa on the lake', 'Sir Christopher Carstairs will remain here for another month at least', 'This is my brother, Sir Arthur Studley', 'Janet, we shall pack up and leave tomorrow morning', etc., etc., the person addressed invariably echoing with subdued horror, 'This morning!', 'Tomorrow afternoon!' 'In *that* villa!' and so on.[1]

Shaw's strictures are not undeserved, but Sardou was not really a playwright in the Ibsenian sense of the work; he was, rather, a carpenter, a constructer of vehicles for famous actors and actresses, among them Sarah Bernhardt for whom he wrote *Théodora* (1885) and *La Tosca* (1887), and Sir Henry Irving for whom he created *Robespierre* (1902) and, in collaboration with Émile Moreau, *Dante* (1903). His melodramas, their technique and style based on the prolific Eugène Scribe, were as popular abroad in translation as they were in Paris; Bernhardt's world-wide reputation was achieved largely in works by Sardou, and it was, as we have seen, Bernhardt's Tosca which first directed Puccini's attention to that play.

Sardou's *La Tosca*, produced in Paris on 24 November, 1887, is a play in five acts with a cast of twenty-three characters; Puccini's opera is in three acts, and has only nine characters. Much has, therefore, been lost in the transition from play to opera, and not surprisingly it is the historical sub-plot which has largely disappeared. Puccini was more interested in the personal drama being enacted between Tosca, Cavaradossi and Scarpia than in the historical events which play a much larger part in Sardou's play. The fact that the date of the action is given by Sardou as specifically 17 June, 1800, whereas in the opera it is merely 'June, 1800', is not without significance. The 17th June is three days after the date of Napoleon's victory against the Austrian forces at Marengo (14 June), the news of which reached Rome that evening. Puccini and his librettists make reference to the Napoleonic wars, of course, but history is not an integral part of their drama as it is in Sardou's play.

Sardou was hardly one of the great playwrights of the nineteenth century, but his characters in *La Tosca*, superficially sketched though they may be, have a little more individuality than the puppets displayed for us in Puccini's opera. In *Tosca*, Cavaradossi is just another tenor, and his revolutionary sympathies have to be taken on trust; in *La Tosca*, however, we learn a great deal about him even before he appears, as well as being

[1] George Bernard Shaw, *Our Theatres in the Nineties* (revised edn., 1932).

given much of the political background. The opening scene of Sardou's play, up to the entrance of Cavaradossi, is a conversation between two characters, Gennarino and Eusèbe. Eusèbe appears in the opera, where he is known simply as the Sacristan, but Gennarino, Cavaradossi's servant, is to be found only in Sardou. The play's opening scene begins with the stage direction, 'Gennarino lies asleep, stretched out on the scaffolding under the painting. Eusèbe, approaching from behind, jingles a huge bunch of keys in his ear.' Here is the scene in full:

EUSÈBE: Eh! Gennarino!

GENNARINO: Hein. Plaît-il?

EUSÈBE: Tu dors?

GENNARINO: Oui . . . je dors un peu.

EUSÈBE: Paresseux! Je vais en faire autant, du reste. C'est l'heure de la sieste. Il est temps de fermer les portes . . . Où est ton patron?

GENNARINO: Il est allé jusqu'au quartier des Juifs, acheter une étoffe pour sa peinture.

EUSÈBE: Voilà bien de mon Français, qui court les rues de Rome, au mois de juin, par la grande chaleur du jour, et qui m'oblige à l'attendre!

GENNARINO: Le seigneur Mario Cavaradossi n'est pas français, père Eusèbe, il est romain, comme vous et moi, et de vieille famille patricienne, s'il vous plaît.

EUSÈBE: Bon, je sais ce que je dis. S'il est romain par son père, que j'ai bien connu dans ma jeunesse, il est plus français encore par sa mère, une Parisienne! En voilà bien la preuve: si ton maître était un véritable italien, travaillerait-il à l'heure où tout romain qui se respecte est occupé à faire un somme?[1]

---

[1] EUSÈBE: Hey! Gennarino!

GENNARINO [*awakening with a start*]: What? What is it?

EUSÈBE: Asleep?

GENNARINO [*rubbing his eyes*]: Just a little snooze.

EUSÈBE: Layabout! Still, I'm off now to do the same. It's time for siesta, and for me to shut the doors. Where's your master?

GENNARINO [*taking the palette and cleaning it*]: He's gone to the Jewish quarter to buy some painting materials.

EUSÈBE: That's just like my Frenchman, to traipse around the streets of Rome at the hottest time of a day in June, expecting me to wait for him.

GENNARINO [*now on his feet*]: My lord and master Mario Cavaradossi is not French, Father Eusèbe, he's a Roman just like you and me and, I'll have you know, from an ancient patrician family.

EUSÈBE: Look, I know what I'm saying. If he's Roman on his father's side, a fact I've been well aware of since my youth, his mother – a Parisian! – makes him even more a Frenchman. And here's the proof: if your master were a real Italian, would he keep on working at a time when every self-respecting Roman is having a nap?

GENNARINO: Son Excellence prétend qu'il n'est pas d'heure plus favorable au travail que celle-ci, où, les portes étant closes, il n'est plus distrait par les anglais visiteurs, et leurs ciceroni bavards, par le bourdonnement des prières, le chant des cantiques et les sons des orgues; et que, dans cette solitude et cette fraîcheur silencieuse de l'église, il se sent plus libre, plus inspiré, plus en verve . . .

EUSÈBE: Oui, pour recevoir les visites de certaine dame.

GENNARINO: Vous dites?

EUSÈBE: Rien! Après tout, c'est un généreux seigneur. Il ne quitte jamais la place sans me glisser dans la main trois ou quatre Pauli, en témoignage de son estime. Je regrette seulement, Gennarino, que le cavalier Cavaradossi n'ait pas des sentiments plus religieux.

GENNARINO: Oh! ça!

EUSÈBE: Car enfin, je ne l'ai jamais vu assister aux offices, ni marier sa voix à la nôtre à l'heure des Vêpres. Et, depuis qu'il travaille à cette chapelle, il ne s'est pas confessé une seule fois; pas même au saint jour de Pâques.

GENNARINO: C'est pourtant vrai, père Eusèbe.

EUSÈBE: Un Jacobin, Gennarino, un pur Jacobin. Il a de qui tenir, d'ailleurs. Le papa Cavaradossi passait déjà pour philosophe. Il avait longtemps vécu à Paris, dans la fréquentation de l'abominable Voltaire, et autres malfaiteurs de la même bande. Prends garde, Gennarino, que le contact de l'impie ne te mène droit en enfer.[1]

---

[1] GENNARINO [*preparing the palette*]: It is His Excellency's opinion that there is no time more favourable for work than precisely now, when the doors are closed, with no distraction from English travellers and their chattering guides, without the murmur of prayers, the hymn-singing and the noise of the organ. In the solitude and silent freshness of the church, he feels freer, more inspired, full of verve . . .

EUSÈBE [*grumbling, as he arranges the candles in front of the Madonna*]: Yes, in order to receive the visits of a certain lady.

GENNARINO: What did you say?

EUSÈBE: Nothing! After all, he is a generous gentleman. He never leaves the place without slipping three or four coins into my hand, as a token of his regard. My only regret, Gennarino, is that the Cavalier Cavaradossi doesn't have more feeling for religion.

GENNARINO [*nodding*]: Oh, that! [*He places the palette, freshly primed with new paint, on the steps, and cleans the brushes.*]

EUSÈBE: Because, you know, I've never seen him taking part in a service, or blending his voice with ours at Vespers. And, all the time he's been working in this chapel, he hasn't been to confession once. Not even on the holy day at Easter.

GENNARINO: That's certainly true, Father Eusèbe.

EUSÈBE: A revolutionary, Gennarino, nothing but a revolutionary. And it's all too easily understood. Old Cavaradossi, his father, passed for a philosopher. He had lived for a long time in Paris, often keeping company with the abominable Voltaire and other evil characters of the same type. Just be careful, Gennarino, that your association with such blasphemous creatures doesn't put you on the path to Hell.

GENNARINO: Pensez-vous, père Eusèbe, que l'on y dorme, en enfer?

EUSÈBE: Si l'on y dort?

GENNARINO: Oui.

EUSÈBE: Au fait . . . y dort-on? J'avoue, garçon, que ta question me prend au dépourvu. Il faut que j'interroge sur ce point le père Caraffa, lumière de notre Église. Toutefois, je pencherais plutôt pour l'insomnie, qui est un supplice bien fait pour les damnés.

GENNARINO: Oh oui!

EUSÈBE: Tu devrais au moins corriger un peu ce que la conduite de ton maître a de répréhensible, en lui suggérant l'idée d'offrir pour le sacrifice de la messe quelques flacons de ce Marsala que je vois dans ta corbeille.

GENNARINO: Ce n'est pas du Marsala . . . c'est du Gragnano.

EUSÈBE: Tu m'étonnes, mon enfant. À la couleur, je parierais pour du Marsala.

GENNARINO: Vous perdriez, père Eusèbe.

EUSÈBE: Parbleu, j'en aurai le cœur net.

GENNARINO: Hé là donc!

EUSÈBE: Tu as raison, mon fils . . . c'est du Gragnano, et du meilleur.

GENNARINO: Et puis le patron dira que c'est moi!

EUSÈBE: Bon! Il est trop amoureux pour y prendre garde. D'ailleurs, il me doit bien ce dédommagement pour le temps qu'il me fait perdre à ne pas dormir.[1]

---

[1] GENNARINO [*yawning, and dropping to his knees*]: Do you think, Father Eusèbe, that one is able to sleep in Hell?

EUSÈBE: Able to sleep?

GENNARINO: Yes.

EUSÈBE: Well . . . to sleep . . . I confess, my son, that your question has caught me off guard. I shall have to have a word about that with Father Caraffa, who is a leading light of our church. Meanwhile, I'd plump for insomnia, which is a punishment fit for the damned.

GENNARINO [*to himself*]: Oh, yes!

EUSÈBE: You could at least go some way towards making amends for your master's reprehensible behaviour by suggesting to him that he might offer up, for Mass, a few of those flagons of Marsala that I see in your basket. [*He takes the basket.*]

GENNARINO [*without looking around*]: It isn't Marsala, it's Gragnano.

EUSÈBE [*taking out one of the flagons, and examining it*]: You astonish me, my child. From its colour I'd have bet it was Marsala. [*He uncorks a flagon and sniffs it.*]

GENNARINO: You would have lost, Father Eusèbe.

EUSÈBE [*pouring some wine into a goblet*]: I say, I'll get to the bottom of this. [*He takes a large gulp.*]

GENNARINO: That's the way!

EUSÈBE [*making a clacking noise with his tongue*]: You're right, my son. It is Gragnano, and the very best.

GENNARINO [*snatching the flagon and goblet away from him*]: And now my master will blame me for this. [*He rinses the goblet with water from a jug.*]

EUSÈBE: He's far too lovesick even to notice. [*He looks at his watch.*] Anyway, it's small enough recompense for the time he keeps me from my siesta.

GENNARINO: Il se sera arrêté à voir les préparatifs de la fête au palais Farnèse.
EUSÈBE: Cette fête-là n'est pas pour le charmer, puisqu'elle célèbre une nouvelle victoire de nos armes sur les troupes françaises.
GENNARINO: Quelle victoire?
EUSÈBE: Bon Dieu! Se peut-il que tu n'aies pas entendu parler de la reddition de Gênes?
GENNARINO: Vaguement.
EUSÈBE: C'est-à-dire que le chevalier te laisse volontairement dans l'ignorance de nos triomphes. Sache donc, enfant, que les français sont battus sur tous les points, et que le général Masséna, enfermé dans Gênes, a dû capituler et céder la ville aux troupes de Sa Majesté Impériale.
GENNARINO: Ah!
EUSÈBE: Voici d'ailleurs ce que dit la gazette! Écoute ceci, mon garçon. 'Nous recevons de nouveaux détails sur la reddition de Gênes. Le général Masséna est sorti de la ville avec huit mille hommes seulement, plus ou moins éclopés et hors d'état de tenir la campagne. Le général Soult, prisonnier, est grièvement blessé. Les trois quarts des généraux, colonels, officiers français de tout grade, sont captifs comme lui, ou blessés, ou morts.
'C'est un affreux désastre pour ces bandes indisciplinées qui s'intitulent effrontément l'armée française'.
Et ceci à la suite: 'Sa Majesté Napolitaine la Reine Marie-Caroline, auguste fille de l'Impératrice Marie-Thérèse, soeur de l'infortunée Marie-Antoinette, digne et glorieuse épouse de Sa¹

¹ GENNARINO [replacing flagon and goblet in the basket]: He will have stopped to look at the preparations for the festivities at the Farnese Palace.
EUSÈBE: Not that the festivities will bring much joy to his heart, since they're to celebrate yet another victory over the French troops.
GENNARINO: What victory?
EUSÈBE: Good Heavens! Can you not have heard of the surrender of Genoa?
GENNARINO: Vaguely.
EUSÈBE: What you mean is that your master deliberately leaves you in ignorance of our triumphs. Well, just learn this, my child: that the French are utterly defeated on all sides and that General Masséna, besieged in Genoa, has had to surrender the city to the troops of His Imperial Majesty.
GENNARINO: Ah!
EUSÈBE [sitting on a stool, and pulling from his pocket a newspaper and his spectacles]: And what's more, here's the newspaper account. Listen to this, my son. [Gennarino sits on the steps dangling his legs. Eusèbe reads.] 'We have received more details of the surrender of Genoa. General Masséna retreated from the city with only eight thousand men, nearly all injured and incapable of holding the terrain. General Soult was captured, seriously wounded. Three-quarters of the French Generals, Colonels and officers of all grades have, like General Soult, been captured, or wounded, or are dead. It is a dreadful disaster for the undisciplined mobs that have the effrontery to call themselves the French Army.' And then there's this, further on: 'Her Neapolitan Majesty, Queen Marie-Caroline, august daughter of the Empress Marie-Thérèse, sister of the unfortunate Marie-Antoinette, gracious

Majesté Napolitaine Ferdinand IV, *notre victorieux protecteur,
est venue tout exprès de Livourne où elle était de passage, allant
à Vienne, pour donner, ce soir, 17 juin, une grande fête au palais
Farnèse, en l'honneur de cette victoire. Il y aura concert suivi de
bal, avec illumination à giorno sur la place Farnèse, et
musique . . .*'

GENNARINO: Et musique?

EUSÈBE: '. . . *et musique à tous les carréfours avoisinant le palais. On
ne pourra regretter, à cette solennité vraiment patriotique,
que l'absence de Sa Majesté Ferdinand retenue à Naples par
l'obligation d'y effacer les derniers vestiges de l'infâme
République Parthénopéenne. Ajoutons qu'aux dernières
nouvelles, M. de Mélas concentrait toutes ses troupes à
Alexandrie. Avant peu, nous pourrons fêter une dernière et
décisive victoire.*' Avec M. de Mélas, Gennarino, cela n'est pas
douteux. Il y a bien ce petit général Bonaparte qui serait,
dit-on, à Milan; mais prendrais-tu ce général Bonaparte au
sérieux, Gennarino?

GENNARINO: Moi, je ne sais pas; mais le patron, oh oui!

EUSÈBE: Voilà encore de mon Jacobin! Passe encore pour l'ancien
Bonaparte, le vrai. Mais celui-là qui est faux . . .

GENNARINO: Faux?

EUSÈBE: Parfaitement. Je tiens de source certaine, que le général
Bonaparte est mort en Égypte, noyé dans la mer Rouge comme
Pharaon, et que celui-ci n'est autre que son frère Joseph que[1]

---

[1] and glorious spouse of His Neapolitan Majesty King Ferdinand IV,
our victorious protector, has come expressly from Livorno, where
she was en route to Vienna, in order to give, this evening, 17 June, a
great celebration at the Farnese Palace in honour of the victory.
There will be a concert, followed by a ball, with the Farnese Square
specially illuminated, and music . . .'

GENNARINO [*excited*]: Music?

EUSÈBE: . . . music in all the public places adjoining the palace. Our only
regret, at such a truly patriotic and impressive ceremony, is that His
Majesty, King Ferdinand, will be absent, detained in Naples and
obliged to efface the last vestiges of the notorious Parthenopian
Republic. Add to that the latest news that Monsieur de Mélas is con-
centrating all his military forces at Alexandria. Before long, we shall
be celebrating a final and decisive victory.' With Monsieur de Mélas,
Gennarino, there can be no doubt of the outcome. [*He returns the
newspaper to his pocket.*] There are still some who say we shall see this
little General Bonaparte in Milan, but do you really take him
seriously, Gennarino?

GENNARINO: I really can't say for myself, but my master certainly does.

EUSÈBE: Just as you'd expect from our revolutionary! Of course the old
Bonaparte, the real one, was another matter. But this false one . . .

GENNARINO: False one?

EUSÈBE: Exactly. I have it from a very reliable source that General Bonaparte
died in Egypt, drowned in the Red Sea like the Pharaoh, and that this
other one is merely his brother Joseph whom they represent as the

l'on donne pour le défunt, afin d'inspirer confiance aux soldats français, si découragés qu'ils refusent de se battre!

GENNARINO: Ainsi voyez!

EUSÈBE: Oui, mon garçon, voilà où ils en sont à Paris. Et ce n'est pas tout. Sais-tu ce qu'il a imaginé, ce farceur-là? . . .

GENNARINO: Joseph?

EUSÈBE: Joseph! Il fait courir le bruit qu'il a franchi les Alpes avec tous ses canons! Les Alpes! Non, c'est à mourir de rire.

GENNARINO: Voici le patron.[1]

Sardou's Floria Tosca is a considerably more interesting creature than the opera's prima donna, her jealousy more to the fore and her past revealed in some detail. In Sardou's Act I, Cavaradossi and the escaped prisoner Angelotti appear to have time for a very leisurely chat, despite the fact that Angelotti is anxious to escape from Rome before the alarm can be given. Cavaradossi describes his mistress in a long speech, as though he were gossiping at his club, with not a care in the world:

CAVARADOSSI: Connaissez-vous la Tosca?

ANGELOTTI: Floria Tosa? La cantatrice?

CAVARADOSSI: Oui.

ANGELOTTI: De renommée seulement. C'est elle?

CAVARADOSSI: C'est elle! L'artiste est incomparable, mais la femme . . . ah, la femme! . . . Et cette créature exquise a été ramassée dans les champs, à l'état sauvage, gardant les chèvres. Les Bénédictines de Vérone, qui l'avaient recueillie par charité, ne lui avaient guère appris qu'à lire et prier; mais elle est de celles qui ont vite fait de deviner ce qu'elles ignorent. Son premier maître de[2]

---

[1] real one so as not to demoralize the French troops. They're already so dispirited that they're refusing to fight.

GENNARINO: You don't say!

EUSÈBE: Yes, my boy, that's what they're like in Paris. And that's not all. Do you know that he, that play-actor . . .

GENNARINO: Joseph?

EUSÈBE: Yes, Joseph. He has put it about that he has crossed the Alps with all his cannons! The Alps! No, it's enough to make one die from laughing.

GENNARINO: Here comes my master.

[2] CAVARADOSSI: Do you know Tosca?

ANGELOTTI: Floria Tosca? The singer?

CAVARADOSSI: Yes.

ANGELOTTI: Only by repute. It is she [who is your mistress]?

CAVARADOSSI: It is she! The artist is incomparable, but the woman! Ah, the woman! And that exquisite creature was first discovered, an untamed savage, guarding goats in the fields. The Benedictine nuns in Verona, who had taken her in out of charity, had hardly taught her much more than to read and pray. But she was one of those people who guess instinctively at what they don't know. Her first

musique fut l'organiste du couvent. Elle profita si bien de ses leçons qu'à seize ans elle avait déjà sa petite célébrité. On venait l'entendre aux jours de fête. Cimarosa, amené là par un ami, se mit en tête de la disputer à Dieu, et de lui faire chanter à l'opéra. Mais les Bénédictines ne voulaient pas la céder au diable. Ce fut un beau combat. Cimarosa conspirait, le couvent intriguait. Tout Rome prit parti pour ou contre, tant que le défunt pape dut intervenir. Il se fit présenter la jeune fille, l'entendit et, charmé, lui dit en lui tapant sur la joue: 'Allez en liberté, ma fille, vous attendrirez tous les cœurs, comme le mien, vous ferez verser de douces larmes . . . et c'est encore une façon de prier Dieu.' Quatre ans après elle débutait triomphalement dans la Nina et, depuis, à la Scala, à San-Carlo, à la Fenice, partout il n'y a qu'elle. Quant à notre liaison, elle a été improvisée ici à l'Argentina où elle chante en ce moment. Une de ces recontres où l'on se sent à première vue l'un pour l'autre, l'un à l'autre, où deux êtres se reconnaissent sans s'être jamais vus. C'est lui! C'est elle! Et tout est dit.[1]

Angelotti, too, is a much more colourful character in Sardou's play than in Puccini's opera. In the same scene in Act I, he describes an adventure he had twenty years earlier in London:

Il y a vingtaine d'années, j'étais à Londres, uniquement soucieux alors de mes plaisirs. Un soir, au Waux-Hall, je fus accosté par une de ces créatures qui rôdent, à la nuit, dans ces jardins publics, en quête d'un souper. Celle-là était prodigieusement belle. Notre liaison dura huit jours: puis je partis, ne[2]

---

[1] music teacher was the convent organist. She profited greatly from his lessons, and by the age of sixteen had already acquired a certain celebrity. People came to hear her on Holy Days. Cimarosa, who had been brought by a friend, decided he'd wrest her away from God and have her sing at the Opera, but the Benedictines didn't want to lose her to the Devil. It was a fine battle. Cimarosa schemed, the convent intrigued. All Rome took part, either for or against, and the late Pope himself had to intervene. He had the girl brought before him and heard her sing, then tapping her on the cheek he said: 'Take your freedom, my daughter. You will move hearts as you have mine, you will cause tears to flow, and that itself is another way of making an offering to God.' Four years later, she made her triumphant début in *Nina*, and since then, at La Scala, the San Carlo, the Fenice, she has been the only star. As for our affair, it began here at the Argentina where she is singing at present. One of those meetings when one feels, at first sight, that each is made for the other, when two people recognize each other without ever having met before. It is he! It is she! And everything is said.

[2] Twenty years ago I was in London, purely for pleasure. One evening, at Vauxhall, I was accosted by one of those creatures who prowl the public gardens at night in search of a supper. This particular one was exceedingly beautiful. Our liaison lasted for eight

gardant de cette aventure que le souvenir qu'elle méritait. Des années se
passent: mon père meurt, et le partage de ses biens me fait propriétaire de
terres considérables dans les environs de Naples, et, par suite, habitant de
cette ville. J'y arrive un jour après une assez longue absence. Le prince Pepoli,
chez qui je dîne, me dit: 'Venez ça que je vous présente à l'ambassadeur
d'Angleterre, sir Hamilton, et à sa délicieuse femme qui révolutionne ici
toutes les têtes.' Et dans lady Hamilton, jugez de ma stupeur, je reconnais ma
facile conquête du Waux-Hall.[1]

Even the villainous Scarpia has more opportunity in Sardou to
explain, if not to excuse, his villainy. At the point where, in Puccini's Act
II, he sings his arioso 'Già mi dicon venal', he is given this speech by
Sardou:

Fi donc, Tosca. Vous me connaissez bien mal. Vous m'avez vu féroce, implacable, dans l'exercice de mes devoirs; c'est qu'il y allait de mon honneur et
de mon propre salut: la fuite d'Angelotti entraînant forcément ma disgrâce.
Mais, le devoir accompli, je suis comme le soldat qui dépose sa colère avec ses
armes; et vous n'avez plus ici devant vous que le baron Scarpia, votre
applaudisseur ordinaire, dont l'admiration va pour vous jusqu'au fanatisme,
et même a pris cette nuit un caractère nouveau. Oui, jusqu'ici, je n'avais su
voir en vous que l'interprète exquise de Cimarosa ou de Paisiello. Cette lutte
m'a révélé la femme – la femme plus tragique, plus passionée que l'artiste
elle-même, et cent fois plus admirable dans la réalité de l'amour et de ses
douleurs que dans leur fiction! Ah, Tosca, vous avez trouvé là des accents, des
cris, des gestes, des attitudes! . . . Non, c'était prodigieux, et j'en étais ébloui
au point d'oublier mon propre rôle, dans cette tragédie, pour vous acclamer
en simple spectateur, et me déclarer vaincu!
(TOSCA: Plût à Dieu!)[2]

---

[1] days; then I left, retaining of this adventure only the memories it deserved. Years went
by, my father died, and the sharing-out of his estate made me the owner of considerable
properties near Naples, and thus an inhabitant of that city. One day, after a fairly long
absence, I arrived back, and Prince Pepoli at whose place I was invited to dine said 'Do
come, so that I may introduce you to the English Ambassador Sir Hamilton [sic] and his
ravishing wife who is making all local heads turn.' And imagine my shock when, in Lady
Hamilton, I recognized my easy conquest of Vauxhall.

[2] Shame on you, Tosca. You really don't know me. You've seen me fierce, implacable
in the exercise of my duty; that is because my honour and my well-being are involved;
Angelotti's escape has, of course, brought disgrace upon me. But, when my duty is ac-
complished, I'm like a soldier who lays aside his anger together with his arms. You have
before you only Baron Scarpia who has always applauded you, whose admiration for
you borders on the fanatical and tonight even takes on a new character. Yes, until now I
saw you only as the exquisite interpreter of Cimarosa or Paisiello. This affair has
revealed to me the woman – a woman more tragic, more passionate even than the artist,
and a hundred times more admirable in the reality of love and its sorrows than on the
stage. Ah, Tosca, you found accents there, cries, gestures, attitudes . . . No, it was pro-
digious, and I was carried away to the point of forgetting my proper role in this tragedy,
applauding you simply as an audience and declaring myself conquered!
[TOSCA: I wish to God it were so.]

Mais savez-vous ce qui m'a retenu de le faire? C'est qu'avec cet enthousiasme pour la femme affolante, grisante, que vous êtes, et si différente de toutes celles qui ont été miennes, une jalousie, une jalousie subite me mordait le coeur. Eh! quoi, ces colères et ces larmes au profit de ce chevalier qui, entre nous, ne justifie guère tant de passion? Ah! fi donc! Plus vous me conjuriez pour lui, plus je me fortifiais dans la volonté tenace de le garder en mon pouvoir, pour lui faire expier tant d'amour et l'en punir, oui, ma foi, l'en punir! Je lui veux tant de mal de son bonheur immérité. Je lui envie à ce point la possession d'une créature telle que vous, que je ne saurais le lui pardonner qu'à une condition . . . C'est d'en avoir ma part.[1]

Sardou's five acts have been skilfully compressed into three by Puccini and his librettists, though much that is clear in the play seems, as a result, muddled in the opera. Act I in Puccini is almost identical with Sardou's opening act, but Sardou's Act II, the reception at the Farnese Palace (which Verdi would surely have seized upon as providing magnificent opportunities for great ensembles), does not exist in the opera. Puccini took from it merely the performance of the cantata (heard 'off-stage' in the opera's second act) and the episode in which the unexpected news of Napoleon's victory is announced. Nor does Sardou's Act III, set in Cavaradossi's villa, have its exact equivalent in the opera, though Puccini combines part of it with Sardou's Act IV (a room in the Castel Sant' Angelo) for his Act II, set in Scarpia's study in the Farnese Palace. The two scenes of the play's Act V, the chapel for the condemned in the Sant' Angelo fortress and the platform where the executions take place, are combined in Act III of the opera, which takes place entirely on the platform of the castle.

III

Tosca begins swiftly, and without orchestral preamble. After the brutal chords, which can be thought to characterize either Scarpia or the atmosphere of violence which pervades the opera, are blared out *fortissimo*, the curtain rises immediately as Angelotti (bass) staggers into the church, the music now indicating his desperation, the urgency of his movements and, momentarily, his exhaustion. To his own sprightly little theme, the Sacristan enters. To emphasize that he is a comic character, he is given an occasional nervous twitch, which is even

[1] But do you know what held me back? It is that, together with this enthusiasm for the distracting, intoxicating woman that you are, so different from all the others who have been mine, there is a jealousy, a sudden jealousy that bites into my heart. What, should these rages and these tears be for that Cavalier who, between ourselves, is not worthy of such passion? Shame on you. The more you plead with me for him, the more you fortify me in my determination to keep him in my power and make him pay for so much love. Yes, believe me, I want to punish him for it. I hate him for his undeserved good fortune. I envy him so much the possession of a woman like you that I shall pardon him only on one condition – that I have my share of you.

marked in the score. Ostensibly for baritone, the Sacristan's role is usually sung by an opera company's buffo bass, since his utterances are mostly comic ejaculations or expressions of surprise, annoyance or fear. When the Angelus rings, he kneels to chant, on the monotone of F, accompanied discreetly by strings, flutes and harp: at the conclusion of his prayer, Mario Cavaradossi (tenor) enters.

The mood of the music now becomes more lyrical. Snatches of themes which will later be associated with the Marchesa Attavanti and with the love of Tosca and Cavaradossi are heard in the orchestra as the painter uncovers the picture on which he has been working. While the Sacristan grumbles to himself *sotto voce*, Cavaradossi sings a suave and reflectively lyrical aria, 'Recondita armonia' (Recondite harmony), whose harmonies are themselves far from recondite; an aria in praise of differing types of beauty but especially the dark beauty of Tosca, celebrated with the tenor's (usually sustained) high B flat. The Sacristan's mutterings continue through the aria's postlude; then, after more dialogue, he makes his exit to the jaunty tune which accompanied his entrance.

Cavaradossi's scene with Angelotti is interrupted, almost as soon as it is begun, first by the off-stage voice of Tosca, and then by her entrance which she makes to an *andante* melody on solo flute and solo cello with a pizzicato arpeggio accompaniment on violins and violas. 'Non lo sospiri la nostra casetta . . .?' (Do you not long for our little cottage?) [Ex. 21], the quasi-aria in which Tosca tries to bring Cavaradossi's thoughts

Ex. 21

non la so - spi - ri la no-stra ca - set - ta che tutta a-sco - sa nel ver— de ci a-spetta?

back to her and to their little cottage in the country, succeeds in rousing him to such an extent that he bursts in at its climax, capping Tosca's high A flat with his B flat. Tosca now becomes suspicious of the model Cavaradossi has used for his painting, and, when she recognizes the Marchesa Attavanti, Puccini irrelevantly sounds Angelotti's theme in the orchestra.

The love duet proper ('Qual'occhio al mondo': What eyes could be more beautiful) is begun on Cavaradossi's part, in an attempt to make Tosca leave. Its central tune [Ex. 22] will be heard on other occasions

Ex. 22

Mia To - sca i-do - la - tra - ta, o - gni co - sa in te mi pia - ce;

throughout the opera, sometimes to dramatic purpose and sometimes not. After the duet, and Tosca's departure, the Cavaradossi–Angelotti scene is reconvened: Scarpia's chords are heard when Angelotti mentions the dreaded Chief of Police. The Sacristan's cheerful tune returns, incongruously, in the orchestra after the cannon shot from the Castel Sant' Angelo and while Angelotti and Cavaradossi are making their escape. When the Sacristan enters, he is soon joined by a crowd of choristers and acolytes, with whom he joins in a carefree chorus which is suddenly cut off by Scarpia's theme and the entrance of Scarpia himself.

During Scarpia's exchanges with Tosca, a religious atmosphere begins to be built up by the tolling of the church bells, woven into the orchestral texture. Tosca's F sharp minor arioso, 'Ed io venivo' (Either I come), brings a portentous note of foreboding to the scene, but the finale to the act is formally begun only after her exit, with Scarpia's instructions to Spoletta ('Tre sbirri, una carozza': Three agents, a carriage). Violence and lust are combined in Scarpia's musings, while behind him the Cardinal's procession begins: Puccini's timing here is masterly, and his sense, if not of drama then certainly of melodrama, cannot be faulted. At the choral climax of the *Te Deum*, Scarpia suddenly comes to, and 'con entusiasmo religioso' joins in the chant. His theme is thundered out by the full orchestra, *tutta forza*, as the curtain falls.

Act II begins with Scarpia soliloquizing in his study, after a brief exchange of dialogue with Sciarrone, behind which can be heard the sound of an eighteenth-century gavotte being played elsewhere in the palace by a flute, supported by a viola and harp. The arioso sometimes referred to as Scarpia's 'Credo', 'Ha più forte sapore la conquista violenta' (I relish violent conquest more [than soft consent]) is brief and unmemorable, its empty rhetoric quite ineffective as musical characterization. Indeed, with the exception of his participation in the Act I finale, Scarpia's music is disappointing throughout the opera. After Spoletta's account of his search for Angelotti, there is heard briefly on the flutes a mournful theme [Ex. 23] which will recur again and again

Ex. 23

during the interrogation and torture of Cavaradossi. Until, during the initial questioning of Cavaradossi, Scarpia orders the window to be shut, the sound of a choir singing a cantata can be heard, with the voice of Tosca in the solo part soaring to her high C. (In Sardou, the cantata is by Paisiello who conducts the performance: Puccini had considered using music by Paisiello, but finally decided upon pastiche.) Scarpia's questions and Cavaradossi's answers are set in a recitative which is closely integrated into the orchestral fabric, their exchanges punctuated by orchestral comment in turn menacing, violent or grimly dolorous.

When Cavaradossi is removed to the adjacent torture chamber, Scarpia at first assumes a suave manner for his scene with Tosca, and the music momentarily takes on a misleadingly lyrical character. Slowly but

inexorably the brutality emerges. It is this scene which is both the most
effective and the most sickening in *Tosca*, as Puccini, in his musical
equivalent of *grand guignol*, piles on the agony. Cavaradossi's off-stage
cries of pain, the nerve-grating orchestral phrases which depict the
application of physical torture, Scarpia's cat-and-mouse manner with
Tosca, her shrieks of desperation and despair, all combine to increase
the tension until, in a phrase [Ex. 24] which will reappear in her aria later
in the act, Tosca confesses that she can bear no more, and soon
afterwards reveals Angelotti's whereabouts to Scarpia.

Ex. 24

Cavaradossi's cry of defiance, 'Vittoria! Vittoria! L'alba vindice
appar' (Victory! The avenging dawn appears) is musically poor stuff and
dramatically risible, but it provides a welcome relief after the musical
quasi-pornography of the preceding scene, and gives the tenor a chance
to show off his dramatic range and his ringing A sharp before he is
knocked unconscious and dragged away. Scarpia at first attempts to
resume his suave manner with Tosca, but then reveals his passion for her
in 'Già, mi dicon venal' (They already call me venal), which is perhaps
not one of Puccini's most original arias but which is, in context, quite
effective. Tosca's aria, 'Vissi d'arte, vissi d'amore' (I have lived for art, I
have lived for love) has achieved popularity beyond the confines of the
opera, a broadly flowing lyrical *andante* which is welcome after the
violent non-lyricism of Act II up to this point. After its opening phrase
[Ex. 25], the aria is based on the music to which Tosca had made her first

Ex. 25   Andante lento appassionato   ♩ = 40

entrance in Act I, the theme being heard only in the orchestra while
Tosca sings a kind of descant to it.

   'Vissi d'arte' ends with two bars of music which are virtually never
performed. Scarpia asks 'Risolvi?' (Have you decided?), to which Tosca
replies 'Mi vuoi supplice ai tuoi piedi?' (Do you want me to kneel at your
feet?). Conductors invariably make a *fermata* or pause after the
soprano's 'Perchè me ne remuneri così?' in order to encourage
applause for her, which is sometimes forthcoming and sometimes not.
(The absence of applause at this moment does not necessarily indicate
that the performance has been ineffective: a dramatically affecting 'Vissi
d'arte' does not invite applause.) After the applause or non-applause,

the performance usually takes up again two bars later, at the *allegro agitato*. This unworthy practice can be understood, if not condoned, when resorted to in the opera house. Oddly, however, it has spread to gramophone recordings of the opera, most of which omit the Scarpia–Tosca question and answer.[1]

After Scarpia has given his instructions to Spoletta for an execution 'come Palmieri' (just like Palmieri), Spoletta makes his exit, repeating 'come Palmieri' meaningfully, and sometimes so meaningfully that one is surprised that Tosca suspects nothing. She and Scarpia are now left alone, and the finale of Act II is approached at an inexorable pace, its inevitability and, somehow, its tragic outcome emphasized by the *andante sostenuto* theme [Ex. 26] played by muted violins on the G string as

Ex. 26

Scarpia proceeds to write out a safe-conduct pass for Tosca and Cavaradossi; the mood of portentous unease of this theme does something to elevate the stature of the opera at this point, when what we are, in fact, about to witness is an act of savage brutality. The orchestral turmoil as Tosca stabs Scarpia was thought by Ernest Newman to be 'curiously suggestive of the furious outburst that follows the slow movement of the Ninth Symphony';[2] it is followed, as Scarpia breathes his last, by a return of the Ex. 26 theme which now seems to be almost a threnody to the passing of the old order. Tosca's phrase, 'E avanti a lui tremava tutta Roma' (And before him the whole of Rome trembled), is written to be sung in a monotone on middle C. Most sopranos substitute a melodramatic spoken delivery of the line, but Puccini's version is to be preferred.

After Tosca's words, whether spoken or sung, the act ends quietly, as wisps of earlier themes are played softly, to dissolve in a slow sequence of chords separated by pauses. There is a sudden *forte* in the orchestra when a distant drum-roll brings a reminder of urgency and a presage of Cavaradossi's fate, but the final bars are little more than a whisper of sound, to accompany Tosca's stealthy departure.

The curtain rises on Act III after a 16-bar passage played by four horns in unison, a tune which will later be sung in unison by Tosca and Cavaradossi. As the horns fade into silence, an orchestral prelude

---

[1] These two bars are missing even from the much-acclaimed recording conducted by De Sabata, with Callas and Gobbi. Anyone curious to hear them will find them in the RCA recording conducted by Zubin Mehta, with Leontyne Price as Tosca and Sherrill Milnes as Scarpia.

[2] Newman, op. cit.

begins, accompanying the stage picture of the castle platform in the last moments before dawn with a musical portrait of the approach of day. A boy (soprano) singing to his sheep, the jangle of sheep bells and of church bells, these idyllic sounds are disturbed by framents of themes reminiscent of Scarpia, Tosca and Cavaradossi and their passionate involvement. Slowly, the music, in the strings, begins to speak more of the human drama than of the Roman dawn, and a gaoler appears on the stage to await the arrival, under escort, of Cavaradossi, whose entrance is accompanied by the orchestra's statement of what will become the melody of his aria, 'E lucevan le stelle'.

Before Cavaradossi begins his aria, four solo cellos play the theme [Ex. 22] of the Act I love duet as he mentions a person dear to him whom he leaves behind, and violins later join in a further statement of the theme when he sits to write his farewell to Tosca. A solo clarinet introduces the tune of 'E lucevan le stelle' above which the tenor's phrases are recited in a quasi-monotonous recitative. Then, at the words 'O dolci baci' (O sweet kisses), the tenor takes up the melody with the strings doubling it 'con grande sentimento'. Though it can easily be vulgarized by overhysterical performance, this aria of despairing self-pity is exquisitely written and constructed with a simplicity and ease which make it one of Puccini's finest lyrical pieces.

The love theme is heard again in the orchestra as Tosca enters with Spoletta, and fragments of other themes recur as Tosca describes to Cavaradossi how she has secured his release. At the words 'Lì presso luccicava una lama' (Close at hand there glittered a blade), her vocal line alludes, rather oddly, to the melody of Ex. 26; an exultant high C celebrates her fatal thrust of the knife. Cavaradossi's lyrical 'O dolci mani' (O gentle hands) [Ex. 27], derived from a tune salvaged by Puccini

Ex. 27 *teneramente*   p

O dol - ci   ma - ni   mansuete e pu - re.

from the discarded Act IV of *Edgar*, also quotes momentarily from Ex. 26. It is followed by Tosca's not so lyrical instructions in the art of pretending to fall dead, and by the duet 'Amaro sol per te' (The sting of death for thee), which is unremarkable except for two bars in the orchestra which suddenly sound as though they have strayed in by mistake from *Madama Butterfly* or *Turandot*, both operas yet to be composed. The first part of the phrase did, in due course, turn up in *Turandot*. A unison passage at the conclusion of the duet is sung to the music heard at the very beginning of the act played by horns before the rise of the curtain.

The sinister march to which the firing squad enters and leaves is quickly followed by the final bars of the opera, some undistinguished 'flurry' music as Tosca is pursued by the soldiers, and the wildly inappropriate statement by the full orchestra, 'tutta forza con grande slancio', of Cavaradossi's 'O dolci baci, o languide carezze' from his aria 'E lucevan le stelle'. The theme from the love duet or even the fateful Ex. 26 would have made a more suitable conclusion. Even better would have been the Scarpia theme with which the opera began.

Tosca can hardly be described as its composer's finest creation: its lyrical pages are, with one or two exceptions, not among Puccini's most successful, and its dramatic music rarely rises above a workaday level. The fact remains, however, that it is one of Puccini's most popular operas, and would stand high on any list of popular operas. An American professor[1] has called it a 'shoddy little shocker', and Benjamin Britten wrote of becoming 'sickened by the cheapness and emptiness' of Puccini's music.[2] *Tosca* is popular with audiences not because of the quality of its music, but because its melodramatic plot is tautly constructed, and its three leading roles give their interpreters ample opportunity to shine vocally (Cavaradossi), dramatically (Scarpia) and both vocally and dramatically (Tosca). And, of course, it contains in 'Vissi d'arte' and 'E lucevan le stelle' two highly effective arias.

[1] Joseph Kerman, in *Opera as Drama* (New York, 1956).
[2] In *Opera* (February 1951). Britten was referring specifically to *La Bohème*, but the context makes it clear that his comment is intended to apply to Puccini's music generally.

VI

Madama Butterfly

a Japanese tragedy in two acts

Dramatis personæ:

Madama Butterfly (Cio-Cio-San)	(soprano)
F. B. Pinkerton, Lieutenant in the United States Navy	(tenor)
Suzuki, Butterfly's servant	(mezzo-soprano)
Sharpless, United States Consul at Nagasaki	(baritone)
Goro, a marriage broker	(tenor)
The Bonze, Butterfly's Uncle	(bass)
Kate Pinkerton	(mezzo-soprano)
Prince Yamadori	(baritone)
Imperial Commissioner	(bass)
Yakuside	(baritone)
The Official Registrar	(baritone)
Butterfly's Mother	(mezzo-soprano)
Butterfly's Aunt	(mezzo-soprano)
Butterfly's Cousin	(soprano)

LIBRETTO by Giuseppe Giacosa and Luigi Illica, based on *Madame Butterfly*, David Belasco's dramatization of a story by John Luther Long

TIME: 1904
PLACE: Nagasaki, Japan

FIRST PERFORMED at the Teatro alla Scala, Milan, on 17 February, 1904, with Rosina Storchio (Butterfly), Giovanni Zenatello (Pinkerton), Giuseppe de Luca (Sharpless), Giuseppina Giaconia (Suzuki), conducted by Cleofonte Campanini. Revised version first performed in Brescia, at the Teatro Grande, on 28 May, 1904, with the same conductor and cast, except for Butterfly, who was sung by Salomea Krusceniski.

Madama Butterfly

EVEN BEFORE TOSCA had been successfully launched in Rome in January, 1900, Puccini began to search for a suitable subject for his next opera. A number of plays and novels were considered, among them Maeterlinck's *Pelléas et Mélisande* (although, or perhaps because, Puccini knew that Debussy was already at work on his opera based on the play), Victor Hugo's *Les Misérables* and Alphonse Daudet's *Tartarin de Tarascon*. It was not until he went to London in the summer of 1900 in connection with the first English production of *Tosca* that Puccini found what he was looking for: a one-act play, *Madame Butterfly*. The composer's London friends Alfredo and Maria Angeli drew his attention to the play, and when Puccini attended a performance at the Duke of York's Theatre he was deeply impressed by what he saw: by what he saw rather than by what he heard, for his English was too poor for him to understand much of the dialogue. He was greatly struck by the performance of Evelyn Millard as Butterfly, and also by the production and staging by David Belasco, who had adapted the play from a story by John Luther Long. Belasco, in an autobiographical article[1] which is probably no more trustworthy than the general run of theatrical memoirs, tells how Puccini rushed into the green room after the performance, embraced him, and begged for permission to use the play as the basis of his next opera. 'I agreed at once,' wrote Belasco, 'and told him he could do anything he liked with the play, and make any sort of contract, because it was impossible to discuss arrangements with an impulsive Italian who has tears in his eyes and both his arms round your neck.'

Tears notwithstanding, on his way back to Italy from London Puccini stopped off in Paris where he consulted Émile Zola about the possibility of using Zola's novel, *La Faute de l'abbé Mouret*, for his next opera. And some weeks later he was considering Marie Antoinette as a subject. However, in a letter to Giulio Ricordi in November, after mentioning various other suggestions, Puccini admits he has not yet found his subject:

I despair of it and am tormented in spirit. If at least some reply would come from New York [i.e. from David Belasco]. The more I think of *Butterfly* the

[1] Published in *Harper's Magazine*, 1914–15.

more irresistibly am I attracted. Oh, if only I had it here that I might set to work on it! I think that instead of one act I could make two quite long ones: the first in North America and the second in Japan. Illica could certainly find in the novel everything that is wanted.[1]

'The novel' is, of course, John Luther Long's story, which is not even long enough to be called a novella. When he read the story in Italian, Puccini realized that it was vastly inferior to the play which Belasco had fashioned from it. The play is set entirely in Japan, and takes place within a twenty-four hour period, but it retains much of Long's dialogue, and adds to it, sometimes none too happily (Belasco has Butterfly die in Pinkerton's arms, murmuring, 'Too bad those robins did 'n' nes' again').

It was not until April of the following year, 1901, that negotiations were completed with Belasco for the use of *Madame Butterfly*. (In the intervening months, Italy's greatest composer, Giuseppe Verdi, had died in his eighty-eighth year, and Puccini had attended his funeral as the official representative of the town of Lucca.) As soon as a contract had been signed with Belasco, Puccini's collaborators Giacosa and Illica, the librettists of *La Bohème* and *Tosca*, set to work on the play. (It was to be their third and last Puccini opera: Giacosa died in 1906 and, although Puccini subsequently often considered using Illica either alone or with a partner, he did not, in fact, do so.) As usual, it was Illica's task to plan the dramatic structure and draft the dialogue, which Giacosa would turn into verse. Puccini had by now abandoned his idea of a two-act opera, one act of which would be set in America, and his librettists proceeded to prepare a work in three acts, all of which were set in Japan.

Shortly after beginning work on the libretto, Illica wrote to Ricordi: 'In this first act there are even too many opportunities for music. However, I shall leave them all in, and later we can see which to keep and which not, for all are beautiful.' By the end of the summer, Puccini had received two acts from Illica, but it was June of the following year, 1902, before he was to have the complete libretto, in Giacosa's Italian verse. He had begun to compose the music, but was having second thoughts about the three-act structure. At the end of November, Illica and Giacosa agreed reluctantly to drop the second of the three acts, and Puccini was now able to begin in earnest the composition of the opera.

At the same time he immersed himself in *japonaiserie*, consulting a well-known Japanese actress who happened to be in Milan, and acquiring Japanese folk-songs through the wife of the Japanese Ambassador. His curiosity even extended to the Gilbert and Sullivan Japanese operetta, *The Mikado*, a vocal score of which was still to be seen in his library at Torre del Lago in recent years, with an attempt at Italian translation of two of the numbers pencilled in.

[1] Adami, op. cit.

Work on *Butterfly* was interrupted and slowed down for some months when Puccini's splendid new automobile skidded off the road near Lucca on a wet and foggy night in February, 1903, and plunged down a 15-foot embankment. Puccini was thrown out of the vehicle, and suffered a compound fracture of the right shin bone, from which it took him several months to recover. The fracture was badly set, and had to be broken again and reset, leaving him with a permanent limp. It was to be more than two years before he was able to walk unaided. In May, 1903, he wrote in a state of deep depression to Illica: 'Addio tutto, addio Butterfly, addio vita mia!' But the following month he began slowly to resume work, and by the end of the year the orchestration of *Madama Butterfly* was completed.

On 3 January, 1904, Elvira's husband having finally died, Puccini was able to marry her, thus legitimizing their eighteen-year-old son, Antonio. Three days later he travelled to Milan to supervise preparations for the première of the opera, which took place at La Scala on 17 February.

Everything augured well for the first night: a splendid cast had been assembled, led by Rosina Storchio as Butterfly, Giovanni Zenatello as Pinkerton, and Giuseppe de Luca as Sharpless. The producer of the opera was Giulio Ricordi's son Tito, the décor was by the highly regarded French scenic designer, Lucien Jusseaume, and the conductor was the experienced Cleofonte Campanini. Puccini himself felt confident of success. But the première turned out to be a fiasco, due probably in large part to organized opposition by the composer's enemies. The Act I love duet was greeted with hisses and catcalls, 'Un bel dì' was heard in apathetic silence, and when Butterfly's kimono accidentally billowed up in front of her, a cry of 'Butterfly is pregnant' amused the audience considerably. At the end of Butterfly's vigil, Tito Ricordi had arranged an imitation of birdsong to greet the dawn: this elicited loud bird and animal cries from the audience. The newspaper headlines the following morning included 'Puccini Hissed', 'Fiasco at La Scala', and 'Butterfly, Diabetic Opera, Result of an Accident'.

Puccini withdrew the opera immediately after its first performance, and returned to the Scala management his fee for the production rights. Four days later, he wrote to a friend:

> I am still shocked by all that happened – not so much for what they did to my poor Butterfly, but for all the poison they spat on me as an artist and as a man . . . They have printed all kinds of things! Now they say that I am going to rewrite the opera and that it will take me six months! I am not rewriting anything or, at least, very few details. I shall make a few cuts, and divide the second act into two parts – something which I had already thought of doing during the rehearsals, but it was then too near the first performance. . . . That first performance was a Dantean Inferno, prepared in advance.[1]

[1] Ibid.

Pinkerton arrested him with a savage snort.

'You are usually merely frivolous, Sayre; but today you are silly.'

Without manifest offence, Sayre went on:

'When I was out here in 1890 – '

'The story of the Pink Geisha?'

'Well – yes,' admitted Sayre, patiently.

'Excuse me, then, till you are through.' He turned to go below.

'Heard it, have you?'

'A thousand times – from you and others.'

Sayre laughed good-naturedly, and passed Pinkerton his cigarette-case.

'Ah! Ever heard who the man was?'

'No.' He lighted his cigarette. 'That has been your own little mystery – apparently.'

'Apparently?'

'Yes; we all knew it was yourself.'

'It wasn't,' said Sayre, steadily. 'It was my brother.' He looked away.

'Oh!'

'He's dead.'

'Beg pardon. You never told us that.'

'He went back; couldn't find her.'

'And you advise me also to become a subject for remorse? That's good of you.'

'It is not quite the same thing. There is no danger of you losing your head for – ' he glanced uncertainly at Pinkerton, then ended lamely – 'any one. The danger would probably be entirely with – the other person.'

'Thanks,' laughed Pinkerton; 'that's more comforting.'

'And yet,' mused Sayre, 'you are hard to comfort – humanly speaking.'

Pinkerton smiled at this naïve but quite exact characterization of himself.

'You are,' continued Sayre, hesitating for the right word, 'impervious.'

'Exactly,' laughed Pinkerton. 'I *don't* see much danger to myself in your prescription. You have put it in rather an attractive light. The idea cannot be entirely disreputable if your brother Jack used it. We lower-class fellows used to call him Agamemnon, you remember.'

'It is not my prescription,' said Sayre, briefly, leaving the deck.

Long's story is competently told, in a plain, unvarnished prose. His attitude to his heroine is one of delicately balanced ironic sympathy:

But Pinkerton not only got himself married; he provided himself with an establishment, creating his menage in quite his own way and entirely for his own comfort.

With the aid of a marriage broker, he found both a wife and a house in which to keep her. This he leased for nine hundred and ninety-nine years. Not, he explained to his wife later, that he could hope for the felicity of residing there with her so long, but because, being a mere 'barbarian', he could not make other terms. He did not mention that the lease was terminable, nevertheless, at the end of any month, by the mere neglect to pay the rent. Details were distasteful to Pinkerton; besides, she would probably not appreciate the humour of this.

Some clever Japanese artisans then made the paper walls of the pretty
house eye-proof, and, with their own adaptions of American hardware, the
openings cunningly lockable. The rest was Japanese.

Mme Butterfly laughed, and asked him why he had gone to all that trouble
– in Japan.

'To keep out those who are out, and in those who are in,' he replied, with
an amorous threat in her direction.

She was greatly pleased with it all, though, and went about jingling her new
keys and her new authority like toys – she had only one small maid to
command – until she learned that among others to be excluded were her own
relatives.

Less expert with dialogue, at any rate with the speech of his non-
Americans, Long has Butterfly utter a most unconvincing pidgin English
which seems frequently to take on something of the speech-patterns of
the American Negro stereotype, as in this scene with her maid, after
Pinkerton's departure:

'Aha, ha, ha! Aha, ha, ha! What you thing, liddle maiden? Tha's good
song 'bout sorrow, an' death, an' heaven? Aha, ha, ha! What – you – thing?
Speak!'

She tossed the samisen to its place, and sprang savagely at the maid.

'If that Mr B. F. Pikkerton see us doing alig those – ' ventured the maid in
the humour of her mistress.

'O-o-o! You see his eye flame an' scorch lig lightening! O-o-o! He snatch
us away to the house – so – so – *so!*'

The baby was the unfortunate subject for the illustration of this. He began
to whimper.

Rog-a-by, bebby, off in Japan,
You jus' a picture off of a fan.

This was from Pinkerton. She had been the baby then.

'Ah, liddle beggar, he din' know he go'n' make those poetries for you! He
don' suspect of you whichever. *Well!* I bed you we go'n' have some fun when
he *do*. Oh, Suzuki! Some day, when the emperor go abroad, we will show
him. You got say these way' – she changed her voice to what she fancied an
impressive male basso: '"Behole, heaven-descended-ruler-everlasting-
great-Japan, the first of your subjecks taken his eye out those ver' blue heaven
whence you are descend!" Hence the emperor loog on him; then he *stop* an'
loog; he kin naever git enough loogs. Then he make Trouble a large prince!
An' me? He jus' say onto me: "Continue that you bring out such sons." Aha,
ha, ha! What you thing?'

The maid was frankly sceptical.

'At least you can do lig the old *nakodo* wish you – for you are most
beautiful.'

Cho-Cho-San dropped the baby with a reckless thud, and sprang at her
again. She gripped her throat viciously, then flung her, laughing aside.

'Speak concerning marriage once more, an' you die. An' tha' 's 'nother thing. You got to know at his United States America, if one is marry one got stay marry – oh foraever an' aever! *Yaes!* Nob'y cannot git himself divorce, aexcep' in a large courthouse an' jail. Tha's way with he – that Mr B. F. Pikkerton – an' me. If he aever go'n' divorce me, he got take me at those large jail at that United States America. Tha's lot of trouble; hence he rather stay marry with me. Also, he *lig* be marry with me. Now loog! He leave me a 'mos' largest lot money in Japan; he give me this house for live inside for nine hundred an' ninety-nine year. I cannot go home at my grandmother, account he make them outcast me. Sa-*ay*, you liddle foolish! He coming when the robins nest again. Aha! What you thing?'

The maid should have been excused for not being always as recklessly jubilant as her mistress; but she never was. And now, when she chose silence rather than speech (which was both more prudent and more polite), she took it very ill.

John Luther Long's Butterfly attempts to kill herself, but survives. Long's writing is at its best in the description of her suicide attempt, which he handles with tact and a sensitive observation: the final sentence at the end of his story is all the more effective for its objectivity.

She sat quite still, and waited till night fell. Then she lighted the andon, and drew her toilet-glass toward her. She had a sword in her lap as she sat down. It was the one thing of her father's which her relatives had permitted her to keep. It would have been very beautiful to a Japanese, to whom the sword is a soul. A golden dragon writhed about the superb scabbard. He had eyes of rubies, and held in his mouth a sphere of crystal that meant many mystical things to a Japanese. The guard was a coiled serpent of exquisite workmanship. The blade was tempered into shapes of beasts at the edge. It was signed, 'Ikesada'. To her father it had been honour. On the blade was this inscription:

To die with honour
When one can no longer live with honour.

It was in obscure ideographs; but it was also written on her father's *kaimyo* at the shrine, and she knew it well.

'To die with honour – ' She drew the blade affectionately across her palm. Then she made herself pretty with vermilion and powder and perfumes; and she prayed, humbly endeavouring at the last to make her peace. She had not forgotten the missionary's religion; but on the dark road from death to Meido it seemed best to trust herself to the compassionate augustnesses.

Then she placed the point of the weapon at that nearly nerveless spot in the neck known to every Japanese, and began to press it slowly inward. She could not help a little gasp at the first incision. But presently she could feel the blood finding its way down her neck. It divided on her shoulder, the larger stream going down her bosom. In a moment she could see it making its way daintily between her breasts. It began to congeal there. She pressed on the sword, and a fresh stream swiftly overran the other – redder, she thought. And then suddenly she could no longer see it. She drew the mirror closer. Her hand was heavy, and the mirror seemed far away. She knew that she must hasten. But even as she locked her fingers on the serpent of the guard, something within her cried out piteously. They had taught her how to die, but he had taught her how to live – nay, to make life sweet. Yet that was the reason she must die. Strange reason! She now first knew that it was sad to die. He had come, and substituted himself for everything; he had gone, and left her nothing.

The maid softly put the baby into the room. She pinched him, and he began to cry.

'Oh, pitiful Kwannon! Nothing?'

The sword fell dully to the floor. The stream between her breasts darkened and stopped. Her head drooped slowly forward. Her arms penitently out-stretched themselves toward the shrine. She wept:

'Oh, pitiful Kwannon!'

The baby crept cooing into her lap. The little maid came in and bound up the wound.

When Mrs Pinkerton called next day at the little house on Higashi Hill it was quite empty.

Long's story created a great deal of interest in America, and more than one leading actress approached the author for permission to have it adapted for the stage. But it was David Belasco to whom Long agreed to grant the dramatic rights and who alone, and not (as one often reads) in collaboration with Long, wrote the play which he also directed both in New York and London.[1]

David Belasco (1859–1931) was one of the most colourful characters in the American theatre of his day. Descended from a family of Por-tuguese Jews who emigrated to England in the sixteenth century to escape religious persecution, and whose nineteenth-century descen-dants travelled to California in 1848 in search of gold, Belasco was born in San Francisco. By the age of eighteen he was acting in theatre com-panies in California, and soon progressed to producing and adapting plays, and eventually to writing them. Though he could hardly be described as a major dramatist, he strongly influenced American theatre in the direction of greater naturalism, and, as a producer, specialized in stage pictures of an almost cinematic realism. Belasco's best-known plays include a Civil War story, *The Heart of Maryland* (1895), and *The Girl of the Golden West* (1905) which in due course was to provide Puccini with the scenario of *La fanciulla del west*.

The play, *Madame Butterfly*, billed as 'by David Belasco from John Luther Long's Japanese story', was constructed in one act and was produced in a double bill with a farce, *Naughty Anthony*, also by Belasco, at the Herald Square Theatre, New York, on 5 March, 1900.

The farce had been playing there since early January, but audiences

[1] Belasco and Long did collaborate, the following year, in writing a play, *The Darling of the Gods*.

were falling off and Belasco needed a short play to add to the bill to warrant *Naughty Anthony* continuing its run. His attention drawn to John Luther Long's story, Belasco adapted it for the stage, supervised the construction of the scenery and put *Madame Butterfly* into rehearsal, all within a fortnight, and indeed before a contract had been drawn up with Long.

Belasco recognized, in adapting the story, that it would not provide material for a full-length play, but he also saw that at one point it required some halting of the action to denote the passage of time. He regarded this as a challenge to his technical ingenuity, and came up with the episode of Butterfly's vigil which Puccini carried over into his opera. In his book *The Theater Through its Stage Door* David Belasco wrote:

> I have been asked many times what I consider my most successful achievement in stirring imagination through the agencies of acting. I invariably reply that the scene of the passing of an entire night in *Madame Butterfly* has been my most successful effort in appealing to the imaginations of those who have sat before my stage. In that scene, the little Japanese heroine is waiting with her child for its father, Lieutenant Pinkerton, to come from the American ship. The vigil represented an entire night. To portray this episode, Blanche Bates was compelled to hold the stage for fourteen minutes without uttering a word. So, to keep an audience's imagination stirred – to persuade it that what it was witnessing was real – it was necessary to have a scene of changing beauty. There was not a dissenting voice in the criticism of that scene. My experiment was hazardous, but it succeeded, and its success was due entirely to its imaginative appeal. The secret of its fascination lay in my use of lights.[1]

Belasco did not adapt the whole of Long's story: the entire action of his play takes place two years after Pinkerton has sailed away, indeed on the eve and the actual day of his return. (Puccini and his librettists went back to the original story for material for their Act I.) The English dialogue Belasco writes for Cho-Cho-San and Suzuki is no more convincing than Long's: for the most part he makes use of Long's actual words. Here is the scene which, when Giacosa and Illica produced their Italian paraphrase of it, inspired Puccini to write his most famous aria, 'Un bel dì' (One fine day):

MADAME BUTTERFLY (*laughing*): 'Aha, that's 'Merican way sayin' good-bye to girl. Yaes, he come back w'en robins nes' again. Shu'h! Shu'h! (*She claps her hands with delight. Suzuki, with a look of unbelief, starts to go.*) Sa-ey! Why no 'shu'h' on you face for? Such a fools! (*Looking towards the windows.*) O look! Suzuki – a robins. The firs' these spring! Go, see if he's stay for nes'.

SUZUKI (*looking*): It *is* a robins, O Cho-Cho-San!

MADAME BUTTERFLY (*running to the window*): O! O!

[1] David Belasco, *The Theater Through its Stage Door* (New York, 1928).

SUZUKI:	But he's fly away.
MADAME BUTTERFLY:	O! How they are slow this year! Sa-ey, see if you don' fin' one tha's more in-dus-trial an' domestics.
SUZUKI (*looking out*):	There are none yet.
MADAME BUTTERFLY:	But soon they nes' now. Suzuki, w'en we see that ship comin' in – sa-ey – then we goin' put flowers aevery where, an' if it's night, we goin' hang up mos' one thousan' lanterns – eh-ha?
SUZUKI:	'No got moaney for thousan'.
MADAME BUTTERFLY:	Wael, twenty, mebby; an' sa-ey, w'en we see him comin' quick up path – (*imitates*) so – so – so – (*lifts her kimono and strides in a masculine fashion*) to look for liddle wive – me – me jus' goin' hide behind shoji (*making two holes with her wet finger in the low paper shoji and peeking through*) an' watch an' make believe me gone 'way; leave liddle note – sayin': 'Goon-bye, sayonara, Butterfly.' . . . Now he come in. . . . (*Hides.*) Ah! An' then he get angery! An' he say all kinds of 'Merican languages – debbils – hells! But before he get too angery, me run out an' flew aroun' his neck! (*She illustrates with Suzuki, who is carried away and embraces her with fervour.*) Sa-ey! You no flew roun' his neck – jus' me. (*They laugh in each other's arms.*) Then he'll sit down an' sing tha's liddle 'Merican song – O, how he'll laugh. . . . (*She sings as though not understanding a word of it.*)

> 'I call her the belle of Japan – of Japan,
> Her name it is O Cho-Cho-San, Cho-Cho-San!
> Such tenderness lies in her soft almond eyes,
> I tell you, she's just "ichi ban."'

(*Laughs.*) Then I'll dance like w'en I was geisha girl.

Some weeks after the first New York performances of *Madame Butterfly*, David Belasco took his production of another play (*Zaza*, with Mrs Leslie Carter) to London, and it was during this engagement that arrangements were made for the initial British production of *Madame Butterfly*, which was given as an afterpiece to Jerome K. Jerome's four-act comedy *Miss Hobbs*,[1] already enjoying a successful run at the Duke of York's Theatre, St. Martin's Lane. An English cast was engaged, headed by Evelyn Millard as Butterfly and Allan Aynesworth as Lieutenant Pinkerton, with one member of the original American cast, Claude Gillingwater, repeating his portrayal of Sharpless, the American Consul.

Of *Madame Butterfly*, the London *Times* said that 'in any other than an exotic setting, this dramatic episode would be intolerably painful.

---

[1] Not *Miss Nobbs*, a misprint which Puccini commentators have been copying from one another for the past half-century or more.

Redeemed as it is by delicate grace and, above all, by strangeness of
detail, the little play proves by no means as distressing as a bald recital
may suggest, but tear-compelling merely. A tragedy, to be sure, but a toy
tragedy.' Those were the days when the entire Japanese population was
no more real to the average Westerner than Cho-Cho-San to Kate
Pinkerton. ('KATE: Why you poor little thing . . . who in the world could
blame you or . . . call you responsible . . . you pretty little plaything.
MADAME BUTTERFLY (softly): No – playthin' . . . I am Mrs Lef-ten-ant B. F.
– No – no – now I am, only – Cho-Cho-San, but no playthin'.')

Belasco's major contribution to the story of the geisha and her
western lover lay in his introducing the tragedy of Butterfly's suicide,
and bringing Pinkerton back at the moment of her death. His feat as
producer, in staging the silent scene in which the passage of twelve hours
is conveyed in fourteen minutes through changing lighting effects to
simulate dusk, the starry night sky, dawn and sunrise, is remembered as
a *coup de théâtre*.

When Puccini's *Madama Butterfly* was staged at the Metropolitan
Opera, New York, on 11 February, 1907, 'I loaned my models for the
décor and sent over my electricians,' Belasco told his biographer.[1] Of
Geraldine Farrar as Cio-Cio-San he said that he thought a great
dramatic artist was submerged in the opera singer.

When Illica began work on the libretto of *Madama Butterfly*, he had
only Long's story from which to work: it was several weeks before he was
to see a translation of the Belasco play. Thus, the shape of the opera
follows Long, and its Act I takes place before Pinkerton's desertion of
Butterfly, in fact on the day of their wedding. The second half of the
opera leans more heavily on Belasco who, in adapting Long for the
stage, had already done more than half of Illica's work for him. The
librettist had as we have seen planned a work in three acts, the first and
last of which would be set in Butterfly's house, and the second in the
American Consulate at Nagasaki, Acts I and II being derived primarily
from the story, and Act III from the play. (A letter from Illica to Ricordi,
however, makes it clear that, during the weeks in which the librettist had
been working from Long's story, he had not bothered to read it to the
end!) When he received a draft of the first two acts, Puccini expressed
dissatisfaction at parts of the Consulate act, but it was only after Illica
had completed the three-act draft and Giacosa had turned it into verse,
that the composer realized the structure was not to his liking. On 16
November, 1902, Puccini wrote to Ricordi:

> For two days I have been in an absolutely miserable state of mind. Why?
> Because the libretto, as it stands, is not good from the end of Act II onwards,
> and the realization of this has been very painful. Now, however, I am con-
> vinced that the opera must be in two acts! Don't let this frighten you!

[1] William Winter, *The Life of David Belasco* (New York, 1918).

The Consulate scene was a great mistake. The action must move forward to the end without interruption – rapid, effective and terrifying! In arranging the opera in three acts I was heading for certain disaster. You will see, dear Signor Giulio, that I am right . . . Do not be worried about the two acts. The first lasts a good hour, the second well over the hour, perhaps an hour and a half. But how much more effective!

With this arrangement, I am sure of holding my public and not sending them away disappointed. And at the same time we shall have a new shape of opera and a performance that is quite long enough.[1]

After the first-night fiasco in Milan in February, 1904, composer and publisher withdrew their opera, and certain changes were made before its second production three months later in Brescia: deletions, additions, alterations, and the division of Act II into two parts by an intermission. Puccini continued to make occasional changes after the Brescia performances (vocal scores published in 1906 and 1907 differ from the Brescia version of 1904 and from each other), but the opera as we know it today is basically the work as it was heard in Brescia. Although the division of Act II into two parts effectively turned *Madama Butterfly* into a three-act opera, Puccini preferred to describe it as a two-act work, referring to the three scenes as Act I, Act II, part 1, and Act II, part 2.

Madama Butterfly is one of those rare cases of an opera libretto which is an improvement upon its original source. The plot is slight, the situation alone having to carry the emotional weight of the subject, but the writing of the dialogue is considerably better than it is in either Long or Belasco. In particular, Butterfly's embarrassingly inept pidgin English, invented by Long and retained by Belasco, has been turned not into an impossible Japanese-Italian, but into literate and direct Italian. It is Butterfly's simple and, to western minds, 'quaint' thought-processes which convey her foreignness. Compare the examples of dialogue from story and play, quoted above, with the following exchange between Cio-Cio-San (to give the geisha her Italian spelling) and Suzuki in the opera:

BUTTERFLY:	Perchè dispone che il Console
	provveda alla pigione, rispondi, su!
	Perchè con tante cure
	la casa riforni di serrature,
	s'ei non volesse ritornar mai più?
SUZUKI:	Non lo so.[2]

---

[1] Adami, op. cit.

[2] BUTTERFLY:　Why did he arrange for the Consul to see to the rent? Answer that! Why with such care did he fit the house with locks, if he intended never to return again?
SUZUKI:　I don't know.

BUTTERFLY: Non lo sai?
              Io te lo dico: per tener ben fuori
              le zanzare, i parenti ed i dolori,
              e dentro, con gelosa
              custodia, la sua sposa,
              la sua sposa che son io – Butterfly!
SUZUKI: Mai non s'è udito
              di straniero marito
              che sia tornato al suo nido.
BUTTERFLY: Ah! taci, o t'uccido.
              Quell' ultima mattina:
              'Tornerete, signor?' gli domandai.
              Egli, col cuore grosso,
              per celarmi la pena, sorridendo rispose:
              'O Butterfly, piccina mogliettina,
              tornerò colle rose
              alla stagion serena
              quando fa la nidiata il pettirosso.'
              Tornerá.
SUZUKI: Speriam.
BUTTERFLY: Dillo con me: Tornerà.
SUZUKI: Tornerà.[1]

Lieutenant Pinkerton poses a problem. He is clearly no clean-cut, conventional hero; at least, not in the context of his involvement with Cio-Cio-San, for he behaves most callously to her. This comes across less decisively in the original story where the author has opportunities to comment upon Pinkerton's actions, explaining if not actually condoning them, but it is clear enough in Belasco's play, in which Pinkerton plays only a minor part, entering on page 16 of the play's 20 pages, and uttering but six lines of dialogue, not enough to enable charm of personality to mitigate caddishness of character. In the opera, Pinkerton's easy-going philosophy is presented with a disarming frankness in his Act I scene with Sharpless, the Consul, but in the Butterfly–Pinkerton duet at the end of the act, it must be admitted that Giacosa and Illica did not give Puccini any encouragement to treat Pinkerton as other than a

---

[1] BUTTERFLY: You don't know? I'll tell you: to keep mosquitoes, relatives and troubles outside, and inside, jealously guarded, his bride – his bride – me – Butterfly!
SUZUKI: But it's unknown for a foreign husband to come back to his home.
BUTTERFLY: Ah, be quiet, or I'll kill you! That last morning I asked him: 'Will you come back, my lord?' He, with heavy heart, trying to hide his sorrow from me, answered with a smile: 'Oh Butterfly, my darling little wife, I shall return with the roses, in that happy season when the robin makes his nest.' He will return.
SUZUKI: Let us hope so.
BUTTERFLY: Say it with me: He will return.
SUZUKI: He will return.

typical Italian tenor hero, romantically in love. This tends to make the Lieutenant's desertion of his Japanese child-bride seem all the more brutal.

Lieutenant Pinkerton's given names are Benjamin Franklin: in the story, Butterfly calls him 'Mr Ben-ja-meen Frang-a-leen Pikkerton'. In the opera as we know it today, although Pinkerton has retained his names – in the marriage ceremony the Imperial Commissioner addresses him as 'Benjamin Franklin Pinkerton, Luogotenente nella cannoniera "Lincoln", marina degli Stati Uniti, America del Nord' (Lieutenant Benjamin Franklin Pinkerton of the gunboat *Lincoln*, Navy of the United States, North America) – Butterfly continually refers to herself not as Mrs B. F. Pinkerton, but as Mrs F. B. Pinkerton. Perhaps this inconsistency is retained, at least in English-speaking countries, merely in order to avoid a laugh at B. F. (for 'bloody fool'), but Illica's original sketch of his libretto refers throughout to 'F. B. Pinkerton', and in the marriage ceremony actually spells out his full name as the highly unlikely '*Sir Francis Blummy* Pinkerton'. After the first Scala performances, Francis Blummy was dropped, and the original Benjamin Franklin returned, stripped of his extremely un-American knighthood. But, for whatever reason, or simply by oversight, elsewhere in the opera he remains F. B. Pinkerton. Easier to explain is the custom in German-speaking countries of changing Pinkerton's name to Linkerton, for the German verb 'pinkeln' means 'to piss', and Pinkerton would sound as comically in German ears as Piddleton or Pissington would in English. (Mosco Carner's suggestion[1] that Linkerton was used because Pinkerton 'happened to be the name of a famous American detective agency' is as unconvincing as it is unnecessary.)

Puccini was surely correct in his decision not to include an act set at the Consulate, even though, in deciding thus, he lost the touching little scene in Long's story in which Cho-Cho-San visits the Consul and discovers accidentally and shockingly that Pinkerton has an American wife:

A woman entered.

'Mr Sharpless – the American Consul?' she asked, while crossing the threshold.

The Consul bowed.

'Can you reach my husband at Kobe – by telegraph?'

'I think so. Who is your husband?'

He took up a writing-pad as he spoke.

'Lieutenant Pinkerton of the ——.'

'One moment, for God's sake!'

It was too late. The eyes of the little woman in the chair were fixed on his. They even tried to smile a little, wearily, at the poor result of his compassionate lying. She shook her head for silence.

[1] In *Puccini*.

'I beg your pardon; I'm – I am – *ill*,' said the Consul, roughly. Insufficient as the explanation was, he made no other. 'Proceed.'

'I should like you to send this telegram: "Just saw the baby and his nurse. Can't we have him at once? He is lovely. Shall see the mother about it tomorrow. Was not at home when I was there today. Expect to join you Wednesday week per *Kioto Maru*. May I bring him along? ADELAIDE."'

As she advanced and saw Cho-Cho-San, she stopped in open admiration.

'How very charming – how *lovely* – you are, dear! Will you kiss me, you pretty – *plaything*!'

'No,' said Cho-Cho-San, staring at her.

'Ah, well,' laughed the other, 'I don't blame you. They say you don't do that sort of thing. I quite forgive our men for falling in love with you. Thanks for permitting me to interrupt you. And, Mr Sharpless, will you get that off at once? Good day!'

She went with the hurry in which she had come. It was the blonde woman they had seen on the deck of the passenger steamer.

Cho-Cho-San rose, and staggered toward the Consul. She tried again to smile, but her lips were tightly drawn against her teeth. Searching unsteadily in her sleeve, she drew out a few small coins, and held them out to him. He curiously took them on his palm.

'They are his, all that is left of his beautiful moaney. I shall need no more. Give them to him. I lig if you also say I sawry – no, no, no! glad – glad!' She humbly sighed. '*Me?* I – I wish him that happiness same lig he wish for himself – an' – an' – me.'

Her head drooped for a moment. When she raised it she was quite emotionless, if one might judge from her face.

The action of *Madama Butterfly* takes place in Nagasaki in the early 1900s, in a Japanese house and terrace on a hill overlooking the harbour.

Act I. The marriage broker Goro (tenor) is showing the house to Lieutenant Pinkerton of the United States Navy (tenor) who is about to enter into a form of marriage with the geisha Cio-Cio-San. Goro describes the sliding doors and other practical arrangements, and introduces the three servants, among them Suzuki (mezzo-soprano). Pinkerton is amused by Goro's description of the relatives of Cio-Cio-San who can be expected to attend the ceremony. Sharpless, the American Consul (baritone) arrives, and Pinkerton expounds his hedonistic philosophy in general, and his light-hearted attitude to his forthcoming marriage in particular. The marriage contract is for 999 years, but there is, explains Pinkerton, a monthly get-out clause. Sharpless, who has met Cio-Cio-San, or Butterfly as she is known in English, and has been moved by her sincerity, attempts to warn the Lieutenant that his bride-to-be is taking the marriage much more seriously, but when Pinkerton proposes that Sharpless drink with him to 'the day when, in a real ceremony, I marry a real American bride' the two men drink a toast. Goro reappears to announce that Butterfly (soprano) and her friends have just reached the top of the hill.

As she arrives, Butterfly tells her friends that she is the happiest girl in Japan, indeed in the whole world. In conversation with Sharpless, she reveals that her family, once wealthy, lost their fortune, which was why she had to become a geisha; that her father is dead; and that she, Butterfly, is fifteen years old. Pinkerton makes amused and derisory remarks about the crowd of relatives, and Butterfly shyly displays to him her treasures including the dagger with which, at the command of the Emperor, her father had committed *hara-kiri*. She explains to Pinkerton that, in preparation for her marriage, she has been visiting the Christian mission to receive instruction in his religion, and Sharpless again warns his fellow countryman that he must take care, for Butterfly trusts him and loves him.

The brief wedding ceremony is performed by the Imperial Commissioner (bass), who then leaves with his officials and with Sharpless. Pinkerton suggests to Butterfly that they must shortly find a polite way to get rid of the relatives when, suddenly, the festivities are interrupted by the arrival of Butterfly's uncle, a Buddhist priest or Bonze (bass). Furious that Butterfly has renounced her Japanese gods, the Bonze curses her, at which her relations also denounce her. Pinkerton orders them off the premises and, left alone with Butterfly at last, he comforts her. They sing a love duet, Butterfly at first hesitant and shy but finally responsive to Pinkerton's ardour. He draws her inside the house as the curtain falls.

Act II, Part 1. Three years have passed since Pinkerton's ship has left Nagasaki, but, even though Suzuki has her doubts, Butterfly is confident that Pinkerton will return, for he promised her that he would come back 'with the roses, in that happy season when the robins nest again'. In the aria, 'Un bel dì' (One fine day), Butterfly sings with confidence of the day when Pinkerton's vessel will appear again in the harbour, and he will make his way up the hill to greet her. 'All this will happen,' she tells Suzuki, though she is really attempting to convince herself. 'Dispel your fears. With unshakeable faith, I shall await him.' ('Tienti la tua paura. Io con sicura fede l'aspetto.')

Sharpless arrives with Goro, and attempts to read to Butterfly a letter he has received from Pinkerton whose ship will shortly be arriving again in Nagasaki but who will not want to see Butterfly, for he has since married his American sweetheart. Butterfly, however, misunderstands and hears only what she wants to hear, which is that Pinkerton will soon be back. She is overjoyed. When Goro presses his client, the wealthy Japanese Prince Yamadori (baritone), upon her, and Yamadori offers to marry her, Butterfly rejects him politely but firmly, explaining that she is already married to Lieutenant Pinkerton. In desperation, Sharpless asks Butterfly what she would do if Pinkerton were not to return to her. Shocked at such a suggestion, Butterfly replies that she could become a geisha again, or, better, she could die. Sharpless advises her to accept Yamadori's proposal, at which Butterfly rushes out, returning immediately with Pinkerton's child in her arms. She tells the child, who is too young to understand, what Sharpless has said to her. Sharpless, as he leaves, promises to inform Pinkerton of the child's existence.

Goro, who has been telling people that no one knows who the father of Butterfly's child can be, is angrily chased away by Butterfly and Suzuki. Suddenly, a cannon shot is heard, announcing the arrival of a ship which, through her telescope, Butterfly makes out to be Pinkerton's. With Suzuki's help, she joyously decorates the house with flowers from the garden and, as night falls, she, Suzuki, and the child sit, watching through holes she makes in the paper wall, to await Pinkerton's return. As they begin their vigil, the sound of voices humming can be heard in the distance.

Act II, Part 2. After an orchestral intermezzo which accompanies Butterfly's night-long vigil and the coming of dawn, the curtain rises. It is now daylight. The child and Suzuki are asleep, but Butterfly still watches. As Suzuki awakens, Butterfly picks up the sleeping child and takes him off to the next room. Pinkerton and Sharpless arrive, but Suzuki is shaken to see a western woman in the garden, and horrified when she is told that it is Pinkerton's American wife. Sharpless explains to Suzuki that they have come to take the child, for whom the Pinkertons are willing to assume responsibility. Overcome not only with nostalgia at seeing the house again, but also with guilt and remorse, Pinkerton rushes away, leaving his wife Kate (mezzo-soprano) to cope with the situation.

When Butterfly returns, she at first cannot believe that Pinkerton is not present somewhere, perhaps hiding to tease her, but finally she accepts the truth, that Kate is Pinkerton's wife and that she has come for the child. Butterfly agrees to part with her child in half an hour, if Pinkerton himself will come to take him. The visitors leave, and Butterfly collapses in tears. Ordering Suzuki to stay with the child, she takes her father's dagger, reads its inscription, 'He dies with honour who can no longer live with honour' ('Con onor muore chi non può serbar vita con onore'), and is about to stab herself when Suzuki pushes the child into the room in a vain final attempt to dissuade her. Butterfly sits the child on a mat, puts into his hands an American flag and a doll, and persuades him to play with them while she gently blindfolds him. Then she goes behind a screen, kills herself and, in her dying moments, attempts to crawl towards her child, as Pinkerton's voice calling 'Butterfly' is heard outside. Pinkerton and Sharpless rush into the room and run towards Butterfly who points feebly towards the child and dies. Pinkerton kneels over her body, while Sharpless takes the child in his arms.

III

The opera begins with a brief and bustling orchestral prelude, in which two themes which will be heard several times during Act I are presented. The first, highly animated and energetic, is offered in the form of a fugue, while the second is a figure of four chords which will later reveal itself to be associated with the town of Nagasaki, and which, since the stress lies on the third of the four chords, may well be attempting to say to its hearers, 'Na-ga-*sa*-ki.' The curtain rises, and the introduction leads directly into the scene in which Goro describes the 'quaint' Japanese house to an amused Pinkerton, the sprightly theme continuing to be heard in the orchestra beneath the conversational exchanges of the two men. The bustle subsides momentarily as Goro introduces Suzuki and two other servants, to be replaced by a more graceful little theme, but Goro's description of the guests expected to appear for the wedding ceremony produces a new theme for Butterfly's relations, at first announced somewhat comically on the solo bassoon.

The arrival of Sharpless, the Consul, is accompanied by a lyrical phrase on the first violins which suggests the Consul's sympathetic personality: as he and Pinkerton indulge in small talk, the tiny, impressionistic motifs already heard are offered again, but a broader, larger manner, presumably Occidental as opposed to Oriental, emerges quite suddenly with a quotation from the American national anthem, 'The Star-Spangled Banner' scored for woodwind and brass only, and the scene expands into a lyrical duet, launched by Pinkerton with an expansively phrased arietta, 'Dovunque al mondo' (Wherever in the world) [Ex. 28]. Gustav Kobbé wrote: 'The use of the "Star-Spangled Banner"

Ex. 28

motif as a personal theme for Pinkerton always has had a disagreeable effect upon me, and from now on should be objected to by all Americans.'[1] However, this early example of what one might call the Mary Whitehouse syndrome ('What *I* disapprove of *you* shall not enjoy') has never attracted any support: I have yet to meet an American who finds Puccini's use of 'The Star-Spangled Banner' offensive. (It would not be surprising, surely, if Japanese were to find the entire opera offensive, but that is another matter.)

Pinkerton interrupts his own lyrical flow to ask the Consul whether he would prefer 'Milk-Punch o Wisky', and then resumes his aria, with occasional interjections and comments from Sharpless whose part in the duet is subsidiary throughout, though he makes effective use of the *cantabile* phrase which was first heard on the cellos immediately after the 'Star-Spangled Banner' quotation (bars 6 to 8 following Ex. 28). After the two men have drunk a toast to 'America forever', the phrase sung in English, the music relapses into a conversational style again, until Pinkerton's brief aria, 'Amore o grillo' (Love or fancy), a somewhat characterless

[1] *The Complete Opera Book* (New York, 1919).

allegretto moderato in which he sings of his infatuation with Butterfly. The closing pages of the duet are more attractive, and for the first time Sharpless has an equal share of the melodic interest. The two men lapse into parlando again as Pinkerton offers Sharpless another whisky and they toast, this time, Pinkerton's family back home and the girl – 'una vera sposa americana' (a real American wife) – he will one day marry. Pinkerton repeats the climactic phrase from his duet with Sharpless as he sings of his future 'sposa americana'.

His present Japanese bride and her friends are now heard approaching from the distance. Butterfly's voice rises from the soprano chorus of her geisha companions, in an adumbration of the theme which we shall hear again in the love duet at the end of the act [Ex. 29].

Ex. 29

Spi - ra sul ma - re e sul - la ter - ra

This serenely happy ensemble is one of Puccini's most charming and effective numbers, and it is difficult to understand why it should have been greeted with a shout of 'Bohème' at its first performance. There is a certain family resemblance to Musetta's 'Quando m'en vo'' but one would not have expected it to be recognized immediately in the theatre, since the difference of mood and atmosphere surely outweighs the passing melodic similarity. At the end of the ensemble, Butterfly is asked to soar to a sustained high D flat: the alternative phrase for sopranos who do not wish to go above B flat so early in their performance is almost preferable. In the four bars which follow, a delicate theme scored for flute, oboe, harp and bells is heard, which is one of the authentic Japanese tunes Puccini noted and made use of in the opera.

The conversational style returns for the polite exchange of compliments between Butterfly and Pinkerton, in which Sharpless also takes part. In a solo passage, hardly long enough to be called an arietta ('Nessuno si confessa mai nato in povertà': Nobody ever confesses to having been born in poverty), Butterfly is heard at her most Japanese. More often than not, later in the opera, even as early as the love duet which ends Act I, she will sound like Mimi or Tosca, for she quickly and easily falls under the western influence of her American sailor, and is anxious to behave like 'Mrs F. B. Pinkerton'. Here, however, Puccini gives his heroine, to begin with, a chattering vocal line which is meant to sound Oriental to western ears. Twice, the dissonant interval of the augmented fourth – 'the diabolus in musica of medieval music', Mosco Carner reminds us[1] – is heard, and on the second occasion it is in a phrase [Ex. 30], sung to the words 'Ma il turbine rovescia le quercie più robuste' (But the whirlwind uproots the sturdiest oak), which we shall hear again at the moment of Butterfly's greatest suffering. When, in the

[1] In *Madam Butterfly* (Masterworks of Opera series, 1979).

Ex. 30

conversation music, Butterfly mentions her father's death, another sombre theme makes its first appearance, scored here for woodwind instruments in their lowest registers, and punctuated by chords from the trombones.

A few bars of the Japanese Imperial Hymn on the strings are heard as Goro announces the arrival of the Imperial Commissioner, the official from the registry, and the relatives. The relatives' comical bassoon theme accompanies Pinkerton's amused comments to Sharpless, and the relatives chatter away in a lively ensemble, from which there emerges a broad, lyrical melody, perhaps meant to sound somehow more adult than, or superior to these childlike Orientals, in which Sharpless congratulates Pinkerton on his charming bride, but warns him again of the danger of emotionally wounding her. The western and eastern musical styles combine as the relatives continue their chatter behind the conversation of the two Americans in a masterly ensemble, at the climax of which Butterfly joins Pinkerton in his soaring vocal line. The Americanization of Cio-Cio-San has begun.

As the wedding party moves off into the garden for refreshments, Butterfly and Pinkerton converse tenderly, and another Japanese tune, 'The Cherry Blossom', is heard briefly. In a touching arietta, 'Ieri son salita' (Yesterday I went out), Butterfly tells Pinkerton of her desire to be converted to his faith, singing *piano* until the final phrase in which she confesses, in a sudden *forte* outburst, that she loves him. The wedding ceremony is performed, somewhat perfunctorily, and Butterfly's relatives congratulate her, the orchestra offering a theme derived from another Japanese song, 'The Ninon Bashi'. The delicate chorus, 'O Kami! o Kami!', in which Butterfly's family drink to the newly married couple, is interrupted by the arrival of Butterfly's uncle, the Bonze, and by a discordant 'Curse' theme, as he and, after him, the other relatives, renounce Butterfly.

The orchestral din lessens, and Butterfly is comforted by her husband in a tender conversational scene serving to pave the way for the great duet which follows. Lasting nearly fifteen minutes, from Pinkerton's tender 'Viene la sera' (Evening is falling) to the end of the act, this is perhaps Puccini's finest, certainly his longest love duet. Although, at first hearing, its structure may seem rambling, it does in fact progress through several clearly defined moods to its passionate climax. In the section preceding the duet proper, in which Pinkerton consoles the weeping Butterfly, some of the themes heard earlier pass under review, and, in Suzuki's Japanese prayer, the fugal theme from the orchestral introduction to the opera is heard again. The tenderness of the earlier section of the duet begins to move towards passion, at Butterfly's 'Vogliatemi bene' (Love me a little), becomes disturbed when the geisha ponders upon the fate of butterflies whom westerners are known to transfix with a pin, and broadens out into a rapturous finale [Ex. 31],

Ex. 31

which recalls the music of Butterfly's entrance, a semitone lower than when first heard in G flat, the soprano now ending on her high C, the tenor given the option of joining her there or singing a phrase – it is the same phrase that was offered optionally to Butterfly at the climax of her entrance music – which takes him no higher than A. The orchestral postlude dies away, to end on an inconclusive chord.

A miniature *fugato* precedes the rise of the curtain at the beginning of Act II, Part 1, after which the 'Curse' motif reveals the state of Butterfly's mind as she lies on the floor dejectedly, while Suzuki prays. In the scene between Butterfly and Suzuki, when Butterfly sings wistfully of the time when 'the robins build their nest', which is when Pinkerton said he would return, Puccini's orchestra imitates the twittering of birds. Butterfly tries to convince Suzuki that Pinkerton will return, at first by quoting from the love duet. But this does not suffice, and Butterfly tries again, to convince herself as well as Suzuki, in her first full-scale aria in the opera, 'Un bel dì' (One fine day). This is surely the most popular aria Puccini ever composed, and one known to countless thousands who have never attended a performance of the opera for which it was written, or perhaps have never entered an opera house. The vocal line at first displays the calm certainty of Butterfly's conscious mind, but as she becomes agitated in imagining the return of her lover, the voice part takes on an edge of hysteria, until, at her final words, 'Io con sicura fede l'aspetto' (I, with unshakeable faith, will await him), although her words may be confident, the music reveals a frenzied despair. Butterfly's subconscious mind is in a state of fear. The orchestral postlude thunders out, *fortissimo* and *largamente*, the melody of the aria's first eight bars.

Puccini reverts to his conversational vocal style for the scene with Butterfly, Sharpless and Yamadori, with frequent reminiscence in the orchestra of themes previously heard, the fragment of 'The Star-Spangled Banner' and the sound of the twittering robins among them. When Butterfly's suitor Prince Yamadori arrives, he is given a theme of his own, another fragment of Japanese song, familiar to English ears from Sullivan's use of it for the Mikado's entrance in the operetta, *The Mikado*. It is taken from the war song of the imperial Japanese Army.

Butterfly greets Yamadori in phrases full of a tender yearning, though she is supposed to feel nothing but contempt for him. Is this one of those moments when Puccini merely wrote down the notes that came into his head, without considering whether or not they suited the dramatic situation?

Butterfly serves tea to her visitors, to the tune of a 'Valzer lentissimo' or English slow waltz, which seems hardly more appropriate than the melody with which she greeted Yamadori, and which is heard fleetingly as he departs. Sharpless resumes his attempt to prepare Butterfly for the news that Pinkerton will not return to her, and we hear in the accompanying strings a theme which will recur later in the music of Butterfly's vigil. When the Consul asks Butterfly what she would do if Pinkerton were not to return, a sudden *fortissimo* note is struck on the drum and the strings. Sharpless's advice to Butterfly and her reply to it are uttered in dirge-like tones, not unlike the execution music in Act III of *Tosca*. Suddenly, to a triumphant quotation from her entrance music, Butterfly produces her child, to whom she addresses the aria, 'Che tua madre' (That your mother . . .) a noble but melancholy expression of her grief, in a minor key and permeated with a sense of impending tragedy.

After an *allegro vivo* outburst when Suzuki and Butterfly threaten Goro, a distant cannon shot sends Butterfly rushing to look through her telescope at the ship which has arrived in the harbour. The orchestra plays a reprise of the first 16 bars of 'Un bel dì', but its tempo and mood are sadly consolatory, and neither the echoes of 'The Star-Spangled Banner' nor those of the love duet, however confidently they underline Butterfly's excitement, can disguise the fact that disillusion is imminent. However, Butterfly and Suzuki decorate the house with flowers in anticipation of Pinkerton's arrival, as they sing their 'Flower duet', whose closing section in euphonious thirds has something of the voluptuousness of Viennese operetta, à la Lehár [Ex. 32].

Ex. 32

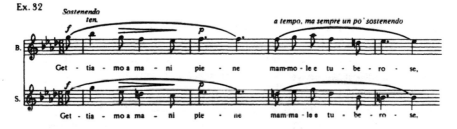

As Butterfly prepares for her vigil, appropriate themes from earlier in the opera are heard occasionally in the orchestra. The scene ends with the instrumental nocturne which accompanies the silent vigil, immediately before which a phrase of great poignancy wells up and dies away again. The music for the vigil is simple, a humming chorus off-stage accompanied by pizzicato strings, but it evokes a mood of poetry and of mystery. (It lasts only for three minutes, not the fourteen minutes of Belasco's scene at this point in the play.)

Act II, Part 2 (which some theatres prefer to call Act III, separating it from the preceding scene by an interval), begins with a long orchestral introduction, or intermezzo, in Puccini's almost Straussian symphonic manner. It takes nearly five minutes to play, and in the theatre always seems awkwardly out of place, an intrusion into the mood and style of the rest of the opera. Without pause, the introduction gives way to the off-stage voices of the sailors calling, and to an orchestral presentation of dawn, complete with those bird whistles which the audience of the Milan première found so hilarious in 1904.

The music in which Butterfly sings to her sleeping child, a theme which we heard when she first showed the child to Sharpless, is touching in its simplicity, and highly effective. Played twice by muted violins in octaves, it is taken up by Butterfly as she carries the child into another room, her voice dying away on a high B, as Suzuki comments 'Povera Butterfly' (Poor Butterfly). Pinkerton and Sharpless now appear, and the grave *largo* theme which accompanies them becomes a duet for tenor and baritone, begun by Sharpless, and then a trio with Suzuki joining in. 'Io so che alle sue pene' (I know that all her sorrows) [Ex. 33] gives Suzuki

Ex. 33

her only chance to participate in an extended lyrical passage. The trio is soon followed by Pinkerton's only solo, the remorse-ridden 'Addio, fiorito asil' (Farewell, flowery refuge), to which Sharpless contributes several phrases, even while the tenor is holding his high B flat at the end. This aria was added by Puccini after the Milan première.

Puccini's fragmented conversational style suffices for the exchanges between Suzuki and Kate Pinkerton, but Butterfly re-enters, and the scene in which slowly the truth dawns upon her consists of an extended arioso solo for Butterfly, with minor contributions from Sharpless and Suzuki. The entire scene is immensely effective in dramatic terms, and Puccini's orchestration is at its most sensitive and communicative: a shortened version of the Curse motif blares forth from three trumpets *fortissimo* as Suzuki tries to prevent Butterfly from encountering Kate Pinkerton; three solo cellos play a softly descending whole-tone scale, to heart-rending effect, as Cio-Cio-San begs Suzuki not to cry, but to answer frankly whether Pinkerton is still alive; the arioso passage beginning 'Sotto il gran ponte del cielo' (Under the great arc of the sky) [Ex. 34] which the heart-broken girl addresses to Kate, and in which she agrees to give up her child, has a grave and tragic beauty. It is here that Butterfly achieves the status of a tragic heroine.

Ex. 34

Sot - to il gran pon - te del cie - lo non v'è don - na di voi più fe - li - ce.

The end comes quickly. As Butterfly takes her father's dagger from its shrine, we hear the Suicide motif growled out roughly in the strings. In a monotone chant, she reads the inscription engraved on the knife, and then, as Suzuki desperately thrusts the child into the room in a vain attempt to deflect her mistress from death, Butterfly utters her farewell to the child she loves. She is already beyond life, and sings with an exalted ecstasy in this final outburst which is one of Puccini's most poignant soprano arias. Her suicide takes place behind a screen, the music dramatically suggesting the exact moment at which she plunges the dagger into her throat. Pinkerton's off-stage cries of 'Butterfly' come too late, for the orchestra is already reminding us, *tutta forza*, of the aria 'Che tua madre' in which Butterfly had said she would die rather than return to her old life. As it does so, the curtain falls on the work of which Puccini later said, 'I am conscious that in it I have written the most modern of my operas.'[1]

More modern than *La fanciulla del west* (not to mention *Turandot* which Puccini had not begun when he made his remark)? Perhaps not. Nor has *Butterfly* the formal beauty of *La Bohème* or the dramatic force of *Tosca*. But, if one responds to Puccini at all, *Butterfly* remains solidly in one's affections.

[1] Specht, op. cit.

VII

La fanciulla del west

an opera in three acts

Dramatis personæ:

Minnie	(soprano)
Jack Rance, Sheriff	(baritone)
Dick Johnson (Ramerrez)	(tenor)
Nick, bartender at the 'Polka' Saloon	(tenor)
Ashby, Wells Fargo agent	(bass)
Sonora	(baritone)
Trin	(tenor)
Sid	(baritone)
Bello	(baritone)
Harry	(tenor)
Joe	(tenor)
Happy	(baritone)
Larkens	(bass)
Billy Jackrabbit, a Red Indian	(bass)
Wowkle, his squaw	(mezzo-soprano)
Jake Wallace, a minstrel	(baritone)
José Castro, a member of Ramerrez's gang	(bass)
Pony Express rider	(tenor)

miners: Sonora, Trin, Sid, Bello, Harry, Joe, Happy, Larkens

LIBRETTO by Guelfo Civinini and Carlo Zangarini, based on the play *The Girl of the Golden West* by David Belasco

TIME: The California Gold Rush of 1849–50
PLACE: A mining camp at Cloudy Mountain, California.

FIRST PERFORMED at the Metropolitan Opera House, New York, on 10 December, 1910, with Emmy Destinn (Minnie), Enrico Caruso (Dick Johnson), Pasquale Amato (Jack Rance), Adamo Didur (Ashby), Dinh Gilly (Sonora), conducted by Arturo Toscanini

La fanciulla del west

I

AFTER THE SUCCESSFUL re-launching of *Madama Butterfly* in Brescia in May, 1904, Puccini began seriously to consider subjects for future operas. He was to spend a considerable amount of time during the following three years in his search for the right play or novel, before alighting on David Belasco again, and his melodrama of the Wild West. One possibility, which the composer mentioned to Illica who thought it would present too many difficulties, was Victor Hugo's *Notre Dame de Paris*, known in English as *The Hunchback of Notre Dame*. Puccini was also in touch with a Florentine dramatist, Valentino Soldani, who made a number of suggestions to him, none of which appealed to the composer. For a time, he was intrigued by the idea of writing three one-act operas on stories by Gorky, in which the great Russian bass, Feodor Chaliapin, would sing the leading roles; this, too, came to nothing, mainly because of Ricordi's opposition to the project, which he thought would be too expensive. The playwright d'Annunzio prepared synopses of two possible subjects for Puccini's approval but this was not forthcoming, due mainly to an incompatibility of styles and temperaments.

With Illica, Puccini also discussed a subject which they had considered in the past, and which was to stay in their minds even after the next opera had been agreed upon: this was Marie Antoinette. In a letter to Sybil Seligman, Puccini described the last days of the ill-fated queen:

A soul in torment – First act, prison; second act – the trial; third act – the execution. Three short acts, stirring enough to take one's breath away. I'm absolutely taken up with this idea of mine. And I have found a title which seems to me fitting and appropriate, because it couldn't be called *Marie Antoinette*, seeing that it deals only with the one episode of her tragic death. The title is *The Austrian Woman (La Donna austriaca)*. What do you think of it?[1]

When Giacosa, who had been ill for some time, died in September, 1906, it became clear that Illica would have to be provided with a new collaborator for any future project, for he was not, in Puccini's opinion, able to produce a satisfactory libretto unaided. Having read and found very much to his taste Pierre Louÿs's *La Femme et le pantin* (The Woman and the Puppet), a sado-masochistic novel written primarily to *épater les*

[1] Seligman, op. cit.

bourgeois, Puccini persuaded Ricordi to procure the rights to it, and Illica was set to work modifying an existing dramatization. But in due course, the composer turned against 'the Spanish whore', as 'La femme' of the title now became in his mind, largely because the reception given to Richard Strauss's *Salome* in New York made him fear that prudery might well cause *Conchita* (which is what *La Femme et le pantin* would have been called in its Italian operatic version) to be banned from a number of theatres, with a consequent drop in income for its composer.

Other possible subjects were considered and eventually rejected. Since he was not at work on an opera, Puccini had time to travel and to participate in the preparation of productions of his operas in various cities. In the summer of 1905, he accepted an invitation to visit Argentina, where five of his operas were being performed, among them *Edgar*. In the autumn of the same year, the composer attended some of the London performances of *Madama Butterfly* at Covent Garden, his South American visit having caused him to miss the London première in July. From London he went to Bologna in October, to attend Toscanini's performance of *Butterfly*. The following year he was present during the entire rehearsal period of the first Paris production of *Butterfly* at the Opéra Comique, and at the beginning of 1907 he sailed to New York where four of his operas were being performed at the Metropolitan Opera House, among them *Manon Lescaut* and *Madama Butterfly* in their Met premières. (*Manon Lescaut* had been staged in Philadelphia in 1898.)

Puccini's main interest during his New York visit was in the première of *Butterfly* on 11 February. A week later, he wrote to Sybil Seligman:

> I've had all I want of America – at the Opera all is well, and *Madama Butterfly* was excellent, but lacked the poetry which I put into it. The rehearsals were too hurried, and the woman [Geraldine Farrar] was not what she ought to have been. Also as regards your God [Enrico Caruso] (*entre nous*) I make you a present of him – he won't learn anything, he's lazy and he's too pleased with himself – all the same his voice is magnificent.[1]

While he was in New York, Puccini took the opportunity to see a number of plays, including no fewer than three by David Belasco: *The Music Master*, *The Rose of the Rancho* and *The Girl of the Golden West*. He enjoyed all three, to the extent that his still limited English allowed him to. But although Belasco claimed that when the minstrel in the last-named play appeared singing 'Old Dog Tray', Puccini cried 'Ah, there is my theme at last',[2] the composer appears not to have been immediately bowled over by *The Girl of the Golden West*, for on the same day that he wrote to Sybil Seligman Puccini also wrote to Ricordi:

> Here too I have been on the lookout for subjects, but there is nothing possible, or, rather, complete enough. I have found good ideas in Belasco, but nothing definite, solid or complete.

[1] Ibid.   [2] Winter, op. cit.

The 'West' attracts me as a background, but in all the plays which I have seen I have found only some scenes here and there that are good. There is never a clear, simple line of development; just a hotch-potch and sometimes in very bad taste and very *vieux jeu*.[1]

In the same letter, Puccini again criticized Geraldine Farrar's performance as Butterfly, this time more specifically: 'Farrar is not too satisfactory. She sings out of tune, forces her voice, and it does not carry well in the large space of the theatre.'

The Girl of the Golden West stayed in Puccini's mind and, when he was in London in May and June, he discussed the play with Sybil Seligman. She procured a copy of the text for him, and proceeded to have it translated into Italian so that Puccini could form a knowledgeable opinion of it. Back at home in Torre del Lago in July, Puccini read Belasco's play and immediately decided that here was his next opera. He wrote to Ricordi's agent in New York to inquire about Belasco's terms, and entrusted the writing of the libretto not to Illica but to a new collaborator, Carlo Zangarini. Zangarini, an experienced dramatist, had the advantage of excellent English, for his mother was an American from Colorado. He was later to collaborate on the libretti for Wolf-Ferrari's *I Gioielli della Madonna* and Zandonai's *Conchita* (Puccini's abandoned Pierre Louÿs project).

By the end of August, agreement had been reached with Belasco, and Zangarini set to work on the libretto while Puccini went off on his travels again: in the autumn he supervised the production of *Butterfly* in Vienna and in the winter he took his wife, Elvira, to Egypt. By April, 1908, Zangarini had still not completed his libretto and Puccini, who now wanted to begin composing, had to insist that he take on a co-librettist. One Guelfo Civinini, from Livorno, was engaged, and proceeded to re-work Zangarini's text for the first two acts and to write his own Act III. Zangarini sulkily took no further part in the work, and the third act, which is less closely based on Belasco than the earlier acts, was written by Civinini along lines suggested by Puccini.

An exact translation of Belasco's title was thought to be too much of a mouthful, so the opera was called *La fanciulla del west* (The girl of the West). Puccini began its composition in May, 1908, and worked on it throughout the summer at his villa in the mountains at Chiatri. On 22 June, he wrote to Sybil Seligman:

I've taken refuge here in order to work, but I'm doing very little; undoubtedly *The Girl* is more difficult than I thought – it's on account of the distinctive and characteristic features with which I want to endow the opera that for the time being I've lost my way and don't go straight ahead, as I should like. I may also be influenced by my physical condition and the appalling boredom of this accursed spot. Lucky you who live in a country of great

[1] Adami, op. cit.

resources – in Italy I can't find a single town that is possible to live in. Wherever you go you see envious faces and you are treated as Cain treated Abel. It's like this in our country especially for anyone who rises above the common level, and to a peculiar degree in the realm of Art.[1]

The physical condition Puccini referred to was throat trouble which led to persistent hoarseness – the first slight warning signs of the approach of the disease which was to cause his death sixteen years later – but what interrupted work on La fanciulla del west far more seriously, for eight or nine months, was a series of events in the composer's domestic life during the autumn and winter.

Puccini's wife Elvira was not only impossibly shrewish but also neurotically jealous of her husband. Surprisingly, since Elvira was also not good at dealing with servants, they had managed to keep the same maid for several years: a local girl, Doria Manfredi. She had begun working at the Villa Puccini in 1903 when the composer was convalescing from his automobile accident and she was still working for the Puccinis in 1908 as a general maid who helped with the cooking, waited on table, and undertook various household chores.

One evening in the autumn of 1908, after Puccini had returned to Torre del Lago, he was talking to the maid, Doria, at the door of his study which led into the garden. Elvira Puccini found them there, and immediately began to scream insults at the girl, accusing her of having an affair with Giacomo, and calling her all sorts of foul names. Doria ran to her room, only to be followed by Signora Puccini who pounded on her door and continued to hurl abuse at her.

The next morning, Doria went home to her parents, while Elvira Puccini made it known to the entire village that the girl had been dismissed because she was a whore and a wrecker of families. Puccini's reputation with girls being what it was, Elvira was believed by a good many of the villagers, and the gossip soon spread. This caused the wretched Doria such distress that she took poison and, after five days of great agony, died on 28 January, 1909. Her family insisted upon an autopsy which proved the girl to be a virgin, and they then brought legal action against Elvira, charging her with persecution and defamation of character.

A horrified Puccini fled to Rome, informing Elvira that he wanted a separation. 'I've written to Ricordi to straighten out Elvira's affairs, but I never, never wish to have anything more to do with her,' he wrote to Sybil Seligman.[2] Meanwhile Elvira, unrepentant and apparently convinced that she had been right about Doria, was determined to defend herself in court. The case dragged on, but in July Elvira Puccini was found guilty, sentenced to five months' imprisonment, fined, and ordered to pay all costs. She appealed against this judgement, and even-

[1] Seligman, op. cit.   [2] Ibid.

tually the matter was settled out of court when Puccini persuaded the Manfredi family to accept a large sum of money in compensation. In September, 1909, Giacomo and Elvira were reunited at Torre del Lago, and Puccini was able to resume work on *La fanciulla del west*. 'The Girl goes well and I've nearly finished the second act – where there's a love duet which seems to me to have come out well . . . In my home I have peace – Elvira is good – and the three of us live happily together,' he told Sybil Seligman.[1]

By the end of the year, Puccini was ready to begin the orchestration of the opera, which occupied him, on and off, for about seven months, the task being finally completed on 7 July, 1910. The première of *La fanciulla del west* was to take place at the Metropolitan Opera House, New York (the first world première in the Met's history), and Puccini and his son Tonio travelled across the Atlantic on the *George Washington*, arriving in New York on 17 November. Rehearsals went well, and the first performance on 10 December, conducted by Toscanini, was a triumphant success. Emmy Destinn as Minnie, the only singer about whom Puccini this time expressed reservations in advance ('not bad but she needs more energy'), Caruso as Dick Johnson, and Pasquale Amato as Jack Rance were all applauded vociferously by the audience, fifty-five curtain calls were taken, and a laurel wreath was presented to the composer. Although he was not officially the producer,[2] David Belasco attended rehearsals and

> found himself a quasi-opera director, for he lent to the Metropolitan rehearsals all the ripe experience he had. He trained Caruso painstakingly; and he found these opera folk – so many of them not real actors in technique – eager to be rehearsed. On the opening night, with Signors Puccini, Toscanini, Gatti-Casazza [General Manager of the Met], this son of the Golden West took his curtain call, recipient of a testimonial album from the Metropolitan directors. This opening represented for Mr Belasco more than one conquest, for had anyone been behind the scenes during rehearsals, they would have witnessed a stage director whose word was uninterrupted law, yet being courteously interrupted by the autocratic baton of Toscanini – and Destinn, Caruso and Amato entering whole-heartedly into the new technique, which was different from that which marks opera. To sing was opera. But to act and sing with equal fervour and excellence was a problem which Mr Belasco went about to solve and to conquer.[3]

Press reviews of *La fanciulla* were generally extremely favourable, though Richard Aldrich in the *New York Times* thought that there was 'certainly far less of the clearly defined melodic luster, outline, point,

[1] Ibid. The 'three of us' were Puccini, Elvira and their son, Tonio.

[2] Tito Ricordi was nominally the producer; the playbill credited a Stage Manager (Jules Speck) and a Technical Director (Edward Siedle).

[3] From the Introduction by Montrose J. Moses to *The Girl of the Golden West*, in the volume, *Six Plays* by David Belasco (Boston, 1928).

and fluency, far less of what is tangibly thematic' than in the composer's earlier operas, and he detected the influence of Debussy on Puccini's harmonic idiom. *La fanciulla del west* was performed at the Met nine times during the season, and a separate production which opened in Chicago on 27 December was given five performances there, before being seen in Baltimore, Philadelphia and St. Louis. Boston staged the opera on 17 January, 1911, and gave seven performances during the season. In all these towns, *La fanciulla* was well received, and the Metropolitan Opera revived it for the next three seasons, after which it was not seen again there until 1929. When the first London performance was given at Covent Garden on 29 May, 1911, Emmy Destinn repeated her New York success with new co-stars, Amadeo Bassi as Dick Johnson and Dinh Gilly, who had sung Sonora in New York, promoted to the role of Jack Rance. Puccini, who had dedicated the score of the opera to Queen Alexandra, was present. The conductor was Cleofonte Campanini.

After its initial warm reception, for many years *La fanciulla del west* lagged well behind the more popular Puccini operas. In recent years, however, new productions in New York, Vienna, London and elsewhere have led to its reappraisal, and it would seem now to have firmly established a place for itself in the international repertoire.

II

It was with one of his favourite actresses, Blanche Bates, in mind that David Belasco wrote *The Girl of the Golden West*. Blanche Bates had created the role of Madame Butterfly in his play of that name, and was touring in another Belasco–John Luther Long play, *The Darling of the Gods*, when, in November, 1904, Belasco wrote to say that he wished to discuss his new play with her. By July, 1905, he was able to send her word that 'it is a *bully* play' and that 'the character of "*the girl*" is sky-high, fits her from her head to her feet'. 'There are some beautiful speeches in the play,' he told her, 'very Batesesque.' *The Girl of the Golden West* was also a play very close to Belasco's heart which he later described as 'my very best'. 'I know the period of Forty-nine as I know my alphabet,' he wrote, 'and there are things in my *Girl of the Golden West* truer than many of the incidents in Bret Harte.'[1] Belasco had been brought up in California, and he had toured its backwoods, and had immersed himself in a way of life which still retained elements of the old days of the gold rush.

The Girl of the Golden West, with Blanche Bates as 'The Girl', opened at the Belasco Theatre, Pittsburgh, on 3 October, 1905, and arrived at the Belasco in New York on 14 November, where it instantly achieved popular success. It now reads melodramatically and quaintly, and is

[1] Quoted in Belasco, *Six Plays*, op. cit.

hardly likely to appeal to audiences without the help of Puccini's music, yet at the time of its first performances it was found immensely moving. The play was in the middle of its New York run in April, 1906, when word was flashed from California of the disastrous San Francisco earthquake and fire. Many in the cast and in the audience had relatives or friends in San Francisco, and that evening, at the Belasco, when Blanche Bates reached the final line of the play, 'Oh, my mountains – I'm leaving you – Oh, my California, I'm leaving you – Oh, my lovely West – my Sierras! – I'm leaving you – Oh, my – my home,' she broke down and cried, and many in the audience wept with her.

Belasco later cashed in on the popularity of the play by making it into a novel, which was published in 1911, the year after Puccini's opera was first given. Though Belasco's descriptive prose in the novel lacks the colourful quality of his dramatic dialogue, certain scenes are even more effective in the novel than in the play, among them the episode in which Rance, about to leave Minnie's cabin, is suddenly made aware that Minnie is harbouring the injured bandit:

With the one thought that she must get rid of him – do anything, say anything, but get rid of him quickly, she forced herself forward, with extended hand, and said in a voice that held out new promise:

'Good-night, Jack Rance – good-night!'

Rance seized the hand with an almost fierce gladness in both his own, his keen glance hungrily striving to read her face. Then, suddenly, he released her, drawing back his hand with a quick sharpness.

'Why look at my hand! There's blood on it!' he said.

And even as he spoke, under the yellow flare of the lamp, the Girl saw a second drop of blood fall at her feet. Like a flash, the terrible significance of it came upon her. Only by self-violence could she keep her glance from rising, tell-tale to the boards above.

'Oh, I'm so sorry,' she heard herself saying contritely, all the time desperately groping to invent a reason; at length, she added futilely: 'I must have scratched you.'

Rance looked puzzled, staring at the spatter of red as though hypnotized.

'No, there's no scratch there,' he contended, wiping off the blood with his handkerchief.

'Oh, yes, there is,' insisted the Girl tremulously; 'that is, there will be in the mornin'. You'll see in the mornin' that there'll be – ' She stopped and stared in frozen terror at the sinister face of the Sheriff, who was coolly watching his handkerchief turn from white to red under the slow rain of blood from the loft above.

'Oho!' he emitted sardonically, stepping back and pointing his gun towards the loft. 'So, he's up there!'

The Girl's fingers clutched his arm, dragging desperately.

'No, he isn't, Jack – no, he isn't!' she iterated in blind, mechanical denial.

With an abrupt movement, Rance flung her violently from him, made a grab at the suspended ladder and lowered it into position; then, deaf to the

Girl's pleadings, harshly ordered Johnson to come down, meanwhile covering the source of the blood-drops with his gun.[1]

Belasco's play is in four acts, Puccini's opera in three. Acts I and II of the opera follow the first two acts of the play quite closely, but it was Puccini's idea to combine Acts III and IV of Belasco into a third and final act of the opera, making it an outdoor scene and showing something of the man-hunt for the bandit Ramerrez. The final moments of the opera actually take in the whole of Belasco's Act IV which is really just an elaborate stage picture with less than two minutes of dialogue. Here is the entire Act IV of Belasco's *The Girl of the Golden West*, as published.

ACT IV

The boundless prairies of the West.
On the way East, at the dawn of a day about a week later.

'Oh, my beautiful West!
Oh, my California!'

The scene is a great stretch of prairie. In the far background are foothills with here and there a suggestion of a winding trail leading to the West. The foliage is the pale green of sage brush, – the hills the deeper green of pine and hemlock. In the foreground is a little tepee made of two blankets on crossed sticks. The tepee is built against a grass mound and is apparently only a rude shelter for the night. Back of the tent is an old tree stump which stands out distinctly against the horizon. Here and there are little clumps of grass, bushes and small mounds of earth and rocks. A log fire is burning to the left of the tepee, a Mexican saddle lies beside the fire.

As the curtain rises, the stage is in darkness. Johnson is lying on the grass, leaning against his saddle, smoking a cigarette. The Girl is inside the tepee. Gradually the dawn begins to break. As the scene becomes visible, The Girl pushes aside the blanket and appears in the opening.

GIRL: Dick, are you awake?

JOHNSON (*turning to her*): Another day . . . the dawn is breaking.

GIRL (*looking towards the unseen hills in the distance*): Another day . . . Look back
. . . the foothills are growing fainter – every dawn – farther away.
Some night when I am going to sleep, I'll turn – and they won't be
there – red and shining. That was the promised land.

JOHNSON (*rising*): We must look ahead, Girl, not backwards. The promised
land is always ahead.

        (*A glimmer of the rising sun is seen on the foliage of the foothills.*)

GIRL: Always ahead . . . Yes, it must be. (*She comes out of the tepee and goes
up the path.*) Dick: all the people there in Cloudy – how far off they
seem now – like shadows in a dream. Only a few days ago, I
clasped their hands; I saw their faces – their dear faces! And now
they are fading. In this little, little while, I've lost them . . . I've
lost them. (*There are tears in her voice.*)

JOHNSON: Through you, all my old life has faded away. *I* have lost that.

[1] David Belasco, *The Girl of the Golden West* (New York, 1911).

GIRL: Look! (*Pointing to the left as she notices the sunrise.*) The dawn is
           breaking in the East – far away – fair and clear.
JOHNSON: A new day . . . Trust me. (*Stretching out his hands to her.*) Trust me . . .
           A new life!
GIRL: A new life. (*Putting her hands in his.*) Oh, my mountains – I'm
           leaving you – Oh, my California, I'm leaving you – Oh, my lovely
           West – my Sierras! – I'm leaving you! – Oh, my – (*turning to Johnson,
           going to him and resting in his arms*) – my home.

CURTAIN[1]

In the last moments of the opera, this feeling of farewell and renewal
is conveyed not a week after Dick Johnson's release but as Minnie and
Dick walk away from the miners who a few moments earlier had been
ready to lynch the bandit:

SONORA (*a Minnie*):   Le tue parole sono di Dio.
                              Tu l'ami come nessuno al mondo.
                              In nome di tutti,
                              io te lo dono.
JOHNSON: Grazie, fratelli!
SONORA (*piangendo*):   Va, Minnie, addio!
TRIN, HARRY, JOE,
BELLO, HAPPY, MINATORI: Mai più ritornerai, no, mai più.
                              Addio!
MINNIE *e* JOHNSON: Addio, mia dolce terra!
                              Addio, mia California!
                              Bei monti della Sierra, nevi, addio![2]

A reading of the text of Belasco's play throws up a few odd divergences
between play and opera, and produces some fascinating background information. One of the miners, Sid, whose nationality is revealed in the
opera only when another miner, angry at Sid's winning at cards, shouts
at him, 'Australiano d'inferno!' (Hellish Australian!), is described by
Belasco as 'fat, greasy, unctuous and cowardly', his name being short for
'Sydney Duck'. Belasco does not explain 'Sydney Duck' but in fact
histories of California and accounts of San Francisco's Barbary Coast in
the Gold Rush days reveal that among the most notorious of the
marauding criminals infesting the camps were two especially vicious

---

[1] Belasco, *Six Plays*, op. cit.
[2] SONORA [*to Minnie*]: Your words come from God. You love him more than anyone
         in the world. On behalf of us all, I give him to you.
   JOHNSON: Thank you, brothers!
   SONORA [*weeping*]: Go, Minnie, goodbye!
   TRIN, HARRY, BELLO, JOE, HAPPY, *and the other miners*: You will never come back, no,
         never. Goodbye!
   MINNIE *and* JOHNSON: Farewell, my sweet country! Farewell, my California!
   Beautiful mountains of the Sierra, snows, farewell!

gangs consisting mainly of Australians, the 'Australian Hounds' and the 'Sydney Ducks'. Most of them were ex-convicts deported from England to Australia, who had somehow made their way to the Californian gold fields where they proceeded to give Australia a bad name.

In the opera, Larkens is homesick for 'la sua vecchia Cornovaglia' (his old Cornwall) and a collection is taken up to send him back there. The miners in the play do not have to contribute towards so expensive a journey, for Belasco's Larkens comes from somewhere closer: 'I want old Pennsylvany . . . I want my folks . . . I'm done!' Minnie is only rarely referred to by her name in the play, most people preferring to address her as 'Girl', and refer to her as 'The Girl', whereas Puccini and his librettists call her Minnie throughout. But it is only in the play, and then but once in an intimate moment with Johnson-Ramerrez, that Minnie reveals her full name, Minnie Falconer.

Most of the opera's brief arias are based on speeches in Belasco's play. Minnie's speech beginning 'You see, I had a home once, and I ain't forgot it. A home up over our little saloon in Soledad' is the basis of the aria 'Laggiù nel Soledad' ('Way back in Soledad when I was small, I had a smoky little room in our tavern, above the kitchen'); Johnson's Act II aria, 'Ma non vi avrei rubato', derives from this speech in the play:

JOHNSON (*in a low voice*): One word – only one word . . . I'm not going to say anything in defence of myself. It's all true – everything is true, except that I would have stolen from you. I am called Ramerrez – I have robbed – I am a vagabond – a vagabond by birth – a cheat and a swindler by profession. I'm all that – and my father was all that before me. I was born, brought up, educated, thrived on thieves' money – but until six months ago, when he died, I didn't know it. I lived in Monterey – Monterey where we met. I lived decently. I wasn't the thing I am today. I only learned the truth when he died and left me with a rancho and a band of thieves – nothing else – nothing for us all – and I . . . I was my father's son – no excuse . . . it was in me – in the blood . . . I took to the road. I didn't mind much after – the first time. I only drew the line at killing. I wouldn't have that. And that's the man I am – the blackguard I am. (*With feeling.*) But, so help me God, from the moment I kissed you tonight, I meant to change. I meant to change.

Here, in tabular form, are Dick Johnson's intended last words in (a) the play, (b) the Italian libretto, and (c) the libretto in English translation:

(a)	(b)	(c)
I'd like her to think that I got away – went East – and changed my way of living. So you jest drag me a long way from here before you . . . and when she	Ch'ella mi creda libero e lontano, sopra una nuova via di redenzione! Aspetterà ch'io torni . . . E passeranno i giorni,	Let her believe me free and far away, on a new road of redemption. She will wait for my return . . . and the days will pass, and I

| grows tired of looking for letters that never come, she will say: 'He has forgotten me,' and that will be about enough for her to remember. She loved me before she knew what I was . . . and you can't change love in a minute. | ed io non tornerò . . . Minnie, della mia vita mio solo fiore, Minnie, che m'hai voluto tanto bene! Ah, tu della mia vita mio solo fior! | shan't return. Minnie, the only flower of my life, Minnie, you who loved me so much! Ah, you, the only flower of my life! |

Belasco prefaced his play with a quotation from a source which he identified only as *Early History of California*:

In those strange days, people coming from – God knows where, joined forces in that far western land, and, according to the rude custom of the camp, their very names were soon lost and unrecorded, and here they struggled, laughed, gambled, cursed, killed, loved and worked out their strange destinies in a manner incredible to us today. Of one thing only are we sure – they lived!

The playwright's descriptions of his characters, written into his stage directions, are still useful today to interpreters of the opera. Of Rance, Belasco writes:

He is the cool, waxen, deliberate gambler. His hands, almost feminine in their whiteness, are as waxen as his face. He has a very black moustache. He wears the beaver hat of the times, and an immaculate suit of broadcloth. His boots are highly polished, long and narrow with high heels, his trousers strapped over them. He wears a white puffed shirt, with a diamond stud held by side chains, and a large diamond flashes on his hand. He smokes the Spanish cigarros.

Minnie is described thus:

The character of The Girl is rather complex. Her utter frankness takes away all suggestion of vice – showing her to be unsmirched, happy, careless, untouched by the life about her. Yet she has a thorough knowledge of what the men of her world generally want. She is used to flattery – knows exactly how to deal with men – is very shrewd – but quite capable of being a good friend to the camp boys.

And this is Dick Johnson:

He is a young man of about thirty – smooth-faced, tall. His clothing is bought in fashionable Sacramento. He is the one man in the place who has the air of a gentleman. At first acquaintance, he bears himself easily but modestly, yet at certain moments there is a devil-may-care recklessness about him. He is, however, the last man in the world one would suspect of being the road-agent, Ramerrez.

The play, effective in its time, made the transition to opera libretto without much intrinsic change. As slightly reshaped by Puccini and his librettists, it is perhaps even more effective, dramatically, than in its original form. Puccini's own comment on his opera is interesting: 'At a first hearing, the drama can get in the way of listening to the music, but at a second or third hearing the action is familiar and the surprises no longer have the same intensity: then the music can be heard. This always happens to operas with exciting libretti.'[1]

The opera is set in the Sierra Nevada mountains of California, during the Gold Rush days of 1849–50.

Act I takes place in the barroom of the 'Polka' Saloon in a mining camp. It is sunset, and when the curtain rises all that can be seen is the lighted tip of the cigar smoked by the Sheriff, Jack Rance. The voices of miners approaching the bar, shouting and singing, are heard as Nick, the bartender, enters to light the lamps. Three miners, Joe, Harry and Bello, arrive and begin to play a game of faro with another miner, Sid, an Australian. Jake Wallace, a travelling minstrel, enters and sings a nostalgic song of home; the miners join in, and one of them, Larkens, bursts into tears. The miners take up a collection to send Larkens home, after which the card game is begun again. Sid is caught cheating by Bello, and the others are about to lynch him when the Sheriff intervenes. He pins a playing card on Sid's chest, a sign that he is branded as a cheat. If he is ever seen without the card, he will be hanged. As Sid is then thrown out of the bar, Ashby, the Wells Fargo agent, arrives, and informs Rance that the bandit Ramerrez is thought to be in the vicinity.

Rance and Sonora are quarrelling over Minnie, the young proprietress of the Polka, whom both want to marry, when Minnie appears and separates them. The miners greet her affectionately, and offer her gifts, after which Minnie produces a Bible and proceeds to hold her regular 'school', reading a psalm to them, and questioning them on it. When the mail arrives with the Pony Express rider, Ashby asks the rider if he knows a certain Nina Micheltorena. Minnie identifies her as 'a phony Spaniard from Cachuca', and Ashby tells the Sheriff that Nina has agreed to lead him that night to the hiding place of her lover, the bandit Ramerrez. Ashby hurries off to keep his appointment, and Rance declares his love to Minnie, offering to marry her. She rejects him, at the same time reminding him that he is already married. Rance tells Minnie something of his past life: he prizes gold above all else, yet he would give a fortune for a kiss from her. Minnie in turn tells him of her parents,

[1] Letter to Carlo Calusetti of 9 July, 1911, in *Carteggi Pucciniani* (Milan, 1958).

poor innkeepers in Soledad, who were happy because they loved each other. She will give her love to a man as honest and worthy as her father was.

A stranger arrives in the bar, announcing himself as Johnson from Sacramento, and asking for 'whisky and water' which is thought a rather sissy request at the Polka where 'si beve il whisky schietto' (we drink our whisky neat). Minnie recognizes Johnson as a man she had once encountered on the road to Monterey, and had hoped to meet again, but the Sheriff is both suspicious and jealous, and tries unsuccessfully to turn the miners against the newcomer. Johnson asks Minnie to dance with him, and while they are waltzing next door in the dance hall Ashby returns with Castro, a member of Ramerrez's band whom he has captured. Noticing his leader's saddle lying on the floor by the door, Castro gives Ashby misleading information and offers to lead a posse to the bandit's hideout. Before he leaves, Castro manages to whisper to Johnson, who is really the bandit, Ramerrez, that the rest of the gang are close by, and that, when he hears a whistle, Ramerrez should summon them with a whistle in response, at which they will help him steal the miners' gold from the saloon where Minnie holds it in safekeeping.

The posse sets off, Nick closes the bar, and Minnie and Johnson are left alone together. He admires her courage in guarding the saloon, and she shows him where the gold is hidden, adding that anyone who tried to steal it would first have to kill her. Attracted to each other, they talk about their past lives and their aspirations; when Johnson hears the signal from his gang hidden near by, he ignores it, accepting an invitation from Minnie to visit her later that evening at her cabin, halfway up the mountain. As he leaves, he tells her she has a good and pure spirit and the face of an angel. She is pleased, but at the same time moved and disturbed by his words.

Act II is set in Minnie's log cabin in the mountains, an hour later. The cabin is a simple room, with an indoor ladder leading up to a loft. As the curtain rises, Billy Jackrabbit, an Indian, enters and speaks to his squaw, Wowkle, who is Minnie's maid-of-all-work. Wowkle is crooning a lullaby to their papoose, and Billy reminds her that Minnie wishes them to marry in order to legitimize the baby. (There is much use of the word 'Ugh' as an all-purpose exclamation.) Minnie enters, dismisses Billy, and orders Wowkle to tidy up the cabin, as she is expecting a visitor. Minnie dresses in her best clothes to receive Johnson, so noticeably that Johnson, when he arrives, embarrasses her by asking if she is going somewhere. When she asks him if he came to the Polka Saloon earlier because he wanted to see her, or because he had mistaken the road to Nina Micheltorena's place, Johnson answers evasively, complimenting her on her cabin and asking her about her life in the mountains and the miners' camp. Soon, however, they are confessing their love for each other: Johnson thinks he ought to leave, but Minnie points out that it is snowing and that he will not find the trail. Three pistol shots are heard, and Minnie suggests it could be the bandit, Ramerrez. Johnson agrees to stay, and Minnie gives him her bed while she curls up in front of the fire, covered in a bearskin. As they try to sleep, Johnson is aware, through the howling blizzard, of the sounds of men shouting.

There is a sudden knock at the door, and the voice of Nick the bartender calls out that Ramerrez has been seen in the vicinity. Minnie hides Johnson behind the bed curtains, and opens the door to admit Nick, Sheriff Rance, Ashby and Sonora. Rance has the satisfaction of telling Minnie that her dancing partner that evening at the Polka was none other than Ramerrez. Minnie tries not to believe him, but Rance shows her a photograph of Ramerrez which his former mistress Nina Micheltorena has given them. Nick notices in the ashtray a cigar which he identifies as one of Johnson's and, without saying anything to his companions, quietly offers to stay with Minnie. She refuses, and the four men leave.

Confronted by Minnie, Johnson confesses that he is indeed Ramerrez, but claims that he was forced into a life of crime. His father had been a bandit, but Johnson only discovered the fact when, on his father's death, he 'inherited' the gang, the only means of support for his mother and brothers. Since he has met Minnie, however, he has dreamed of becoming an honest man in order to be worthy of her love. Minnie replies that she can forgive him for being a bandit but not for having stolen from her the first kiss she has given any man. She orders him to leave, and he rushes out into the blizzard. A moment later, a shot is heard, followed by the sound of a body falling against the door. Minnie drags the wounded Johnson inside, and stops him from staggering out again only by confessing that she loves him still. She helps him climb up the ladder to hide in the loft, as Rance knocks at the door and enters with gun in hand. Rance hurriedly searches the cabin, then tries to kiss Minnie who, threatening him with a bottle, orders him to leave. As he stands in the doorway, a drop of blood suddenly appears on his hand, and Rance realizes that Ramerrez is hiding in the loft. He orders him to come down, and Minnie helps Ramerrez to a chair at the table where he faints from loss of blood.

To save the bandit's life, Minnie appeals to Rance's gambling instincts, and proposes a game of poker with the bandit as prize. If Rance wins, he can take both the prisoner and Minnie, but if he loses, he is to allow Ramerrez to escape. Rance agrees. While his attention is momentarily diverted, Minnie stuffs some cards into the top of her stocking. They begin to play. Each wins a hand, but when Rance reveals his third hand of three kings, Minnie pretends to swoon and asks for a drink. While Rance is looking for bottle and glass, she quickly removes the cards from her stocking and substitutes them for those in her hand. She can now top his three kings with three aces and a pair. Looking at her cards, Rance merely utters a cold 'Good night', and departs, while Minnie's hysterical laughter turns into tears as she embraces the unconscious Ramerrez.

Act III takes place some days later, at dawn in a clearing in the forest not far from the mining camp. Rance and Nick sit by the fire, while Ashby and some of the miners are asleep on the ground near their tethered horses. Nick compliments Rance for having kept his word to Minnie not to pursue Ramerrez, and Rance exclaims bitterly that he cannot understand what she can see in such a man. Suddenly, voices are heard shouting and a group of miners rushes in to announce that Ramerrez has been seen close by, and is likely to be captured at any moment. The miners leave again, and Ashby goes with them, after remarking to Rance that he is puzzled by the present behaviour of the Sheriff who seems to have given up his pursuit of Ramerrez. Left alone with Nick, Rance expresses his delight that the bandit is about to be captured. Miners continue to rush in and out, commenting on the imminence of Ramerrez's capture, until the sound of a galloping horse is heard, and Sonora rides up to announce that Ramerrez has now been taken. The miners gleefully anticipate a lynching party.

Billy Jackrabbit begins to prepare a noose, but Nick bribes him to take his time over it, and hurries off to find Minnie. Ramerrez is led in, dishevelled and bleeding, and Ashby formally hands him over to the Sheriff for sentencing. When the miners accuse him of murder as well as theft, Ramerrez swears that, though he is a thief, he has never committed murder. He is then accused by the miners of having stolen not only gold but the affections of Minnie, and the cry goes up to hang him immediately. Clearly he is resented as much because Minnie loves him as because he and his gang have plundered the countryside.

Ramerrez asks his captors to kill him quickly but to allow Minnie to think that he has escaped and is leading a new life far away. In a fit of jealous anger, Rance strikes the bound captive, to the disapproval of the miners. As the noose is slipped over Ramerrez's head, Minnie's voice can be heard calling from the distance. When Minnie arrives, on horseback, she dismounts quickly, runs to Ramerrez and shields him with her body. Drawing a gun, she holds the miners at bay. Rance hysterically orders the men to proceed with the lynching, but Minnie reminds them of all that she has done for them in the past, insists that they are in her debt, that Ramerrez has repented of his crimes, and that she loves him. Sonora is the first to relent, and adds his voice to hers. Minnie throws down her gun, and pleads with the men. Eventually, they are won over, and Johnson is set loose. Arm in arm he and Minnie slowly leave, bidding farewell to California, while the miners express their sorrow that they are likely never to see Minnie again.

III

Puccini commentators usually refer to a falling-off of inspiration in *La fanciulla del west*, which they tend to attribute to the difficulties the composer was undergoing in his private life at the time he was at work on the opera; specifically, the tragedy of the Puccinis' maid, Doria. I am unable to go along with this view, not only because I believe the relationship between an artist's life and his work to be somewhat more complex than that kind of reasoning suggests but also because I fail to discern any creative decline in *La fanciulla del west*. A sunny and blameless life devoid of unpleasant incident does not necessarily lead an artist to produce works which radiate contentment and joy, nor does a turbulent personal life preclude the possibility that he may produce such works. The point, surely, need not be laboured. Those who consider that *La fanciulla* is lacking in Puccinian tunes or think that it is a poor opera *because* it lacks such tunes are those who also fail to recognize that Verdi's *Falstaff* is not a less great work than his *Rigoletto* but a different kind of great work.

The fact that, in *La fanciulla*, the arias are shorter, fewer, and more closely integrated into the fabric of the composition as a whole than previously merely makes it somewhat more difficult for the commentator to describe the music without indulging in close analysis at great and, for the general reader, tedious length. I shall attempt to avoid this pitfall while nevertheless aiming to draw the reader's attention to a number of points in each act where it may be helpful to know what the composer is doing and why.

A short 34-bar orchestral prelude makes an exhilarating start to Puccini's Wild West opera, alternating themes suggesting the excitement and the lyrical grandeur of the mountainous California landscape, and a syncopated, unmistakably 'American' phrase at the end encapsulating the character of the bandit, Ramerrez, though at the same time it betrays its indebtedness to Debussy's 'Gollywog's Cake Walk'. The prelude ends, and there is a silent bar during which the curtain rises. From the distance is heard the sound of men's voices greeting one another as they approach the 'Polka' Saloon, and a baritone voice singing a fragment of a nostalgic tune which will shortly be heard in full. The music becomes livelier as the miners arrive on stage, with their cries of 'Hello' in English. Two of them, Joe and Bello, sing a couple of phrases to the words 'Dooda, dooda, day', which might lead one to suppose that Puccini is quoting musically from the Stephen Foster song, 'The Camptown Races'. He is not, perhaps for the good reason that much of the music of Stephen Foster (1826–1864) was still in copyright in 1910. (At the beginning of Belasco's play, a miner does sing the Stephen Foster song, accompanying himself on the concertina, and Belasco quotes the words in full:

Camptown ladies, sing this song,
  Dooda! Dooda!
Camptown race track, five miles long,
  Dooda! Dooda! Day.
G'wine to run all night,
G'wine to run all day,
Bet my money on a bob-tail nag,
Somebody bet on the bay.

La fanciulla is an opera which wastes little time on lyrical expansion, and the bustling music to which the miners shout their comments as they settle down to play cards calls for no detailed comment. When Nick, the bartender, suggests that the men might care to dance in the ballroom next door, four bars of elegant dance music are heard. The card game has now become somewhat quieter, allowing the voice of the travelling minstrel, Jake Wallace (baritone), to be heard singing [Ex. 35] as he ap-

Ex. 35   Andante tranquillo ♩ = 46
        (interno. molto lontano)

Che fa - ran - no i vec-chi miei là lon - ta - no,   là lon - ta - no?   che fa-ran - no?

proaches the 'Polka'. This is the voice and this the song already briefly heard a few bars after the rise of the curtain. The melody, used by Puccini to portray the nostalgic home-sickness of the miners who have come from all parts of the world to search for gold in California, is that of an old American song, 'Old Dog Tray'. ('Would angel mother know me, if back there I did roam? Would old dog Tray remember me?')

When Jake Wallace arrives, still singing, the miners take up the song and join in with him. This is the first moment of lyrical repose in the opera, and it is moving despite the abject sentimentality of both words and music. The miners become positively lachrymose as they remember the old folks at home, and they beat the tables with their fists in deep emotion when they think of their childhood pets. (Their thumps on the table are marked in the score.) The song builds up into an ensemble of plaintive beauty, quoting in its final bars from another American song, 'Dear Old House', reducing one of the miners, Larkens, to tears of self-pity and acute homesickness. It is all the more effective for Puccini's direction that it be sung 'with great feeling and never in full voice' ('con molto sentimento et *mai* a piena voce').

When Larkens breaks down, Sonora takes up a collection from the other miners to allow him to return home, and the orchestra bursts out with a *fortissimo* account of Jake Wallace's song. Jake mutters his thanks and leaves, while the miners hum a wordless cadence and the music fades into silence. But only momentarily, for the card game noisily begins again, and a fight breaks out when Sid is caught cheating.

Nothing of great moment occurs musically until the entrance of Minnie, with her sumptuous theme [Ex. 36]. After she has accepted the homage

Ex. 36

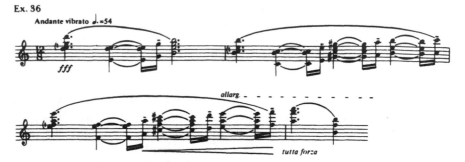

and the simple gifts the miners offer her, Minnie begins her Bible class, in which she teaches the men an Old Testament psalm. This charming interlude is introduced and punctuated by a curious little theme scored for piccolo, glockenspiel and celeste. The orchestra momentarily imitates the braying of an ass when Harry refers to the ass's jawbone in his attempts to answer a question about the biblical David, but the lesson continues its gentle path with Minnie reading and commenting upon the psalm, the orchestra stealing in with Jake Wallace's song [Ex. 35] as she finishes.

The orchestra suggests a trotting rhythm when the Pony Express rider arrives with the mail, and for the next few minutes the action is advanced in music which is always apposite to the situation and to the actual text but which is neither memorable nor intended to be. Much more than in any of his earlier operas, Puccini in *La fanciulla* uses his music to underline and advance the action rather than to express the feelings of his leading characters. To a large extent, the nature of Belasco's play and the libretto fashioned from it require him to adopt such a method, but he would hardly have chosen this terse, action-filled play had he not wanted to attempt something new in opera. When those few moments arrive in which Minnie or Jack Rance or Dick Johnson reflect on their feelings, they are kept as brief as possible. The only aria to have become popular out of context is the tenor's in Act III though sopranos and baritones do occasionally record their own quasi-arias from Act I.

These two quasi-arias for Rance and Minnie are now heard, as the sheriff and the saloon-keeper are left alone on stage. Rance's 'Minnie, dalla mia casa son partito' (Minnie, I left my home) begins gloomily, orchestra and voice brooding darkly, Rance's suppressed bitterness finally bursting forth at its climax at the top of the baritone's range [Ex. 37]. 'L'amore è un altra cosa' (Love is another matter), Minnie comments, and immediately begins her own account of the events which have shaped her life and her feelings, in 'Laggiù nel Soledad' (Way back in Soledad), a lightly scored conversational piece about her childhood,

Ex. 37

Or   per un ba - cio   tu - o   get - to un te - so - ro!____

with a solo violin prominent in the accompaniment and an ardently
lyrical conclusion [Ex. 38] containing a high C to emphasize her determination to find true love.

Ex. 38

S'a - ma - van   tan - to!   S'a - ma - van   tan - tó!   Ah!   Anch'io vor -

re - i   trovare un   uomo: e   cer - to   l'a - me - re - i

Dick Johnson's syncopated theme from the prelude is heard as the
hero-bandit enters. He and Minnie converse in gentler phrases than we
have been hearing so far in Act I's conversational music, and Rance
makes his jealous annoyance felt in loud, angry outbursts. Invited to
waltz by one of the miners, Johnson prefers to dance with Minnie, and
does so to a swaying waltz tune sung by the miners [Ex. 39], interrupted

Ex. 39

La,   la,   la,   la,   la,   la,   la,   la,   la,   la,   la,____

by an *allegro feroce* tumult when a captured member of Ramerrez's gang is
dragged in.

The first tentative love scene between Minnie and Johnson begins
after Rance and the miners have left in search of Ramerrez. The waltz
tune is heard on the oboe as 'Mister Johnson' wanders about the saloon.
Minnie enters, and he and she resume their tender discovery of each
other. In a touching solo, 'Io non son che una povera fanciulla' (I'm
only a poor girl) [Ex. 40], Minnie tries to articulate her half-formulated
aspirations and yearnings, and the orchestra's strings shimmer in their

Ex. 40

Io   non   son   che u - na   po - ve - ra   fan - ciu - lla____   o -

- scu - ra e   buo - na a   nul - la:

highest registers at 'su, su, come le stelle' (up, up, as high as the stars).
Johnson responds sympathetically with the tune of the waltz they danced
[Ex. 39]. Later, when Minnie expresses her determination not to allow
the miners' gold to be stolen, and Johnson reassures her, the orchestra
supports the singers with a new warmth and fervour. Minnie's confidence in herself wavers, and two solo violins refer to the opening
phrase of her 'Io non son che una povera fanciulla' [Ex. 40] but her
theme [Ex. 36] accompanies Johnson's final words of tender feeling, not
only in the orchestra but hummed off-stage by fifteen tenor voices. As
the curtain falls on Act I, the final chord fades slowly, the number of
players diminishing until the nine notes of the chord are played by only
nine instruments, and the humming voices can hardly be heard. So ends
one of Puccini's most delicately written scenes, which is not a love duet
in the conventional sense, but a duet scene in which two people slowly
discover their attraction for each other.

Act II begins with a brief scene for the Indian couple with their baby,
in which Wowkle sings a few bars of a lullaby based on an authentic
Indian tune. Phrases from Act I are heard as Minnie announces that she
will wear her best clothes for Johnson's visit; when Johnson enters,
despite the orchestra's encouraging reprise of the waltz theme, it is some
time before their conversational exchange broadens lyrically into a love
duet. Before it does, Minnie has told Johnson of the joys of living alone
in the mountains, in an arietta, 'Oh se sapeste come il vivere è allegro'
(Oh, if only you knew how happy life is), an uncharacteristic piece of
clumsy and un-Puccinian coloratura with a lightly sparkling accompaniment and an enthusiastic high B at the end as Minnie likens the
heights of her beloved Sierras to the gates of heaven.

The love duet begins prosaically enough, and *andante calmo*, as Minnie
asks Johnson if he will have a 'biscotta alla cream', but it really gets
under way as Wowkle, the Indian, goes out into the snow, and the
orchestra brings the tempestuous weather into consideration at the
moment that the tempest of love enters Minnie's heart. Johnson gives
out the leading theme of the duet [Ex. 41] which he then repeats in
unison with Minnie. After they have sung the word 'eternamente' (eternally), there is a passage of 15 bars which Puccini added in 1922, twelve

Ex. 41

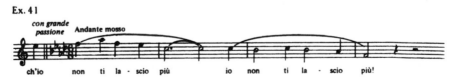

years after the opera's première, as a climax to the duet. The additional
15 bars, in which the soprano and tenor continue to sing in unison, were
written for a Rome production, but were not performed then, as the
singers found the climactic high C too difficult. This additional passage

was first heard the following year in a performance at Puccini's local theatre, the Politeama at Viareggio, and it remains in the score, but is almost invariably cut in performance. The music is excessively trite and its omission is no loss.

The arrival of Rance with Nick, Ashby and Sonora, in search of Ramerrez, is dealt with in effective recitative, and it is only when they have departed again, and Minnie confronts Johnson with her knowledge of his identity, that the music reasserts itself. Johnson's aria in which he attempts to justify his lawless way of life, 'Ma non vi avrei rubato' (But I wouldn't have robbed you), extracts less easily from its context than his Act III aria, but is in itself a stirring and immensely exciting solo.

From here to the end of the act, events move swiftly, carried forward by Puccini's music at its most dramatic, especially in the game of poker in which Johnson's life is the prize. Though the score contains little that is memorable in itself, it is not only thoroughly effective but also, in context, quite moving, as Minnie fights to save the man who, bandit though he may be, has awakened her heart to love. As music for the theatre, the final pages of this act are among the finest Puccini ever composed.

Acts I and II of *La fanciulla del west* play for about an hour and three-quarters of an hour respectively. Act III is much shorter, less than 26 minutes. In its opening bars, the orchestra paints a sombre picture of dawn breaking over a mountainous forest in California. Puccini's means are simple, but highly effective. The atmosphere he seeks is immediately and swiftly evoked, and is sustained in the conversation between Rance and Nick, to be dispelled only by the off-stage cries of the chorus of miners and by the change of tempo as Ashby rushes in to announce that the miners are hot on the trail of Ramerrez. When Sonora announces that Ramerrez-Johnson has been captured, the orchestra excitedly offers, for no very good reason, the theme of the love duet from Act II.

Excitement mounts to fever pitch as the bandit is dragged on-stage to face the taunts and accusations of the miners. Allowed a few last words before he is to be lynched, Johnson proceeds to sing his big aria, 'Ch'ella mi creda libero e lontano' (Let her believe me free and far away) [Ex. 42],

Ex. 42   Andante molto lento

Ch'el - la mi cre - da   li - be - ro e lon-ta - no,   so - pra u-na nuo-va via_____ di re-den-zio - ne!

a grave and restrained lament which consists of an 11-bar melody played twice. The first time, Johnson sings it while the orchestra accompanies; the second time, he shares the tune with the orchestra. (This aria was, on one occasion, sung by Italian soldiers on the Macedonian front in World War I, to keep their spirits up.)[1]

[1] Seligman, op. cit.

A fanfare-like passage leads to the preparations for Johnson's execution, which are interrupted by the off-stage voice of Minnie, as she rides to her lover's rescue, her theme resounding in the orchestra. The final ensemble is begun solo by Minnie, who appeals to her old friends to forgive Johnson. As the ensemble progresses, she wins them over, and finally, to the tune of Jake Wallace's song from Act I [Ex. 35], the miners sing their sad farewell to Minnie as she and Johnson walk away into the distance, uttering their own farewell to California ('Addio, mia California'). The curtain descends slowly over the final sustained chord, diminuendo, on the orchestral strings, with the celeste also in evidence, and a pianissimo note from the bass drum.

La fanciulla del west, one of the most fascinating of Puccini's operas, works remarkably well in the opera house, and grows on one's affections with repeated hearings, not only because of the subtlety of its orchestration and the modernity of its harmonies, but also because its music serves the libretto faithfully and somehow ennobles it. As a piece of musical theatre, La fanciulla del west is the equal of La Bohème, lacking only the earlier score's fresh melodic prodigality.

VIII

La rondine

an opera in three acts

Dramatis personæ:

Magda de Civry, Rambaldo's mistress	(soprano)
Ruggero Lastouc, a young man from the provinces	(tenor)
Rambaldo Fernandez, a wealthy Parisian banker	(baritone)
Lisette, Magda's maid	(soprano)
Prunier, a poet	(tenor)
Yvette ⎫	(soprano)
Bianca ⎬ friends of Magda	(soprano)
Suzy ⎭	(mezzo-soprano)
Périchaud ⎫	(baritone)
Gobin ⎬ friends of Rambaldo	(tenor)
Crébillon ⎭	(bass)
Georgette ⎫	(soprano)
Gabriella ⎬ *grisettes*	(soprano)
Lolette ⎭	(mezzo-soprano)
Rabonnier, a painter	(bass)
A Student	(tenor)
Majordomo	(bass)

LIBRETTO by Giuseppe Adami, based on an original libretto in German by Alfred Maria Willner and Heinz Reichert

TIME: The 1850s; the Second Empire of Napoleon III
PLACE: Paris and the Riviera

FIRST PERFORMED at the Monte Carlo Opera, on 27 March, 1917, with Gilda Dalla Rizza (Magda), Tito Schipa (Ruggero), Ines Maria Ferraris (Lisette), Francesco Dominici (Prunier), Gustave Huberdeau (Rambaldo), conducted by Gino Marinuzzi

La rondine

EVEN BEFORE *La fanciulla del west* reached the stage in New York, Puccini had begun to search for his next libretto, listening to suggestions from Sybil Seligman and others, reading plays and novels, but unable to find (as he put it when rejecting Hermann Sudermann's *Johannisfeuer*) 'something loftier, more musical and more original'. Another German play which Puccini considered for a time was Gerhart Hauptmann's *Hanneles Himmelfahrt* (Hannele's Ascension), and other projects which came to nothing included Oscar Wilde's *A Florentine Tragedy*, the Richard Blackmore novel *Lorna Doone*, Ferencz Molnár's *Liliom*, and a Spanish comedy, *Anima Allegra* (The Cheerful Soul), by the brothers Joaquin and Serafin Quintero. *Anima Allegra*, though it went the way of the other abortive projects, brought Puccini into contact with a young playwright, Giuseppe Adami, who wasted several months of his time preparing a libretto from the Spanish play, but who later was to be involved as librettist in three Puccini operas.

D'Annunzio suggested, and indeed wrote for Puccini, a libretto based on the Children's Crusade of 1212, but when he had read the script, Puccini dismissed it, commenting in a letter to Sybil Seligman that 'D'Annunzio has given birth to a small, shapeless monstrosity, unable to walk or live . . . Is there nothing to be seen in London at the theatres?'[1] A typical Puccinian situation developed over another possibility, a story by the romantic novelist, Ouida, called *The Two Little Wooden Shoes*, known in its Italian translation as *Due zoccoletti*. Puccini's enthusiasm for it waxed and waned, and waxed again when he read an announcement that Mascagni intended to use it for his next opera. Ouida having died intestate in 1908, the question of rights became a somewhat tangled one, and a tenacious Puccini pursued the matter legally until the Italian courts decreed that a public auction should be held on behalf of Ouida's creditors. Puccini's publishers made the winning bid, to the dismay of Mascagni, but, having won, Puccini immediately lost interest in the project. (Mascagni composed the opera, renamed *Lodoletta*, which was staged in Rome in 1917.)

For some years, Puccini had occasionally toyed with the idea of composing three one-act operas for production together on a single

---

[1] Written from Milan, 27 January, 1913; Seligman, op. cit.

evening, and by June, 1913, he thought he had found his three subjects. One of these, based on a French play, did in due course become *Il tabarro*, the first of his *Trittico* operas. However, in October, Puccini paid a visit to Vienna on the occasion of the Austrian première of *La fanciulla del West* at the Hofoper (or the Staatsoper, as it was renamed after the fall of the Austrian monarchy). It was in Vienna that the project which was to lead to the composition of his next opera, *La rondine*, was first mentioned to Puccini.

He had gone, one evening, to the Carl Theater in the Praterstrasse,[1] to attend a performance of a Viennese operetta. In the course of the evening he was approached by the directors of the theatre, Heinrich Berté[2] and Otto Eibenschütz, with the proposal that he compose an operetta for them for a very large fee (variously reported as between 200,000 and 400,000 Austrian crowns, at that time between £10,000 and £20,000). Less music would be needed than for an opera: Puccini would be required to compose no more than eight or nine self-contained musical numbers – songs, duets, perhaps a waltz or two. It was a tempting offer, and Puccini expressed cautious interest, asking a Viennese friend, Baron Eisner von Eisenhof, to act as his intermediary, the composer's German being no more fluent than his English.

Within a few weeks, a libretto was concocted and submitted to Puccini, who turned it down. In December, the proposal seemed doomed, for the composer wrote to Baron von Eisenhof, 'I shall never compose an operetta. A comic opera, yes, like *Rosenkavalier*, but more amusing and more organic.'[3] Some months later, however, the Viennese impresarios came up with a second libretto, the work of Alfred Willner and Heinz Reichert,[4] and in March, 1914, Puccini accepted the new libretto, on the strength of its first act alone, and signed a contract to write, not an operetta, but a light or comic opera. A Viennese quartet consisting of Berté, Eibenschütz, Willner and Baron von Eisenhof had travelled to Milan to conduct the final negotiations with the composer, and professed themselves delighted with the arrangements made. The first production of the work, still described as an operetta, was to be given in Vienna in the German language, but Puccini was to retain Italian and South American rights, and an Italian version of the libretto would be made by a dramatist of the composer's choice.

Giuseppe Adami was engaged to work on the Italian version of the text, and was allowed a reasonably free hand where any question of adaptation as opposed to direct translation might be called for. Puccini

---

[1] A leading operetta house between 1847 and 1929, the Carl Theater was severely damaged by bombs in 1944, and was finally demolished in 1951.

[2] Berté is better known as the composer-arranger of *Das Dreimäderlhaus* (Lilac Time), the operetta based on music of Schubert. A pupil of Bruckner, he composed at least six ballet scores and twelve operettas.

[3] *Carteggi Pucciniani*, op. cit.

[4] They were shortly to write the libretto of *Das Dreimäderlhaus* for Berté.

was to compose to Adami's text, which would then be retranslated into German for the première in Vienna. Composer and librettist set to work.

Writing more than twenty years after the event, Adami gave the impression[1] that the entire concept of the work altered during the course of composition: that Puccini began to compose a handful of musical numbers to be inserted into a play with dialogue, and that what in due course was completed was a full-scale opera, its music composed throughout, with no spoken dialogue. It is clear from Puccini's letters, however, that, although the work, when first spoken of, was intended to be an operetta, the decision against an operetta or *opéra comique* format, with spoken dialogue, had been taken before the composer began to set Adami's text.

By the autumn of 1914, Act I of *La rondine* had been completed. Also by the autumn of 1914, much of Europe was at war, with Austria and Italy on opposing sides (although Italy did not declare war on Austria until May, 1915). The least political or public-minded of men, Puccini harboured no strong anti-Austrian sentiments (nor, a decade later, did he feel very strongly one way or the other about Mussolini and Fascism), but he was worried about the effect of the war upon his current plans. 'Tell me,' he wrote to Baron von Eisenhof, 'given the present frightful state of things due to this horrible war, what will happen to this opera?'[2] Having already composed one act of it, he did not want to have to abandon the work he described to Sybil Seligman as 'a light, sentimental opera with touches of comedy . . . agreeable, limpid, easy to sing, with a little waltz music and lively and fetching tunes . . . a sort of reaction against the repulsive music of today'.[3]

During the early spring of 1916, *La rondine* was completed. As Italy and Austria were at war, there could be no question of a première in Vienna, and, after a meeting with Berté on neutral ground at Interlaken in Switzerland, Puccini was granted permission to arrange for the publication and first performance of the work in Italy. His own publisher Tito Ricordi having rejected the opera ('He said that I had written an opera that hadn't come off, and that was bad Lehár!' Puccini later told Sybil Seligman[4]), the composer offered *La rondine* to a rival firm, Sonzogno. In view of the conditions prevailing in Italy due to the war, Sonzogno thought it best to arrange for the opera to have its première in nearby, peaceful Monte Carlo, and so *La rondine* was revealed to the world on 27 March, 1917, at the Opera House in the casino at Monte Carlo, with Gilda Dalla Rizza and Tito Schipa in the leading roles, and Gino Marinuzzi conducting.

[1] In his *Puccini* (1935), op. cit.
[2] *Carteggi Pucciniani*, op. cit.
[3] Seligman, op. cit.
[4] Ibid.

The opera was enthusiastically received in Monte Carlo, both by the public and by the press, the *Journal de Monaco* calling it 'une comédie musicale variée, vivante . . . exquise'. Soprano and conductor, with a new tenor, the American Charles Hackett, performed it two months later in Buenos Aires, again with great success. But the first Italian performances, in Bologna in June, attracted disappointing reviews, and the Milan production at the Teatro dal Verme in October, with a totally new cast including the young Toti dal Monte as the maid, Lisette, did even less well with the critics, although it was well received by audiences. Vienna eventually saw *La rondine* after the war, in 1920 (in German, as *Die Schwalbe*), when Felix Weingartner conducted it at the Volksoper. It was not performed at the Metropolitan Opera until 1928 (with Lucrezia Bori and Beniamino Gigli), and has still to be staged at the Royal Opera House, Covent Garden. The first London production was a semi-amateur affair in Fulham in 1965, but the English Opera Group staged the work professionally in 1974 at Sadler's Wells Theatre, with June Bronhill leading an excellent cast, and Meredith Davies conducting. Puccini had predicted, in a letter to Sybil Seligman, that *La rondine* would 'go well in London because it's a melodious opera and the subject is a moral one'.[1]

II

La rondine is set in France in the 1850s, the Second Empire of Napoleon III. Act I takes place in an elegantly furnished salon in the home of Magda de Civry in Paris. Magda (soprano) is the mistress of Rambaldo Fernandez (baritone), a wealthy banker, and when the curtain rises Magda and Rambaldo are seen entertaining a group of their friends, among them three men, Périchaud, Gobin and Crébillon, who are friends of Rambaldo; three young women, Yvette, Bianca and Suzy, friends of Magda; and Prunier, a young poet (tenor). They have just finished dinner. The men are talking to Rambaldo, and the women to Prunier, as Magda pours coffee which is handed round by the maid, Lisette (soprano).

The three young women are amused when Prunier claims that romantic love is coming back into fashion in Paris, and even the maid Lisette tells him he is talking nonsense. Magda, however, is willing to consider his remarks seriously. When Prunier, who appears to be a musician as well as a poet, sits at the piano and performs for the assembled company his latest song, as yet unfinished, about a girl called Doretta, Magda goes to the piano and accompanies herself in an improvised ending in which she envisages Doretta rejecting the advances of the king because she is in love with a poor student. All her guests are charmed by Magda's performance, Rambaldo so much so that he

[1] Ibid.

presents her with a pearl necklace which he had intended, but had forgotten, to give her before dinner. After admiring the necklace, the three male guests go off to the conservatory to smoke, and Lisette rushes in to announce to Rambaldo that a stranger who had earlier been inquiring for him is at the door again, having been loitering in the street outside for an hour or more in the hope of speaking to him. Rambaldo asks Magda's permission to receive the stranger, whom he identifies as the son of an old school friend.

Lisette hurries out, and Prunier asks Magda how she can put up with having a veritable whirlwind as a maid. Magda replies that, though inclined to be cheeky, Lisette is a good girl and a ray of sunshine in her life. When Bianca, Yvette and Suzy express their envy of Magda's relationship with the wealthy Rambaldo, Magda wistfully recalls a romantic flirtation of her youth with a young man whom she encountered one evening at Bullier's Restaurant, with whom she danced and drank bock beer for an hour or two, before fleeing in confusion, never to see him again. The girls mockingly suggest that Prunier should use the escapade as the subject for a song, but he replies that he prefers more perverse heroines such as Galatea, Berenice, Francesca or Salome. He takes the girls to one side to read their palms, predicting that, like the swallow, Magda will migrate across the sea towards a bright land of dreams, towards the sun and towards true love.

During the hand-reading, the stranger has been admitted by Lisette and greeted by Rambaldo. He is Ruggero Lastouc, and a letter of introduction from his father reveals to Rambaldo that the young man, who comes from the country, is visiting Paris for the first time. Rambaldo asks the assembled company where he should send a young man on his first evening in Paris, and Prunier advises an early night in bed, as the romantic idea of one's first evening in Paris is nothing but an idle legend. Lisette indignantly refutes this: a true Parisienne, she is keen to defend the city's reputation. One's first evening in Paris, she says, is comparable to one's first sight of the ocean. Her suggestion is that Ruggero should be sent to Bullier's Restaurant. Given the address, Ruggero rushes off to Bullier's, and Rambaldo and the others soon depart as well.

Magda tells Lisette she will be remaining at home, and Lisette reminds her mistress that this is her evening off. Left alone, Magda remembers Prunier's prediction that, like the swallow, she will migrate towards happiness. She glances at a piece of paper left on a table, on which the girls had listed a number of night clubs and restaurants for Ruggero to choose from, and suddenly exclaims 'Bullier's!' As Magda runs into the boudoir, Lisette reappears, and Prunier who has waited for her in the entrance hall embraces the maid as they go off together. Magda comes back, dressed as a simple *griselle*, with her hair arranged differently. Putting a red rose in her hair, she looks at herself in the mirror, murmurs 'Who would recognize me?' and goes out quickly.

Act II takes place later that evening, in the elaborate ballroom at Bullier's Restaurant. Students, artists, shop girls, men-about-town and curiosity-seekers are milling about, flower-girls offer their wares, and waiters flit to and fro between the tables around the dance floor. Several *grisettes*, led by Georgette, Gabriella and Lolette, try to entice Ruggero to join them, but he irritably gestures them away from his table. Magda enters, attracting the attention of most of the men present. She gets rid of them by telling them she has an assignation, and sitting at Ruggero's table, to that young man's surprised delight. Magda and Ruggero go off into the crowd to dance. A few moments later Prunier and Lisette arrive, in the middle of what appears to be a lovers' quarrel, and they too join the dancing.

Magda and Ruggero return to their table, and when he orders bock beer she is filled with memories of her romantic encounter in this same restaurant many years earlier. Magda gives her name as Paulette. They kiss, at which moment Lisette who is passing by with Prunier recognizes her mistress. Prunier, quick to respond to a sign from Magda, persuades Lisette that she is mistaken. They join Ruggero and 'Paulette', and when Prunier notices Magda's lover Rambaldo entering the ballroom, he gets Ruggero and Lisette out of the way by asking Ruggero to keep Lisette from being seen by her employer. Rambaldo comes over to Magda, and asks her to explain her presence. She replies that she has found real love, and gently requests him to leave her. Most of the crowd have gone by now, and Rambaldo leaves with the remaining stragglers. As the first rays of dawn come through the windows, Magda sits alone at her table, listening to the song of a girl in the street outside. Ruggero returns, they confess their love for each other, and leave arm in arm, Ruggero in ecstasy and Magda happy but also apprehensive.

Act III takes place some months later at the villa of Magda and Ruggero on the Riviera. It is late afternoon on a day in spring, and the lovers are taking tea on the terrace. They have been living together happily for several months. Ruggero now tells Magda that he has written to his father not only for money to pay their living expenses but also for the family's consent to his marriage. When he speaks of their future wedded bliss, and his hopes that one day they will have a child, Magda realizes that Ruggero's family will never consent to his marrying her when her former way of life becomes known to them. After Ruggero leaves, she wonders sadly how she can tell him about her past. She goes into the villa, and a moment later Lisette and Prunier come on to the terrace from the garden. Lisette is upset because Prunier's attempt to launch her as an entertainer has ended in disaster at Nice the previous evening, when she was hissed by the audience. She now wants to return to her former job as Magda's maid. Magda appears, and is happy to take Lisette back. Prunier points out that Lisette has found happiness by giving up her illusions and returning to reality, and that Magda should do likewise. He hints that Rambaldo is ready to take her back whenever she wishes to return. Magda sends him away, but before going Prunier makes an assignation for later that evening with Lisette who has reappeared in her maid's uniform.

Ruggero comes out on to the terrace with a letter from his mother who has given her consent to his marriage, on the assumption that the girl is a virtuous maiden. Unable to keep silent any longer, Magda confesses her past to Ruggero, telling him she could have continued to be his mistress but never his wife, for she comes to him contaminated by her past. In vain he pleads with her, but she insists on leaving him so that, one day, he will be able to make a suitable marriage. Ruggero collapses into a chair, overcome with grief, while Magda, supported by Lisette, walks sadly away from true love and back to her former way of life.

Clearly, although it is ostensibly an original work by Willner and Reichert, there are elements in the plot of *La rondine* which derive from *La traviata* (the courtesan who attempts to find true love but finds herself defeated by the moral attitudes of society) and *Die Fledermaus* (maid and mistress meeting at a party in Act II, the maid wearing her mistress's dress, the mistress unrecognized by the maid). Details of the plot were altered during the course of composition by Adami and Puccini, and even after the première musical and textual changes were made, at first for the Vienna production and then later for an Italian production. The version in print and in use today is, however, the original one, i.e. the opera as it was first performed in Monte Carlo.

Although the libretto in its final state leaves much to be desired in structure and characterization, as well as being weakly plotted, Puccini's letters to his librettist reveal that a great deal of thought and care had been expended upon it. As early as September, 1914, Puccini was writing to Adami:

I do not say that Act II is ugly, slovenly, or untheatrical. No, not that. But I do say that it is not . . . very beautiful, that in form it is not very perfect, that it is not . . . super-drama as it should be. As I read the review of Labiche's vaudeville, *Le Chapeau de paille*,[1] my heart was wrung. Why? Because our work lacks vitality and the varying intrigue and the changing vicissitudes which are essential if we are to interest and amuse the public. We must amuse the *organ-grinder*, my dear Adami. If not, we fail utterly, and that must not happen. Act I is good, and Act III will be excellent. But Act II won't do at all, *tout cru*! Let's send Bullier to the devil! Let's find another scene, more alive, more varied, more full of colour, if possible. I have nothing to suggest offhand; but I judge from that feeling which weighs upon my spirit as I work that our labours are not prospering. I am not happy, I am not laughing, I am not

---

[1] *Le Chapeau de paille d'Italie* (The Italian Straw Hat) by Eugène Labiche.

interested. We need something better than this, dear Beppino, in our weary world! . . . We need, that is, a second act.[1]

Bullier's Restaurant was, however, to remain as the scene of Act II, and Puccini did his best to provide musically what was lacking dramatically. On 11 November, 1914, he wrote to Adami:

We must keep this plot, but we must make it less harsh. So I am going ahead, and as I find that in the second act there is too little animation and none of the gaiety and cheerful noise that there should be, considering where the scene is laid, I have had the idea of lengthening the waltz by adding some music which will be livelier and have more *entrain* in it. This music I have, in fact, composed. It now only wants the *mise en scène*. This lively music must have its counterpart in some scene of unrestrained gaiety. And we need words. At a certain point the two lovers break into the love song in waltz time, and this, I think, is going to fit in well. We have still to consider the third act. Meanwhile I am going ahead. There is an Achilles' heel also in the first act: Magda not seen by Ruggero. When I reread the libretto *I did not like this*. I think, however, that, now that everything else is satisfactorily arranged, it will be possible to add a few words for Magda and make her go out, and come back again at the moment when Lisette is showing Ruggero out.[2]

Eight days later, the composer's optimistic mood changed:

I am utterly discouraged! That third act is tormenting me to such a horrible degree that perhaps *La rondine* will remain, with its two acts only, to be published after the death of the composer. The plot won't do – it doesn't convince me. Where did he find Magda? In a convent perhaps? And so this great love of his dies in an instant as soon as he learns who she is? Anyone who sees and hears such a drama unfolded must remain unconvinced and find the end almost illogical and quite unreal. And when the public is not convinced there isn't a shred of hope for the opera. I am in despair. Even the second act is rather dead. All that crowd of thoughtless revellers say very little, and we nowhere arrive at one of those moments of mad folly which are characteristic of such evenings or nights in the cafés of Paris. But Act III in its present state is quite useless, quite dead. Just the usual duet and an end which violates reason and carries no conviction. What is to be done? Is there any solution?

I can send the contract back to Vienna and start thinking of something else. Believe me, dear Adami, my eyes are wide open and – *La rondine* is a piece of obscene trash (*porcheria*). I curse the day when I made a contract with the Viennese.[3]

Three months later, composer and librettist are still grappling with their problems: 'The quartet is driving me mad', wrote Puccini on 27

[1] Adami, op. cit.
[2] Ibid.
[3] Letter of 19 November, 1914; ibid.

February, 1915. 'I cannot fit in the words of that tiresome pair, the poet and the girl. We must just sit down at the table together and in a good half hour's work settle those words. Tomorrow at five? Does that suit you?'[1]

On 22 August, 1915, Puccini was able to assure Adami that 'the third act is nearing the end and is very good. I have taken out all that dramatic stuff, and the end is approached quietly and delicately without any orchestral blaring or screaming. It is all in keeping.'[2]

Puccini was by now also at work on *Il tabarro*, whose libretto had been provided by Adami, and in a letter dated 'Saturday, Holy Week, 1916' he wrote:

La rondine is absolutely finished! I think the last scene is very good.

I am orchestrating *Il tabarro*.

I have given up composition for the moment, because we shall have to revise the libretto [of *Il tabarro*] in two or three places where it lacks character.

Have you nothing new in the way of subjects? I can find nothing! It is desperate! I search and search. I thought I had found two acts but they have come to nothing.[3]

Although, in the spring of 1916, Puccini may have thought he had finished *La rondine*, and was already lusting after new subjects, he and Adami were to go on tampering with *La rondine* long after its 1917 première in Monte Carlo. The firm of Sonzogno published the score in 1917, but on 5 July, 1918, Puccini wrote to Renzo Sonzogno:

I need the entire full-score of *Rondine*. I have made some valuable accommodations and valid little changes in the first act; Prunier baritone, Lisette raised tessitura, Rambaldo more conspicuous, Ruggero less stupid, and Magda finishes the first act singing effectively. For the second act we will see what is to be done. At least we must change the *mise en scène*, that is, the scenario. As for the third act, there are real problems. It is a great reef [*scoglio*] because the subject is the great enemy.[4]

Some writers on Puccini have interpreted the words 'Prunier baritone' as meaning that the tenor role of Prunier was, in an original version, a baritone role. It was not. The composer is here announcing it as a baritone role as part of the changes he is proposing. During the following weeks, other alterations were proposed and adopted: the action is moved from the nineteenth century to 'the present'; a tenor *romanza* has been added to Act I; some transpositions are made at the ends of Acts I and II. It was this second version of the opera, which also included some changes of detail to the plot of Act III, which was produced at the Vienna Volksoper on 9 October, 1920. Puccini was still dissatisfied with the work and on Christmas Day, 1920, he wrote to a

[1] Ibid.   [2] Ibid.   [3] Ibid.   [4] *Carteggi Pucciniani*, op. cit.

friend, Riccardo Schnabl, to say that he and Adami had reverted to the original versions of Acts I and II, with minor changes, but that he is planning a much altered Act III, with a prelude and 'the woman's voice off-stage', and with Rambaldo making an appearance. These changes, however, appear not to have been made, and the third and definitive edition of *La rondine* differs only on minor points from the first. The changes made for Vienna have been discarded, and Prunier, the poet, is a tenor again, as he was in 1917.

III

With the exception of his two earliest works for the stage, *Le villi* and *Edgar*, *La rondine* is Puccini's least performed opera. It is certainly less well known than any other of his mature works, having been unfairly written off as 'bad Lehár' by Tito Ricordi, who had at least seen the score, and subsequently by a number of writers who had seen neither the score nor a performance of the work. *La rondine* is not 'bad Lehár', nor is it either an operetta or a comic opera. It is a light, romantic opera whose music has sufficient melodic interest, charm, and subtle orchestration to triumph over a rather weak libretto, given a lyric soprano capable of doing justice to the role of Magda and a conductor able to interpret the romantic languor of the score without sinking into post-Romantic heaviness. One might have expected Viennese writers on Puccini, such as George Marek and Richard Specht, to be sympathetic to the Italian composer's attempt to forsake Italian melodrama for Viennese lightness and charm; but Marek finds *La rondine* undistinguished and dull,[1] while Specht says it is 'feeble from beginning to end'.[2] The judgement of Mosco Carner (also Viennese) is less harsh. '*La rondine*', he writes, 'lacks the vital melodic spark and shows fatigue in lyrical invention, though it is by no means devoid of inspiration.'[3]

It *is* an uneven work, with a final act which is anti-climactic both musically and dramatically, but some of the problems of appreciating *La rondine* disappear if one ceases to compare it with works in categories in which it has no wish to compete. Think of *La rondine* as an operatta, and you will rightly conclude that Lehár's *Die lustige Witwe* and *Der Graf von Luxembourg* are better organized and contain music as exquisitely scored as Puccini's, and melodically superior. Decide that it is a full-blown opera, and you immediately have to concede that it pales into insignificance beside Strauss's *Der Rosenkavalier*. Realize that *La rondine* is *sui generis*, and the barriers to its enjoyment are down.

There is no self-contained overture: a lively orchestral prelude, whose jaunty *allegro brillante* gives way after a few bars to the romantic theme

[1] Marek, op. cit.   [2] Specht, op. cit.   [3] Carner, op. cit.

Ex. 43

[Ex. 43] which will occur throughout the opera to convey its heroine's mood of romantic yearning, takes the curtain up on the animated conversation of Magda's guests. Puccini's conversational manner is lightly and fluently employed throughout the opening scene. Magda's three friends, Yvette, Bianca and Suzy, are hardly characterized at all individually – they are almost invariably used as a trio, their voices and phrases complementing one another – but Magda (soprano), her maid Lisette (soprano) and the poet Prunier (tenor) soon reveal their own characteristic tendencies which are respectively towards romanticism, practicality and cynicism.

When Prunier sneers at romantic love, the trio of girls supports him, but, although they are directed to sing 'con esaggerato languore' (with exaggerated languor), the theme they sing is that of Ex. 43, to whose nostalgic cadences we have already succumbed in the orchestral prelude. If Puccini meant us to hear this theme as satire or burlesque, he has miscalculated.

Magda reproaches her friends for teasing the poet, and she does so by making use of the lively opening bars of the prelude, to which Prunier continues to make his case against romance. The girls react with a pert little trio in unison, 'É un microbo sottile che turbina nell' aria?' (Is it a subtle germ that pervades the air?).

With her customary air of tenderness, Magda invites Prunier to perform his latest song, and the 'Amore' theme of Ex. 43 is heard again as the poet sits at the piano. As he begins to play the introduction to his song, a series of arpeggio chords and an adumbration of the opening vocal phrase, at first we hear only the piano. When Prunier begins to sing [Ex. 44], the woodwinds steal in, almost drowning the piano. A solo

Ex. 44   Andantino ($\bf J$ = 52)

Chi il bel   so - gno di Do - ret - ta po - te in - do - vi - nar?

violin, supported by celesta and harp, enters a few bars later, and, when Magda takes over the second stanza of the song, she is accompanied by the full orchestra. This, the first aria in *La rondine*, 'Chi il bel sogno di Doretta pote indovinar?' (Who could divine Doretta's beautiful dream?) is therefore a duet, or rather a solo sung first by tenor and then

by soprano. The poet can only speak over the romantic theme of its
refrain [Ex. 45a], leaving it to Magda to 'complete' his song by singing
the phrase [Ex. 45b], inspiring her audience to spoken murmurs of
'Deliziosa!' When she repeats the phrase, 'with increasing ardour',
Magda soars to her high C, bringing the poet's song to a splendidly
romantic conclusion.

Ex. 45a

Ex. 45b

In the ensuing conversation, the three male guests, Périchaud,
Crébillon and Gobin, are heard for the first time, but they are no more
individually characterized than the girls. Even Magda's lover, Rambaldo, fails to come alive in his almost literally monotonous phrases. If
Puccini meant to portray him as utterly boring and colourless, he certainly succeeded. By responding to Rambaldo's gift of a necklace in a few
bars of waltz rhythm, Magda momentarily goads him into an ironic
comment in waltz-time, but Prunier's intervention, with a reference to
the 'Doretta' theme, followed by the maid Lisette's lively chatter,
quite easily distracts our attention from him. Magda's recitative
('Denaro! Nient' altro che denaro!': Money! Nothing but money) and
aria ('Ore dolci e divine': Sweet and divine hours) provide the musical
peak of Act I. The phrases of Magda's languid recitative are punctuated
by the 'amore' theme in the orchestra, and the aria itself is a nostalgic
remembrance of Magda's one encounter with romantic love, its waltz
themes alternately mellow [Ex. 46a] and lively [Ex. 46b].

The conversation continues, at first to a lilting waltz as the girls
continue to tease Prunier, and then in phrases of Puccini's fluent parlando, until Ruggero enters to the strains of Ex. 46a from Magda's aria.
Clearly, Puccini has Ruggero marked out for Magda, and is telling us so

Ex. 46a

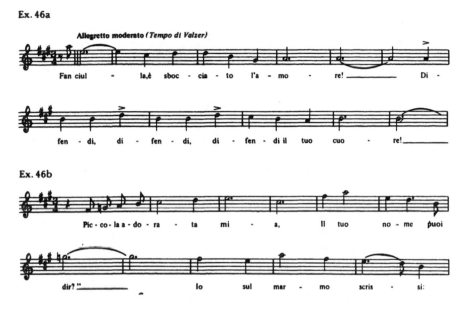

Ex. 46b

immediately. Our attention, however, is diverted from Ruggero, as Prunier begins his fortune-telling, and in a tender little melody compares Magda to the migrating swallow [Ex. 47]. The curiously

Ex. 47

oriental character of Prunier's scene immediately preceding and following the lyrical 'rondine' episode seems to anticipate the music of Ping, Pang and Pong in *Turandot*.

The ensemble in which the others advise Ruggero on how to spend his first night in Paris culminates in a delightful polka begun by the trio of girls, and contributed to by Lisette in a solo passage culminating in her high C, but the rhythm of the waltz returns as the guests depart. When she is left alone, Magda begins to sing softly the 'rondine' theme which is completed by the orchestra. The act is almost over, but there is a surprise to come: the delightful duettino sung by Prunier and Lisette. Though it consists of little more than the repetition of one highly individual phrase [Ex. 48], it has a character of its own, quite different from that of

Ex. 48

the music for the principal pair of lovers which we shall hear in Act II, and with rather more flavour. Like Mimi and Rodolfo at the end of Act I of *La Bohème*, Lisette and Prunier end their duet as they walk off into the night. The orchestra plays Ex. 46a from Magda's aria, and then recalls the Doretta song [Ex. 45b] as Magda speaks her final line and quickly leaves.

The most attractive music in *La rondine* has been heard in Act I. Act II, though lively, is musically less interesting, and Act III is rather arid. This is one of the opera's major drawbacks: if its music improved from act to act instead of deteriorating, *La rondine* might have held the stage more successfully. However, what Act II may lack in musical distinction it compensates for in sheer vivacity throughout its not very extensive length of less than half an hour. The opening chorus is banal but energetic. The tempo slackens at Magda's entrance, as the students attempt to flirt with her. Magda's extended duet scene with Ruggero begins as she introduces herself with the 'rondine' theme. Their waltz tune, 'Nella dolce carezza della danza' (In the sweet caress of the dance), which is taken up by the chorus, is a charming piece of its kind, but it owes a great deal to Franz Lehár. However, the orchestral waltz which follows, though it, too, is Viennese in inspiration, sounds more like Johann Strauss the younger.

Magda and Ruggero express their awakening love in the 'amore' theme [Ex. 43] and then the dancers continue their waltz [Ex. 49]. The

Ex. 49

rhythm of the dance continues under the conversation of Lisette and Prunier and, when Magda and Ruggero re-enter, the 'amore' theme returns with them. The delightful central portion of their duet begins with Magda's 'Perchè mai cercate di saper ch'io sia?' (Why try to discover who I am?). A scene for both pairs of lovers leads to the quartet with ensemble which is the musical climax of the act. It begins with Ruggero's 'Bevo al tuo fresco sorriso' (I drink to your fresh smile), a tender melody which develops into an ensemble and to a climax in a manner more Puccinian and operatic than Viennese and operettish. It is, in fact, reminiscent of the ensembles in Act II of *La Bohème*. Magda's outburst of emotion in which she confesses to Rambaldo that she loves Ruggero is too brief to merit the status of an aria, but it is perhaps her most effective solo passage in the entire opera. It is followed quickly by the exit of the remaining merry-makers, and the little off-stage song sung by a light soprano, the voice part doubled by a piccolo. There is a reprise of the quartet shared by Ruggero and Magda, and the curtain falls on their climactic phrase with its sustained B flat.

After 14 bars of orchestral introduction, Act III begins with another duet for Magda and Ruggero, a slow, rather colourless waltz ('So l'arte strana': I know the strange art), which is followed by a reprise of Ex. 49, one of the waltz themes from Act II, and by a conversational scene which broadens into arioso, as the orchestra softly remembers the Act II quartet. Ruggero's aria, 'Dimmi che vuoi seguirmi alla mia casa' (Tell me you want to follow me to my house), is a gentle but dull piece with which it is difficult for the tenor to make any effect. Unfortunately, it is his only aria in the opera. As he makes his exit, the orchestra plays Ex. 46a from Magda's 'Ore dolci e divine'.

A solo arioso passage for Magda is followed by a scene for Prunier and Lisette, whose liveliness is welcome. Lisette recalls her disastrous début as an entertainer, and the orchestra leaves one in no doubt as to either the level of her performance or the reaction of her audience in Nice the previous evening. It even imitates the whistles with which Lisette's singing had been received. After Magda re-enters, there are echoes of the 'rondine' theme and of the Prunier–Lisette duet from the end of Act I. Restored to her mistress's service, Lisette returns to her cheerful soubrette manner of Act I, but Ruggero's re-entrance with the 'amore' theme leads to a more sombre scene in which Magda reads the letter Ruggero has received from his mother. Puccini's music here is un-distinguished, and fails to rise to the pathos of the occasion. Nor, despite the dramatic support given by the orchestra, does the final duet sufficiently make amends. The ending of the opera, musically as well as dramatically, is anti-climactic.

IX

Il trittico

three one-act operas

Il tabarro

Dramatis personæ:

Michele, barge owner (aged 50)	(baritone)
Luigi, a stevedore (aged 20)	(tenor)
Il 'Tinca', a stevedore (aged 35)	(tenor)
Il 'Talpa', a stevedore (aged 55)	(bass)
Giorgetta, wife of Michele (aged 25)	(soprano)
La Frugola, wife of Il 'Talpa' (aged 50)	(mezzo-soprano)

LIBRETTO by Giuseppe Adami, based on the play *La Houppelande* by Didier Gold

TIME: The beginning of the twentieth century
PLACE: Paris

FIRST PERFORMED at the Metropolitan Opera House, New York, on 14 December, 1918, with Luigi Montesanto (Michele), Claudia Muzio (Giorgetta), Giulio Crimi (Luigi), Angelo Bada (Tinca), Adamo Didur (Talpa), Alice Gentle (Frugola), conducted by Roberto Moranzoni

Suor Angelica

Dramatis personæ:

Suor Angelica (Sister Angelica)	(soprano)
La Zia Principessa (her aunt, the Princess)	(contralto)
La Badessa (the Abbess)	(mezzo-soprano)
La Suora Zelatrice (the Sister Monitor)	(mezzo-soprano)
La maestra delle novizie (mistress of the novices)	(mezzo-soprano)
Suor Genovieffa (Sister Genevieve)	(soprano)
Suor Osmina (Sister Osmina)	(soprano)
Suor Dolcina (Sister Dolcina)	(soprano)
La Suora Infermiera (Nursing Sister)	(mezzo-soprano)

LIBRETTO by Giovacchino Forzano

TIME: The end of the seventeenth century
PLACE: A convent in Italy

FIRST PERFORMED at the Metropolitan Opera House, New York, on 14 December, 1918, with Geraldine Farrar (Angelica), Flora Perini (Principessa), Rita Fornia (La Badessa), conducted by Roberto Moranzoni

Gianni Schicchi

Dramatis personæ:

Gianni Schicchi (aged 50)	(baritone)
Lauretta, his daughter (aged 21)	(soprano)
and the relatives of Buoso Donati:	
Zita (or 'La Vecchia'), cousin to Donati (aged 60)	(contralto)
Rinuccio, Zita's nephew (aged 24)	(tenor)
Gherardo, Buoso's nephew (aged 40)	(tenor)
Nella, his wife (aged 34)	(soprano)
Gherardino, their son (aged 7)	(contralto)
Betto di Signa, brother-in-law of Buoso, (age unguessable)	(bass)
Simone, cousin of Buoso (aged 70)	(bass)
Marco, his son (aged 45)	(baritone)
La Ciesca, Marco's wife (aged 38)	(mezzo-soprano)

LIBRETTO by Giovacchino Forzano, based on some lines in Dante's *Inferno*

TIME: 1299
PLACE: Florence

FIRST PERFORMED at the Metropolitan Opera House, New York, on 14 December, 1918, with Giuseppe de Luca (Schicchi), Florence Easton (Lauretta), Giulio Crimi (Rinuccio), Kathleen Howard (Zita), conducted by Roberto Moranzoni

Il trittico

THE IDEA OF composing two or three short operas for performance
together on one evening had been in Puccini's mind for some years
when, in 1912, a year before the Viennese impresarios suggested the
'operetta' project to him, he saw at the Théâtre Marigny in Paris a one-
act play which impressed him sufficiently for him to inquire after the
rights. This was *La Houppelande* (The Cloak) by Didier Gold, which had
first been produced in 1910. At the time, Puccini's intention was to
produce three short operas, the other two to libretti by d'Annunzio and
the French novelist and playwright Tristan Bernard. However, the d'Annunzio proposal came to nothing, and Bernard's suggestion that he
adapt his own 1907 comedy, *La Peau d'ours* (The Bearskin), did not meet
with the composer's approval. (Bernard's play concerned a Negro who
had once been humiliated by being exhibited to whites in Paris and who,
on his return to his native village, took his revenge by capturing a group
of white explorers and exhibiting them to members of his cannibal tribe,
until such time as they were ripe to be eaten!)

Finding the appropriate companion-pieces to *La Houppelande* was to
prove difficult. Describing Didier Gold's play to Illica, Puccini wrote:
'The subject is *apache* in all its meanings and, even without the almost,
Grand Guignol. But that doesn't matter, It pleases me and strikes me as
highly effective. But this red stain needs something different to contrast
with it, and it is this that I am looking for: something that will be
somewhat elevated, and give me an opportunity to write music that will
take wing.'[1]

Several likely and unlikely subjects were considered, advice was
sought from George Bernard Shaw and from Sacha Guitry, and Adami
began to search through the works of one of Puccini's favourite authors,
Charles Dickens. Meanwhile, the task of adapting *La Houppelande* for
operatic purposes was entrusted to an elderly writer and politician, Ferdinando Martini, who had been suggested to Puccini by the twenty-
nine-year-old playwright and stage director, Giovacchino Forzano.
Martini's work was slow and unsatisfactory, and, when Puccini
attempted to speed him up, he relinquished the task. Giuseppe Adami
took it on, in late 1913, and completed the adaptation within two weeks.

[1] *Carteggi Pucciniani*, op. cit.

By now, Puccini was involved in negotiations for the Viennese project, *La rondine*, whose Italian libretto was to be provided by Adami. For a time, both projects went forward together, until, in due course, Puccini finished *La Houppelande* – which had become, in Italian, *Il tabarro* – and put it aside in order to concentrate upon *La rondine*.

At one point, however, the composer appeared to be attempting to proceed simultaneously on too many fronts. On 23 October, 1915, he wrote from Torre del Lago to 'caro Adamino':

> I have set to work in the meantime on *La Houppelande*. Are you prepared to go over the libretto with me again? I think that if you were here we could settle everything within a week. You could also finish *La rondine*, and we could tackle seriously the question of *Gli zoccoletti*.[1] And we'd settle especially the problem of the third act.[2] I am promising myself again to finish *Il tabarro* in a few weeks, and I think that it will be good. From the point of view of contrast, too, I think that it suits me better just now than *Gli zoccoletti*.[3]

By the end of November, 1916, *Il tabarro* had been completed and set aside. The following January, two or three months before the Monte Carlo première of *La rondine*, Giovacchino Forzano, who had recommended the unsatisfactory Martini to Puccini, showed the composer the sketch of a one-act play he had prepared for a touring company, a piece with an all-female cast, set in a convent. *Suor Angelica* immediately appealed to Puccini as a companion-piece and a strong contrast to *Il tabarro*, and Forzano was encouraged to turn it into an opera libretto. By the beginning of March, the playwright had completed his libretto, and read it to Puccini who expressed his delight and immediately set to work to compose the opera.

While he was at work on *Suor Angelica*, Puccini was offered another subject by Forzano, an idea suggested by a few lines in Dante's *Inferno*, about the Florentine rogue Gianni Schicchi. This appealed to Puccini even more strongly than *Suor Angelica*, and when he received Forzano's completed libretto for *Gianni Schicchi* in the early summer of 1917 he broke off work on his 'nun opera', as he called it, in order to begin on the comedy right away, announcing his intention to Forzano in a piece of doggerel:

> Dopo il *Tabarro* di tinta nera
> sento la voglia di buffeggiare.
> Lei non si picchi
> se faccio prima quel *Gianni Schicchi*.[4]

[1] This was Ouida's *Two Little Wooden Shoes* (see p. 199).
[2] I.e. Act III of *La rondine*.
[3] Adami, op. cit.
[4] (After the black-hued *Tabarro*, I feel a desire to be amusing. Don't be annoyed if I begin on *Gianni Schicchi*.)

Puccini also produced another piece of doggerel, conveying the plot of *Gianni Schicchi* in four lines:

> S'apre la scena col morto in casa.
> Tutt'i parenti borbottan preci
> viene quel Gianni – tabula rasa
> fiorini d'oro diventan ceci.[1]

After beginning *Gianni Schicchi*, however, Puccini returned to the completion of *Suor Angelica*, a task he achieved on 14 September, 1917; he then turned back to *Schicchi*, which he completed in April of the following year. A joint title for all three operas was now required. Puccini, Forzano and a group of friends discarded a number of words such as *triangolo* (triangle), *trinomio* (trinomial, an algebraic expression), *treppiede* (tripod), before agreeing on the misnomer, *Il trittico* (The triptych). A triptych, usually a picture or carving in three hinged sections, ought surely to possess a certain unity of theme. The component parts of Puccini's *Trittico* have nothing in common as a theme except, perhaps, death.

Puccini had hoped that the *Trittico* could have its première in Rome, but this turned out not to be feasible, because of the war. When the Metropolitan Opera, New York, with one Puccini première already to its credit (*La fanciulla del west*), offered to mount the first production of the new one-act operas, Puccini and the firm of Ricordi gave their enthusiastic consent. *Il trittico* was staged at the Met on 14 December, 1918, only a month after the signing of the Armistice. Private international travel was still difficult (and transatlantic travel dangerous because of mines), so for the first time in his life the composer himself was not present at a Puccini première. After the first night, Gatti-Casazza, General Manager of the Met, sent Puccini a cable:

> Most happy to announce the complete authentic success of the *Trittico*. At the end of each opera long very sincere demonstrations more than forty warm curtain calls altogether. In spite of public notice forbidding encores by insistence Lauretta's aria was repeated. Principal strength Moranzoni[2] magnificent. Farrar Muzio Easton De Luca Montesanto Didur incomparable singers and actors. Daily press confirms success expressing itself very favourably on worth of the operas enthusiastically for *Schicchi*.[3]

In fact, press reviews of the first two operas were, on the whole, respectful rather than enthusiastic, and it was only *Gianni Schicchi* which found favour. 'This comedy is so uproariously funny,' the New York

---

[1] The curtain rises on a dead man in the house. All his relatives are muttering prayers. Then Gianni arrives, and makes off with all their hopes of money.

[2] The conductor, Roberto Moranzoni.

[3] A copy of the cable is preserved in the archives of the Metropolitan Opera.

Tribune reported, 'the music so full of life, humour and ingenious devices, that, though there is less singing than in the preceding pieces, it was received with uproarious delight.'

The Rome première of *Il trittico* took place one month later,[1] and again it was only *Schicchi* which was enthusiastically received. The tenor who sang both Luigi (*Il tabarro*) and Rinuccio (*Gianni Schicchi*) on that occasion was the Canadian Edward Johnson (then known as Eduardo di Giovanni), who was later to become General Manager of the Metropolitan Opera. Johnson recalled that, at the end of the performance of the *Trittico* in Rome, Puccini, who always claimed that he was indifferent to applause, turned to him as they were standing in the wings, and whispered 'Tira, tira!' (Pull me, pull me). Johnson did as instructed and dragged the shy, retiring composer out on to the stage to acknowledge the applause.

In Rome, *Il tabarro* was generally regarded as the weakest of the three operas, *Suor Angelica* managing to please some of the critics because of its religious subject matter. It was in Vienna, however, that *Suor Angelica* had its first real success, and this was apparently due to Lotte Lehmann's moving assumption of the title role in the first Viennese performances of the *Trittico* at the Hofoper (now the Staatsoper), eleven days after the first Viennese *Rondine* at the Volksoper. Writing three months later from Milan, Puccini, who had been present at the Vienna performances, told Sybil Seligman:

> I have protested to Ricordi's for giving permission for *Tabarro* and *Schicchi* without *Angelica* – it makes me really unhappy to see the *best* of the three operas laid on one side. In Vienna it was the most effective of the three with the good Lehmann. She's German, it's true, but a fine, delicate artist – simple and without any of the airs of a prima donna, with a voice as sweet as honey.
>
> . . . As to what you say about the 'religiosity' of the subject of *Angelica* which cannot appeal to the English, I permit myself to say that I am not of your opinion. The thing is, and I've said it already, that the opera didn't have time to find its way into the public's ears – because the story is really one of passion and it's only the environment which is religious. And besides, why was Max Reinhardt's *Miracle* at Olympia such a success? There you have Madonnas and churches etc., to your heart's content.[2]

The *Trittico* had been staged in London the preceding summer, at Covent Garden. It had been announced for the summer before that (i.e. 1919), but at that time Puccini objected to Toscanini having been invited to conduct. 'I've heard about Covent Garden', he wrote to Sybil,

[1] Despite his close connection with Puccini, as librettist of three operas, Adami is an unreliable Puccini chronicler. In his edition of the composer's letters, he states that '*Il trittico* was performed for the first time in Rome on the night of 11 January, 1919' and that the Met performances took place 'in the following season . . . with tremendous success.'

[2] Seligman, op. cit.

and I protested to Ricordi's because I don't want that *pig* of a Toscanini; he has said all sorts of nasty things about my operas and has tried to inspire certain journalists to run them down too. He didn't succeed in every case, but one of his friends (of the *Secolo*) wrote a beastly article under his inspiration – and I won't have this *God*. He's no use to me – and I say, as I have already said, that when an orchestral conductor thinks poorly of the operas he has to conduct, he can't interpret them properly. This is the reason from the point of view of Art which I have expounded; there remains the personal question, and I shall do all I can not to have him; I have no need of *Gods* because my operas go all over the world – they have sufficiently strong legs to walk by themselves. If you see Higgins or any of the others, tell them too that I don't want this *pig*; if he comes to London, *I shan't come*, which would be a great disappointment to me – I can't object to this *God* because my contract with Ricordi's doesn't give me the right, but I'll do and say everything I can so that it should be known and so that he should know it himself.[1]

So neither Toscanini nor the *Trittico* appeared at Covent Garden in the summer of 1919. The following year, Puccini travelled to London to supervise rehearsals of the operas, which were conducted by Gaetano Bavagnoli. *Schicchi* was liked, *Tabarro* received with indifference, and *Angelica* generally disliked. King George V and Queen Mary attended the second performance but arrived late, perhaps deliberately, thus missing *Il tabarro*. As Angelica, Gilda Dalla Rizza 'had so little variety of tone at her command, and so often engaged one's attention in wondering which note she really meant to sing, that her performance did not help matters much'.[2] *Suor Angelica* was dropped after the second Covent Garden performance of the *Trittico*, to the annoyance of the composer, while the other two operas were given further performances during the season, either together or as part of a programme of opera and ballet, sharing the evening with Diaghilev's Russian Ballet. 'I very much dislike the *Trittico* being given in bits – I gave permission for two operas, and not *one*, in conjunction with the Russian Ballet,' Puccini wrote to Sybil Seligman[3] when he heard that *Il tabarro*, too, had been dropped, leaving *Gianni Schicchi* to share an evening with the ballet.

After a performance of the complete *Trittico* in 1921 at the opera house in Lucca, Puccini himself accepted that the three operas together made too long an evening (though each plays for under an hour), and became reconciled to their being performed separately. 'How I hate these three operas,' he wrote to Adami in the letter in which he asked for words for a replacement aria for Michele. 'You cannot ever imagine it. At Bologna they seemed to me as long as a transatlantic cable.'[4]

Gianni Schicchi remains the most frequently, and *Suor Angelica* the least

[1] Ibid.
[2] Press comment quoted in Harold Rosenthal, *Two Centuries of Opera at Covent Garden* (London, 1958).
[3] Seligman, op. cit.
[4] Adami, op. cit.

frequently performed of the *Trittico* operas. At Covent Garden, for instance, after the 1920 performances, only *Gianni Schicchi* was seen again:
in 1924 (in English) with a staged version of Bach's cantata, 'Phoebus
and Pan'; in 1926 with Ravel's *L'Heure Espagnole*; in 1931 with *Fedra* by
Romano Romani, the teacher of Rosa Ponselle who sang the role of
Fedra; in 1936 with Strauss's *Salome*; and in 1962 with *L'Heure Espagnole*
and Schoenberg's *Erwartung*. A new production of the complete *Trittico*
was given at Covent Garden in 1965, with Tito Gobbi as Michele in *Il
tabarro* and as Schicchi; but when it was revived, which was not until
1976, it had been reduced to *Il tabarro* and *Gianni Schicchi*: *Suor Angelica*
has really not gained in popularity over the years. There have, however,
been productions of the *Trittico* at several important opera houses in
recent times, among them the Deutsche Oper, Berlin (1975), the
Metropolitan, New York (where a 1974 production of *Schicchi* was joined
in 1975 by its companions), and the Vienna State Opera (1979).

II

Il tabarro

The opera is set in Paris in the early 1900s, and the action takes place on a
barge tied to a landing stage on the Seine. It is twilight. On the barge, its
owner Michele (baritone) stands, watching the sunset, his unlit pipe in
his mouth. His much younger wife Giorgetta (soprano) busies herself
with such tasks as taking down a line of drying laundry, watering the
flowers, and cleaning the bird cage. Stevedores, moving between the
hold of the barge and the quay, are loading sacks of cement on to a
horsedrawn cart on the quay. In the distance, the sound of tugboat
whistles and automobile horns can be heard.

Giorgetta tells Michele that the men have finished unloading the
cargo, and that they should be offered a drink. Michele agrees, and
kisses his wife affectionately, but she draws back from him and he goes
below. Luigi (tenor), youngest of the stevedores, complains of the heat,
and Giorgetta, flirtatiously promising him relief, produces a jug of wine
and glasses for him and the other two stevedores, 'Tinca' and 'Talpa'.
The men drink to her health and, when an out-of-tune barrel organ
begins to play on the quayside, Tinca dances with Giorgetta. Luigi and
Talpa are amused by Tinca's clumsy attempts at dancing, and Luigi
pushes him away and takes his place, at which moment Michele emerges
from the hold, and the merriment suddenly ceases. The stevedores
descend to the hold, while Michele and Giorgetta discuss which of the
men should be paid off when they leave Paris the following week.

A ballad-monger passes along the quay, singing the latest popular
song, the story of the dying Mimi, and is soon surrounded by a group of
seamstresses who listen eagerly to his song. Frugola (mezzo-soprano)
appears, to await her husband, Talpa. She shows Giorgetta the various

bits and pieces she has scavenged during the day, and then sings a song about her old cat. Giorgetta has noticed Michele's distant mood, but cannot get him to reveal what is on his mind. As the stevedores prepare to depart, Michele asks Luigi to come again the following day, to give a hand. Tinca announces that he is going off alone to get drunk, and Luigi agrees with him that, since life is so hard and so hopeless, it is better to drown one's sorrows in drink than to waste time in thought. Frugola reveals that her ambition is to have a little cottage in the country, while Giorgetta and then Luigi sing the praises of Paris and its suburbs.

When the others have left, Luigi remains behind on the pretext of having to speak to the boss. He and Giorgetta recall the ecstasy of their love-making the previous evening, and begin to make plans to meet again later. Michele appears from the hold, and Luigi asks if he can be put ashore at Rouen, for he plans to look for work there. After Michele has gone into the cabin, Luigi and Giorgetta confess their love for each other, and Luigi agrees to return within an hour. He will come aboard quietly, wearing rope-soled shoes, at Giorgetta's usual signal, the lighting of a match.

Luigi leaves quickly, as Michele emerges from the cabin with the lanterns he has lit. When Michele reproaches her for no longer loving him, and refers to their child who died years ago in infancy, Giorgetta tells him that he is mistaken, that nothing has changed except that they are both older. He reminds her of the days when he would shelter her beneath his cloak as they stood on deck in the cool breeze of the evening. Giorgetta claims that she is exhausted, and goes below. Watching her go, Michele calls her a slut. As he hangs the lanterns on either side of the barge, two lovers pass by on the quay, promising to meet again on the morrow. Through the cabin window, Michele sees that Giorgetta is not preparing to go to bed but is obviously awaiting someone. He wonders which of the men it might be, but rejects them all, including Luigi who, after all, has asked to be allowed to leave at Rouen. Miserable with jealousy, Michele imagines the joy of strangling his wife's lover.

In the darkness of the night, Michele takes out his pipe and lights it. On the quay, Luigi mistakes this for Giorgetta's signal, and comes on board. Michele leaps upon him, frightens him into confessing that he is Giorgetta's lover, and strangles him. Aroused by the noise, Giorgetta calls from within the cabin, whereupon Michele quickly draws Luigi's body inside the folds of his cloak. When Giorgetta comes on deck, anxious and frightened, she attempts to make her peace with Michele. He invites her to nestle close to him, inside his cloak. As she approaches, he flings the cloak open, revealing the body of Luigi which falls at her feet. Savagely, Michele presses Giorgetta's face against her dead lover.

The one-act play, *La Houppelande* (The Cloak) by Didier Gold contains not one but two *crimes passionnels*, for there is a sub-plot involving the

stevedore Goujon who stabs his unfaithful wife in a tavern on the
quayside, emerging to brandish the blood-stained weapon at the
moment that Michel is pressing Georgette's face against the dead body
of her lover. Gold's Goujon (or 'Gudgeon') becomes in Adami's Italian
libretto Tinca (or 'Tench'), and his domestic situation is merely hinted
at. The play's La Taupe (Mole) and La Furette (Rummager) are
translated into the opera's Talpa and Frugola, and the names of
Michel, Georgette and Louis are retained in their Italian forms. *La
Houppelande* is an effective piece of low-life melodrama, and Adami's
libretto, though it deletes the sub-plot, deals fairly with the play's atmosphere and characters, the librettist's alterations and occasional
expansions merely romanticizing the situation for operatic purposes.
The libretto is tautly constructed, and smoothly written, though
Adami's Italian verse lacks the flavour of Gold's Parisian argot.

When the Triptych is performed as a unity the order of the operas is (i)
Il tabarro, (ii) *Suor Angelica*, (iii) *Gianni Schicchi*. Puccini asks that the
curtain be raised immediately on *Il tabarro*, indeed before the music
begins, so that one's first impression is a visual one of the Seine at
twilight, the barge at its moorings, the stevedores moving between the
quay and the hold of the barge, Giorgetta attending to various tasks and
Michele, a stationary figure, watching the sunset. Richard Specht
thought that the brooding theme on which the orchestral prelude is
based served to express 'at once the night descending upon Paris, the
hush that falls over the working day, and the stolid, resigned weariness
that reigns on board the tug on the Seine'.[1] Certainly the beginning of
one of Puccini's most advanced, 'impressionist' scores conjures up with
its regular swaying motion a desolate atmosphere which is to pervade
the entire opera, and could be said to do for the Seine what the opening
of *Das Rheingold* does for the Rhine. A certain weariness of spirit is
conveyed by the harmonies and by the muted strings as much as by the
onward movement of the music. The life of the city, both on the river
and in the streets, is suggested by the whistle of a tugboat and the distant
sound of a motor horn. This river theme, which wends its way through
the texture of the first part of the opera, is a musical equivalent of the
lines which preface the original French play, beginning, 'Lumineux, à
grands traits, comme un immense flaque, / Le fleuve s'assoupit à
l'ombre d'un bateau' (Luminous, in general outline like an immense
pool, the river dozes off in the shade of a boat).

During the dialogue between Giorgetta (soprano) and Michele
(baritone), which is carried on in Puccini's usual recitative-like conversational style, the voices of the stevedores (basses, baritones, tenors) can
be heard singing a melancholy work song. The basic *andante moderato
calmo* of the music now quickens to an *allegretto* with the entrance of Luigi
(tenor), and two other stevedores, Il 'Tinca' (tenor) and Il 'Talpa' (bass),

[1] Specht, op. cit.

and the lively little drinking song, 'Èccola la passata', begun by Luigi and taken up by the other two men. There is a brief reference to a theme which is later associated with the love affair of Giorgetta and Luigi, but in general his convivial solo gives a misleading impression of Luigi who is revealed in his later arioso to be a more introspective character.

The waltz played by the organ-grinder on an old, out-of-tune hurdy-gurdy, is wittily saturated in dissonant harmonies, with major sevenths making do for octaves, and scored for two flutes, two clarinets and bass clarinet: it is clear that Puccini has heard the organ-grinder's music in Stravinsky's *Petrouchka* – though if his scoring is Russian his melody is authentically French, the waltz being based on a well-known popular song of the time. With Michele's re-entrance the dancing ceases, and the slightly tense domestic dialogue is resumed, this time accompanied by the song of a ballad-monger and his harpist accompanist, who approach along the quayside. When the ballad-monger gets close enough, his song is revealed to be 'the story of Mimi', and sure enough each verse ends with a deliberate reference to Puccini's *La Bohème* (the beginning of 'Mi chiamano Mimi'). He moves on, followed by a group of seamstresses who have bought copies of his song from him, and are trying it out. (Earlier, when he was announcing his song, the ballad-monger quoted not *La Bohème* but, very briefly, a phrase from the Act I soprano–tenor duet in *Tosca* [Ex. 50]. Was Puccini aware of this?

Ex. 50

Chi vuol l'ul - ti - ma can - zo - net - ta?

Soon after La Frugola arrives on the scene with her repetitive chatter, she has a song, 'Se tu sapessi gli oggetti strani che in questa sacca sono racchiusi' (If you only knew what strange objects are gathered together in this sack), which, like most of the lyrical passages in *Il tabarro*, is so closely woven into the structure of the music that it is hardly identifiable as song or arietta, and so strongly characterized that it would be meaningless as the utterance of anyone but La Frugola. In accompanying her chatter, the orchestra's oboes and violas find themselves imitating La Frugola's cat. Luigi's 'Hai ben ragione' (You are right) [Ex. 51] brings a more sombre mood back into the music: this is Puccini's

Ex. 51

Hai ben ra - gio - ne; me - glio non pen - sa - re, pie-gare il

ca - po ed in cur - var in schie - na.

familiar vein of writing for his *disperato* tenor heroes. The self-pity of
Luigi's lament is no less deeply felt or convincingly expressed for being
less called-for than, for instance, Cavaradossi's 'È lucevan le stelle' or
Dick Johnson's 'Ch'ella mi creda libero e lontano'.

La Frugola's second song of longing for a cottage in the country, 'Ho
sognato una casetta' (I've dreamed of a little house), is a nagging little
piece largely on one note, with stabbing phrases as though La Frugola
would prod her dream into becoming reality. Giorgetta responds to it
with her dream of happiness, 'È ben altro il mio sogno' (My dream is
quite different), a warmly lyrical effusion in praise of the district of
Paris in which she grew up. When she sings of her excursions to the
Bois de Boulogne, the horns naïvely imitate the call of a cuckoo. Luigi,
who was born in the same district, joins Giorgetta in ecstatic praise
of the bourgeois life, perhaps carried away by her (optional) high
C on 'no*stal*gia'. Their outburst has little effect upon La Frugola who
leads Il Talpa away, somehow bullying him into joining her in a
monotonous, oddly grim little song about the pleasures of country life.
The river theme from the very beginning of the opera now returns with
its fog-laden orchestration, sung wordlessly by an offstage sopranino,
answered by a tenorino, to round off this first, expository, atmospheric
half of the opera.

From this point on, the plot or, in the absence of very much plot, the
situation, takes over; the subsidiary characters have departed and we are
left with the three principals. Luigi and Giorgetta are momentarily
alone, but their love duet cannot properly get under way until they are
certain that Michele will not interrupt them. A persistent foghorn is
heard as they begin to converse nervously, urgently. The duet begins
agitatedly as soon as Michele goes below, but then broadens into the
passionate accents of Ex. 52 ('È la gioia rapita': Joy is ruined), only to

Ex. 52

È la gio - la ra - pi - ta   fra spa-si - mi e pa- u   -   re

subside into melodic recitative as the lovers discuss the practical details
attendant upon their meeting again later that evening. The passionate
tone returns in Luigi's final phrases, almost a separate solo ('Folle di
gelosia': Insane jealousy).

The cellos offer a misleadingly comforting *andante* melody as Michele
reappears. His scene with Giorgetta begins prosaically but, at his
'Perchè non m'ami più?' (Why do you no longer love me?) it takes on a
tender, immensely sad mood as he sings of a past whose happiness she
cannot bear to remember. Giorgetta remains unresponsive, the music
dies away as she goes below, and a distant clock is heard to strike nine.

We are brought shockingly back to the present with Michele's snarl of 'Squaldrina' (Harlot), and by the sad irony of the off-stage voices of a pair of lovers, acting as a bridge passage to Michele's savage outburst of jealousy.

The sound of a cornet sounding the retreat is heard in the distance, and then, 'Nulla! Silenzio' (Nothing! Silence), the opening words of the aria which Puccini composed in 1921 to replace the original monologue heretofore heard at this point. The aria, or dramatic scena, is a superb piece of music drama, in which the orchestra plays as important a role as the voice in portraying first Michele's brooding jealousy and then the fury of his almost suicidal despair. In its succession of moods, it calls to mind Rigoletto's great monologue, 'Pari siamo', in Verdi's opera.

'Scorri, fiume eterno' (Rush on, unending river), the gloomy, contemplative aria which formerly occurred at this point, is set to different words, and is also quite different musically in its lyrical middle section; a less interesting, more conventional piece than its replacement. Puccini asked Adami for new words to which he composed the present aria, when he had reached the conclusion that the earlier one was too academic, and weakened the dénouement.

The final pages of the opera are filled with music which moves quickly and dramatically to accompany the murder and Michele's final savage gesture in revealing to Giorgetta the corpse of her lover. Hardly memorable as music, the last minutes of the score nevertheless fulfil their function in carrying the brutal action along with strength and conviction. *Il tabarro* makes an exciting opening to the *Trittico*, and in itself is an excellent piece of *verismo* theatre. Though the entire score plays for no more than fifty minutes, its first half needs especially careful performance if it is not to drag: its second, sturdier half can more or less look after itself!

III

Suor Angelica

The action takes place in the cloisters of an Italian convent, at the end of the seventeenth century. As the curtain rises, the voices of nuns singing an 'Ave Maria' can be heard from within the chapel. When the Sisters emerge from the chapel, the Monitress assigns penances to two who were late for the service: Sister Osmina is sent to her cell for having hidden two scarlet roses in her sleeve in chapel, and Sister Lusilla made to work and to observe silence for having made other members of the choir laugh.

Sister Genevieve (Suor Genovieffa) reminds the others that it is one of the three evenings of the year when the sunlight falls on the fountain at the close of day. She suggests taking a pail of the golden water to the grave of a nun who had died during the year. When the nuns exclaim that the dead sister would like this, Sister Angelica (soprano) exclaims that likes and desires are the flowers of the living and do not bloom for the dead. Sister Genevieve, who used to be a shepherdess, confesses her desire to hold a baby lamb in her arms once more, and the stout Sister Dolcina is about to confess her desire when the others exclaim that they know it to be gluttony. Angelica claims to have no desires, but the other nuns say they know that she has a great desire for news of her family. Of noble birth, Angelica has been in the convent for seven years, having been forced by her family to take the veil as a punishment for some crime or sin unknown to the other nuns.

The Nursing Sister announces that Sister Chiara has been stung by wasps, and asks Angelica, who has a great knowledge of herbs, to concoct a remedy. Two alms-collectors arrive, leading a donkey laden with gifts of food, and report seeing a splendid carriage at the convent gates. Angelica questions them eagerly about the exact appearance of the coach, and the nature of its coat-of-arms, for she hopes it may belong to a member of her family. The Abbess enters, motioning to the other sisters to withdraw, and informs Angelica that her aunt, the Princess, has come to visit her.

The Princess (contralto) enters, a dignified, middle-aged woman of aristocratic features, who walks with the aid of an ebony cane. When they are left alone, the Princess glances coldly at her niece, and extends her hand for Angelica to kiss. She sits, and Angelica kneels before her.

Throughout their conversation, the Princess stares straight ahead of her, rarely looking at Angelica. She informs her niece that the estate of her late parents is to be divided, as her younger sister is about to marry. When Angelica asks whom her sister is to marry, she is told it is a man whose love has enabled him to overlook the disgrace Angelica has brought upon the family. Angelica exclaims that her aunt is inexorable, to which the Princess, offended, replies that Angelica's mother, though dead, still weeps in heaven at the thought of Angelica's sin, for which she, Angelica, must continue to atone. This leads Angelica to beg for news of her baby, the baby son whom she saw and kissed only once before he was taken away from her and she was sent to the convent. She has prayed for news of him these past seven years. What does he look like? What colour are his eyes?

For a moment, the Princess does not reply. She glances at Angelica, then looks away again as she informs her that the child was taken seriously ill and, despite all efforts to save him, died two years ago. Angelica falls to the ground. Thinking that she has fainted, her aunt rises to help her, but when she hears the girl's sobs she restrains herself from displaying any compassion. She turns to a sacred image on the wall, and prays before it. The Abbess and the Portress enter with pen and ink, and

Angelica drags herself to the table to sign the document her aunt had placed there, renouncing her inheritance in favour of her sister. The Abbess and Portress leave, and the Princess takes the document. She moves towards her niece, but Angelica shrinks away from her. The Princess leaves, after a final glance at Angelica from the door.

Night has fallen. In the cemetery the sisters can be seen lighting lanterns on the tombstones. Angelica sobs bitterly as she remembers her child who died without knowing his mother's caresses. She longs to be united with the child, and in a mood of mystical exaltation feels suddenly convinced that she is in a state of grace. As the sisters retire for the night, Angelica emerges again from her cell, carrying an earthenware jar which she puts at the foot of a cypress tree. She collects twigs and branches, lights a fire, adds water to the jar and sets the jar on the fire, brewing a deadly herb. She has been called by her child to join him in heaven, she murmurs in farewell to the sisters as she drinks the poison.

As soon as she has poisoned herself, Angelica experiences a sudden return to reality, and now fears that she will die in mortal sin. She prays to the Virgin to forgive her, for she had momentarily lost her reason because of her love for her child. She seems now to hear the voices of angels interceding for her. The chapel doors swing open, and the chapel, dazzlingly bright, is revealed to be crowded with angels. The Virgin Mary appears in the doorway, leading by the hand a small child whom she gently pushes towards Angelica who dies in a condition of ecstatic bliss.

The libretto of *Suor Angelica*, not an adaptation but an original work by Giovacchino Forzano, is little more than a series of pious vignettes, framing the confrontation scene between the Principessa and Angelica. Other writers on Puccini have suggested that Forzano must have known Massenet's *Le Jongleur de Notre-Dame* or at least its plot, and no doubt he did, though the similarities are not so startling that they cannot be explained by coincidence. Both operas are set in a religious community, and both end with a miracle. Puccini greeted Forzano's libretto with delight, professing himself overjoyed to be offered the mystical subject which he had long dreamed of. He was, however, by no means a religious man, and his initial delight may have been overtaken by other feelings as he came to grapple with the problems of composing appropriate music for Forzano's stage pictures.

The opening of *Suor Angelica* offers a sharp contrast to the violent and melodramatic end of *Il tabarro*.

A four-bar phrase played on the bells off-stage precedes the rise of the curtain, and then is given first to strings and celesta and then to the full orchestra, as the accompaniment to the nuns' chanting of the 'Ave Maria' inside the church: the solo voice of Angelica is briefly heard

during the prayer. In the opening scene, one's ears become accustomed
to the fact that the timbre of the female voices, unalleviated by any male
sound throughout the opera, will be matched by an almost cloying
quality in the orchestral writing, the over-all effect one of sweetness
verging on sickliness.

Although, in the first part of the opera, the stage appears to be filled
with nuns, the only one other than Angelica to emerge as a personality in
musical and dramatic terms is the gentle Sister Genevieve (Suor
Genovieffa) whose gay little arioso [Ex. 53], 'O sorelle, sorelle' (Oh

Ex. 53

O so-rel - le, so - rel - le,_____   io voglio ri - ve - lar - vi _____   che una spe-ra di   so - le ____

sisters, oh sisters), does something to dispel the monotony which
threatens to set in early, a monotony exacerbated by the contrast
between *Suor Angelica*'s serene string-dominated orchestral piety and the
noisy clamour of the preceding opera. Angelica's first extended solo
passage, 'I disiderii sono i fiori dei vivi' (Desires are the flowers of the
living), reaches its climax at the words 'La morte è vita bella' (Death is
beautiful life) with an hysterical orchestral tutti which gives the first hint
of the psychotic behaviour of which the apparently calm Angelica will be
found capable.

Sister Genevieve's amiable solo, 'Soave Signor mio' (My sweet lord), is
quietly charming, despite the naïvely onomatopoeic bleating of the
lamb offered by the woodwind section. A little later, when Sister Clara is
stung by a wasp, Puccini does it again, this time imitating the wasp on
muted trumpets and pizzicato strings, and when a donkey is driven on to
the stage by two nuns it too is portrayed in the orchestra. (The wasp
episode is marked in the orchestral score as an optional cut, but it ought
to be retained, as it reveals Angelica's way with herbs, which is important
since she later kills herself by drinking poison distilled from plants.)

When Angelica is told that a beautiful carriage has drawn up outside
the gates of the convent, we hear in the orchestra a theme which we shall
later understand to be associated with Angelica's past and her noble
family. A note of welcome fervour enlivens Angelica's brief prayer, 'O
madre eletta' (Oh blessed mother), and a solo viola takes up this theme
as Angelica asks the Abbess to reveal the identity of her visitor. The off-
stage voices of the nuns chanting a Requiem intervene before she is
answered. The mood of the scene between Angelica and her Aunt the
Principessa is set by the gloomy unison theme heard in the strings four
times while the Abbess prepares Angelica for this unexpected confrontation. Tension rises as the pitch of the last two notes of the theme rises at
their second and third repetitions.

The key scene of the opera is that in which, for the first time in seven years, Angelica and her aunt, the Princess, meet: a scene which, in its aura of implacable religious suppression, oddly recalls a quite different kind of confrontation between Philip II and the Grand Inquisitor in Verdi's *Don Carlos*. Here, freed from the necessity to paint scenes of piety, and able instead to indulge his gift for dramatic characterization in music, Puccini rises to the occasion with a chilling portrait of the harsh old woman, his orchestra as much as his vocal writing for the Principessa exposing the inhumanity cloaked as religious devotion, and with a warmly sympathetic portrayal of Angelica's agitation. The Principessa's first solo passage, 'Io dovevo dividerlo' (I had to divide it), proceeds to advance the plot in a grave melodic arioso, until she is stung to more excited utterance by her niece's accusation that she is hard-hearted. Her later solo, 'Nel silenzio di quei raccoglimenti' (In the silence of those prayers) [Ex. 54], is the nearest equivalent to a full-scale aria in *Suor*

Ex. 54

Angelica, except for Angelica's 'Senza mamma' (Without a mother) from which it is separated by the dramatic but workaday music which accompanies Angelica's collapse on being told of the death of her child, and the orchestral comment when she signs the document and the Principessa departs.

'Senza mamma' [Ex. 55], Angelica's only aria, has an emotional

Ex. 55

restraint and dignity not always observed by Puccini heroines under stress. A sentimental religiosity is present in text as well as music, but it does not run riot, and the aria's ending on a softly floated high A is perfectly judged. Told that the Virgin has heard her prayer, Angelica is moved to express her happiness in a passage culminating in her high C, a note which she repeats off-stage, soaring above the other nuns who are also at prayer. The second part of 'Senza mamma' is heard in the orchestra to accompany the action which, one realizes only later, is Angelica's preparation for suicide. As she actually drinks the poison, the orchestra thunders out the tutti which we had formerly heard underlining her words 'Death is beautiful life.' A second aria for Angelica, in which she addresses the flowers ('Amici fiori'), asking them to yield their poison to her, was deleted by Puccini after the Scala performances of the opera. An 80-bar-long *andante*, it is printed in the first edition of the complete *Trittico*.

Puccini's interest in the supernatural had never been strong, and had certainly not been expressed in opera since his first work for the stage, *Le villi*. It is, therefore, perhaps not surprising that the music the composer provides at the climax of *Suor Angelica* to accompany 'the miracle' in which the Virgin Mary appears, pushing Angelica's child towards her, fails to rise to the heights of mystical ecstasy required by the situation. Angelica's mortal distress as the poison takes hold is affectingly projected, but her apotheosis lacks conviction. With a final rise to her high C, Angelica cries for salvation, and the hymn to the Virgin, with suitably saccharine accompaniment, is sung by the nuns as she greets her child in death. Musically, the conclusion of the opera remains earthbound.

Suor Angelica was, from the time of the *Trittico*'s première, generally regarded as the weakest of the three operas, and it is much less frequently performed than the other two. It can, however, be effective in the theatre, and never more so than when it occupies its rightful place, offering an hour of sweetness and sentimentality between the brutal tragedy of *Il tabarro* and the not entirely un-brutal humour of *Gianni Schicchi*.

I have tried to describe *Suor Angelica* fairly, but I am conscious of the fact that, temperamentally, I do not warm to the piece, and so, as a corrective balance, I offer the opinion of Mosco Carner, the distinguished biographer of Puccini: '[*Suor Angelica*] is an opera of impeccable craftsmanship and capable of achieving an impact, if carefully staged and if the heroine's part is taken by a singer-actress of warmth and sincerity, like the great Lotte Lehmann.' In a footnote, Mr Carner adds: 'This writer, then a student, recalls Lotte Lehmann's moving interpretation of the Nun, which indeed lent the opera a poignancy he has not experienced since in any other production. It was as though Puccini had written this part especially for her.'[1]

Lehmann was indeed unique, and Puccini himself on several occasions expressed the warmest admiration for her. But if some enterprising management today were to cast Ileana Cotrubas in the title role, I have a feeling that she might well achieve for *Suor Angelica* in the 1980s what her great predecessor achieved in Vienna so many years ago.

Perhaps *Suor Angelica* would find its most appreciative audiences among religious communities in Italy and Ireland. When Puccini had finished composing the opera, he took his manuscript to the nunnery where his sister Iginia lived, and played the music to her and her fellow

---

[1] Carner, op. cit.

nuns. He first explained the story to them, and then played most of the music. At the end, several of the nuns were in tears. When they heard Angelica's cry 'O Madonna, Madonna, save me for the sake of my son,' they were deeply moved, and hastened to offer absolution to their fictional sister.

IV

Gianni Schicchi

The action of the opera takes place in the year 1299, in Florence, in the house of Buoso Donati, a well-to-do landowner who has just died. The curtain rises to reveal his bedchamber, with the corpse of Donati still in the bed, and nine of his relatives gathered, ostensibly to mourn his passing but actually to intrigue over his will. The relatives are Zita (or La Vecchia, 'the old woman'), a sixty-year-old cousin to Buoso Donati; Rinuccio (tenor), Zita's nephew, twenty-four years old and in love with the daughter of Gianni Schicchi; a family group consisting of Buoso's nephew Gherardo (aged forty), Gherardo's wife Nella (thirty-four) and child Gherardino (seven); Betto di Signa, Buoso's brother-in-law, poor and shabbily dressed, and of indefinable age; Simone, a seventy-year-old cousin to Buoso, and Simone's son Marco (forty-five) and daughter-in-law La Ciesca (thirty-eight).

Betto tells the others there is a rumour that Buoso has left most of his estate to the monks at the local monastery: this leads to a desperate search for the dead man's will, which is found by Rinuccio. Before he opens the will, Rinuccio asks his Aunt Zita if, provided they are now all going to be rich, she will agree to his marrying Gianni Schicchi's daughter Lauretta. Zita tells her nephew that, if all goes well for the family, he can marry the devil's daughter if he wants to. Rinuccio quietly asks young Gherardino to run and fetch Schicchi and Lauretta. He then gives the will to his Aunt Zita who proceeds to open and read it. The other relatives cluster around her, reading over her shoulder. As they take in the contents, expressions of anxiety, fury and finally sheer horror appear in their faces, and Simone blows out all the candles they had lit for the soul of the departed, for Buoso has indeed left everything to the monks.

The relatives, after they have given voice to their fury, begin to wonder if Buoso's will can somehow be circumvented. Rinuccio's view is that only Gianni Schicchi could possibly advise them about that. The others are not impressed, and when Gherardino returns to say that Schicchi is on the way, they all begin to speak against Schicchi, whom they consider an upstart from the country. Rinuccio speaks up for the man he hopes will be his father-in-law. He suggests that they put aside their narrow-minded prejudices. The city of Florence, he says, is now flourishing because of newcomers such as Arnolfo, Giotto, Medici and Schicchi, who should be welcomed for the new ideas they bring.

Schicchi now arrives, and at first cannot understand why the relatives look so gloomy, for, as he puts it, they have lost only Buoso, not his estate. They immediately tell him their sad news, and Zita adds that Schicchi and his daughter had better be off, for she will not allow her nephew to marry a girl with no dowry. The young lovers are miserable to see their elders quarrelling, and Schicchi, offended, is about to depart, dragging Lauretta after him, when she pleads with her father to have pity, and help her to marry Rinuccio. If she cannot marry him, she will go to the Ponte Vecchio and throw herself in the river Arno.

Schicchi yields to his daughter's pleading, and agrees to examine the will. After he has thought for a moment, he sends Lauretta out on to the balcony to feed the birds. Upon being assured by the relatives that no one else yet knows that Buoso has died, Schicchi begins to give instructions. The body and the candlesticks are to be taken into an adjoining room, and the bed remade. This has only just been done, when there is a knock at the door: the doctor, Spinelloccio, has come to see his patient. Schicchi hides behind the bed-curtains and the doctor is admitted. Speaking from behind the curtains, Schicchi imitates the voice of the dead man, tells the doctor that he is feeling much better, and asks him to return later in the evening. In his Bolognese accent, the doctor announces that this miraculous recovery is due entirely to the Bologna school of medicine which he represents. He makes his exit, and the relatives congratulate Schicchi on the astonishing accuracy of his impersonation of Buoso.

Schicchi explains that they must now summon a notary, to whom he, Schicchi, posing as Buoso, will dictate a new will, and one which the relatives will find more agreeable than the original. Rinuccio runs off to fetch the notary. As they are helping him dress as Buoso, several of the relatives attempt to bribe Schicchi to favour them in the new will. The items most sought after are the house, a mule, and the mills at Signa, and the relatives begin to quarrel furiously about them. Schicchi reminds everyone that the penalty for falsifying a will entails exile from their beloved city of Florence and the amputation of the right hand. It is vital that they should not be found out.

The relatives are only momentarily disquieted by his reminder, and when Rinuccio returns with the notary and two witnesses Schicchi begins to dictate the terms of the new will. He will leave the monks, he says (and, as he pauses, the relatives are momentarily terrified), the sum of – five lire! (The relatives sink back in relief.) The cash is divided into equal portions, certain estates go to Simone, the farms at Figline are Zita's, the meadows at Prato are left to Betto, and the others get the pieces of property they had expected to get. So far all is well, but now, the relatives tell one another, the three most important items remain to be bequeathed. 'I leave the mule, the best mule in Tuscany,' announces

Schicchi, 'to my devoted friend – Gianni Schicchi.' The relatives, aghast, are about to protest when Schicchi waves the empty sleeve of his night-shirt at them through the bed-curtains, accompanying his gesture with the words 'Addio, Firenze, addio, cielo divino' (Farewell Florence, farewell, heavenly sky).

Schicchi goes on to bequeath the house and the mills at Signa to his 'caro devoto affezionato amico', Gianni Schicchi. The relatives can barely contain themselves until the notary and witnesses have departed. They then turn furiously upon Schicchi, who orders them out of what is now his house. The relatives grab everything they can lay their hands on in the way of silver, table linen and other portable items before they are finally chased out. Rinuccio and Lauretta, on the terrace, are free to declare their love for each other, and Schicchi steps forward to address the audience in the theatre. Could they have suggested a better use for Buoso's money, he asks? But because he, Schicchi, acted thus, he was placed in hell by Dante. Surely the audience will at least concede that there were extenuating circumstances. With a gesture, he encourages them to applaud, and the curtain falls.

The great Italian poet Dante Alighieri (1265–1321), a native of Florence, wrote his *Commedia* during the last fifteen years of his life. (It was not until after the sixteenth century that it became customary to refer to Dante's three-part masterpiece as *La Divina Commedia*, 'The Divine Comedy', the name by which it is now known.)

All one needs to know of *The Divine Comedy* in order to deepen one's appreciation of Puccini's *Gianni Schicchi* is that Giovacchino Forzano's libretto is based on a few lines in the first part of Dante's poem, *L'Inferno* (Hell), in which Dante is conducted through the several circles of hell by the Roman poet Virgil. In the eighth circle, reserved for seducers, sorcerers, thieves, hypocrites and the like, they encounter two spirits:

> Yet Theban or Trojan furies never wrought
>   Such cruel frenzy, even in the maddened breast
>   Of a brute, still less in any of human sort,
>
> As I saw in two shades, naked, pale, possessed,
>   Who ran, like a rutting boar that has made escape
>   From the sty, biting and savaging all the rest.
>
> One of them fell on Capocchio, catching his nape
>   In its teeth, and dragging him prostrate, so that it made
>   His belly on the rough rock-bottom scour and scrape.
>
> The Aretine, left trembling, turned dismayed
>   To me: 'That's Gianni Schicchi, that hell-hound there;
>   He's rabid, he bites whatever he sees', he said.

'So may thou 'scape the other's teeth, declare
Its name', said I; 'prithee be good enough –
Quick! ere it dart away and disappear.'

And he: 'There doth the ancient spirit rove
Of criminal Myrrha, who cast amorous eyes
On her own father with unlawful love,

And in a borrowed frame and false disguise
Went in to him to do a deed of shame;
As he that fled but now, to win the prize

"Queen of the Stable", lent his own false frame
To Buoso de' Donati, and made a will
In legal form, and forged it in his name.'

That translation of Dante's *terza rima* is by Dorothy L. Sayers.[1] In her notes, Miss Sayers identifies Schicchi as 'a Florentine of the Cavalcanti family', and adds:

When Buoso Donati died, his son Simone was haunted with the fear that he might have left a will restoring some of the property he had unjustly acquired. Before making the death known, he consulted Gianni Schicchi, who, being a very clever mimic, offered to dress up as Buoso and dictate a new will in Simone's favour. This he did, taking the opportunity to bequeath himself a handsome legacy and the best mare in the stables. [The 'Queen of the Stable' in the Sayers translation.]

It was on this flimsy framework, and specifically on the final stanza quoted above –

Per guardagnar la donna della torma,
falsificare in se Buoso Donati,
testando e dando al testamento norma

– that Forzano constructed his excellent libretto, building up the action with impeccable timing, and inventing literate and amusing dialogue for the characters he invented.

Puccini's three one-act operas are so constructed that there is little to be gained, in a general *vade mecum* of this kind, from close musical analysis. This applies perhaps even more to the comedy *Gianni Schicchi* than to the two dramatic works in the *Trittico*, for it is essentially a fast-moving piece with rapid changes of dramatic mood and therefore of pace, musical texture and melody. It is sometimes compared to Verdi's comic masterpiece, *Falstaff*, and indeed the influence of the greater opera is clearly apparent. Puccini, however, is not Verdi (any more than

[1] Dante, *The Divine Comedy*, trans. Dorothy L. Sayers (Harmondsworth, Middlesex, 1949, 1955, 1962).

Dante is Shakespeare), though he is a first-rate composer on a slightly lower rung of the ladder of genius; and if we put *Falstaff* out of our minds we shall be able to appreciate *Gianni Schicchi* on its own level of achievement, which is considerable enough.

The opera begins with a high-spirited allegro outburst in the orchestra in which Ex. 56, marked to be played *tumultuoso*, is prominent.

Ex. 56

We shall hear more of it throughout the work. After only 18 bars, the music begins to slacken in pace, to become softer, and indeed funereal, as the curtain rises on the relatives of Buoso Donati, hypocritically mourning his demise. Ex. 56 is still there, in the orchestra, though it is now not at all riotous but dirge-like. The murmured prayers and lamentations of the various members of the family are chanted, mainly in monotones, until the rumour from Signa is whispered around, and the phrases exclaimed by the relatives assume a livelier aspect. With the exception of the young Rinuccio (tenor), the nine relatives are not strongly and individually characterized by the composer, but treated collectively as a family expression of greed and hypocrisy; and, even so, it is the repetition of the slurred descending second in the orchestra which conveys the character of the family, rather than the vocal writing. With Ex. 57, which injects itself into the accompaniment at intervals, we seem to be offered a kind of preview or anticipation of the roguish Gianni Schicchi himself.

Ex. 57

As the relatives begin to search for the will, there is an abrupt change of tempo to *allegro vivo*. When Rinuccio finds the document, he exclaims in a brief solo passage (but longer than anything sung by any of his relatives so far) that now he will be able to marry his Lauretta: the orchestra anticipates a theme we shall later associate with the two lovers [Ex. 58], scored at its first appearance here for violins, flutes, English

Ex. 58

horn and trumpet. The tempo and mood of the opening return as the will is read, and the orchestra repeats a solemn, slightly pompous 'will' theme, heard first on a group of woodwind instruments, then on solo bassoon, and again on solo horn. An *allegro vivo* of rage follows the realization that Buoso's money has been left to the monks. The relatives fulminate, consecutively and then simultaneously in a lively ensemble, which eventually runs out of steam as the disappointed relatives subside in tears of dejection.

Rinuccio thinks of the one man who can help them, and utters his name, 'Gianni Schicchi', in a sprightly little phrase which henceforth becomes Schicchi's musical signature [Ex. 59]. (The child, Gherardino,

Ex. 59

repeats it a few bars later when he announces that Schicchi is on his way.) Rinuccio sings the praises of Schicchi in a passage of recitative, 'Avete torto' (You are wrong), and the praises of the city of Florence in an aria, 'Firenze è come un albero fiorito' (Florence is like a flowering tree). The aria is described in the score as being like a Tuscan *stornello*: the *stornello* is not a musical form but 'a short poem, in lines of eleven syllables each . . . peculiar to and liked by the people in Tuscany'.[1] The words of Rinuccio's brief *andante* aria are in eleven-syllabled lines, and the music has the air of a popular song in the rhythm of a march, but what is most surprising about it is that, between its two stanzas, the orchestra produces a lyrical phrase [Ex. 60] which is very familiar although it

Ex. 60

properly belongs in an aria which occurs later in the opera: 'O mio babbino caro', sung by Lauretta. Why it should occur here, in the middle of a paean of praise to Florence, probably not even Puccini could have told us. Perhaps we are meant to associate it with the broad flow of the Arno, which Rinuccio refers to as 'singing as it kisses Piazza Santa Croce', and into which Lauretta in her aria threatens to throw herself.

As Rinuccio finishes his aria, Schicchi (baritone) enters. He has with him his daughter, Lauretta (soprano), and at her first words the 'O mio babbino caro' theme recurs briefly on clarinet and solo violin. Various

---

[1] According to Tommaseo's Dictionary, as quoted in the 5th edn. of *Grove's Dictionary of Music and Musicians*. (There is no entry for 'Stornello' in *Grove 6*.)

themes pass in review or, rather whisk past, in the ensuing scene as Schicchi is apprised of the situation. A splendid ensemble of confusion, with the relatives hurling insults at each other while, during the pauses, Rinuccio and Lauretta can be heard declaring their love for each other, is followed by the sweetly pathetic little aria in A flat, 'O mio babbino caro' ('O my beloved daddy' in its familiar English translation) [Ex. 61],

Ex. 61

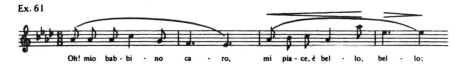

Oh! mio bab - bi - no   ca - ro,   mi pia - ce, è bel - lo,   bel - lo;

a piece known to millions who have heard it on the radio without ever realizing what it is supposed to be about in the context of the opera. It is a charming little song, and there is no reason to think that Puccini intended it as a satire on his own sentimentality. (There is also no reason to think that Lauretta really intends to throw herself into the Arno if she cannot marry Rinuccio; but that is another matter.) Puccini marks the aria *Andantino ingenuo*, whatever one may understand by that.

Twice, Lauretta and Rinuccio sing a sad farewell to their chances of bliss, as twice Schicchi announces that the situation is hopeless. But when he thinks of a scheme, the action races merrily forward again until the next solo passage. This is Schicchi's monologue, 'Si corre dal notario' (You run to the notary), a buffo, parlando piece in which he unfolds his plan of action to the Donati family. Despite its triumphant ending on the baritone's high G, this is not, unlike Rinuccio's and Lauretta's arias, the kind of piece to show off the voice: more than any other role in Puccini, Schicchi is a part for an actor who can sing, as opposed to a singer who can act. (Non-singers, or at least non-operatic singers, have appeared in the role.)

A lively ensemble, with a middle section in which the relatives in solo phrases one by one stake their claim for parts of Buoso's property, follows Schicchi's monologue, but is suddenly interrupted by the tolling of a bell. Gherardo rushes out of the room and down the stairs, his flight illustrated in the orchestra by a rapidly descending chromatic scale, and his return accompanied by an ascending chromatic scale as he reappears, breathless, to announce that it was a false alarm.

The trio for three of the female relatives as they dress Schicchi in the dead man's nightclothes is a charming and agreeable lyrical episode, at whose climax the others join in to hail Schicchi as their saviour. This is the one number in the score worthy of comparison with any page of Verdi's *Falstaff*, its exquisite harmonies almost turning the un-prepossessing women into Wagnerian Rhine maidens, and its lilting melodies reminding us that Rossini was among Puccini's musical forebears.

Schicchi's warning, 'Addio, Firenze', a captivating little melismatic theme [Ex. 62], like a Tuscan folk-song in miniature, is repeated in

Ex. 62

unison by all of the relatives except the young lovers, but before they can reflect further upon the crime they are about to commit, there is a knock at the door and the notary appears, ushered in by Rinuccio. The ensuing action is advanced by the use of a number of themes already heard, including the will and mourning themes and, when he announces himself as the chief beneficiary, Schicchi's own personal phrase [Ex. 59], and his warning theme [Ex. 62] when the relatives attempt to protest. In a final, furious ensemble ('Ladro, ladro': Thief, thief), the relatives indulge in an orgy of pillaging, and run from the house. As the uproar subsides, the young lovers have a final brief duet of lyrical warmth, based on the music of their earlier duet. The opera ends with Schicchi's spoken words, and a final *fortissimo* echo of the fanfare first heard in Rinuccio's aria.

Gianni Schicchi is an amusing opera in its own right, and can seem enhanced when it is heard at the end of a complete performance of the *Trittico*, for it certainly provides a welcome relief after the violent melodrama of *Il tabarro* and the saccharine mood of *Suor Angelica*. Its score is really somewhat too thin for *Gianni Schicchi* to be classed as one of the great comic operas, but it is an enjoyable and amusing piece as long as one is not put off by the oddly bitter and extremely morbid basis of its humour.

X

Turandot

an opera in three acts

Dramatis personæ:

Princess Turandot	(soprano)
Emperor Altoum	(tenor)
Timur, dethroned Tartar King	(bass)
The Unknown Prince (Calaf), his son	(tenor)
Liù, a young slave girl	(soprano)
Ping, Grand Chancellor	(baritone)
Pang, Grand Purveyor	(tenor)
Pong, Chief Cook	(tenor)
A Mandarin	(baritone)

LIBRETTO by Giuseppe Adami and Renato Simoni, based on the play *Turandot* by Carlo Gozzi

TIME: The legendary past
PLACE: Peking

FIRST PERFORMED at La Scala, Milan, on 25 April, 1926, with Rosa Raisa (Turandot), Miguel Fleta (Calaf), Maria Zamboni (Liù), Carlo Walter (Timur), Giacomo Rimini (Ping), Emilio Venturini (Pang), Giuseppe Nessi (Pong), Francesco Dominici (Altoum), Aristide Baracchi (Mandarin), conducted by Arturo Toscanini

Turandot

I

In December, 1918, Puccini celebrated his sixtieth birthday. While he was in Rome for the first Italian performances of his *Trittico* in January, 1919, the composer was approached by the Mayor with the request that he write a hymn to the city of Rome, to commemorate the successful outcome of the war. Given as text a poem by Fausto Salvatori, Puccini produced his 'Inno a Roma' which was given its first performance in Rome in June, 1919, and was later enthusiastically taken up by Mussolini's Fascist regime. During the year 1920, Puccini acquired a new piece of property, the Torre del Tagliata, an old Spanish tower on the promontory of Ansedonia in the Tuscan Maremma, or marshland; but by the end of the following year, 1921, he had disposed of it and had also moved his principal place of residence from Torre del Lago to the nearby seaside resort town of Viareggio. Throughout this period, he was, as usual, also searching for his next libretto.

Among the subjects the composer considered was *Christopher Sly*, based on the character in Shakespeare's *The Taming of the Shrew*, suggested to him by Giovacchino Forzano, his librettist of *Suor Angelica* and *Gianni Schicchi*. In due course, Puccini decided against *Christopher Sly*, but Forzano proceeded to write it as a play for the spoken theatre. It enjoyed success not only in Italy but also, in English translation, in London in 1921, and subsequently was turned by its author into a libretto for the opera *Sly* by Ermanno Wolf-Ferrari (staged at La Scala in 1927).

Gatti-Casazza of the New York Metropolitan Opera sent Puccini a copy of a new David Belasco play, *The Son-Daughter*, but the composer appears not to have considered it very seriously. He had, in any case, asked Giuseppe Adami, the librettist of *Il tabarro* and of *La rondine*, to collaborate with Renato Simoni in a search for possible subjects. Simoni (1875–1952), who had once been the editor of the *Corriere della sera*, was a Gozzi scholar who in 1903 had written a play, *Carlo Gozzi*, so it is perhaps not entirely surprising that, in due course, he and Adami suggested Gozzi's *Turandot*.

At first, however, it seemed that, at the instigation of the composer himself, Adami and Simoni were going to fashion a libretto for an opera to be called *Fanny*, based on episodes in Dickens's *Oliver Twist*, a stage adaptation of which Puccini had seen in London at Her Majesty's Theatre in the spring of 1919. (Fanny was presumably a renamed Nancy.) But Puccini's enthusiasm for this project was short-lived, and in March, 1920, during luncheon in Milan one day with Adami and Simoni, the composer responded to Simoni's proposal that they should consider Gozzi, by agreeing that Gozzi's *Turandot* – which Puccini had seen produced in Berlin by Max Reinhardt, in a German adaptation by Karl Vollmoeller – might well be the subject they were looking for.

A few days after the Milan luncheon, Puccini wrote to Simoni from Rome, whither he had travelled to attend the second Roman production of the *Trittico*. By this time, he had read or re-read *Turandot* and was keen that Adami and Simoni should begin to prepare a libretto, reducing the play's number of acts, slimming it down to make it more effective as an opera and, above all, heightening 'the passion of Turandot who for so long has been suffocated beneath the ashes of her immense pride'. 'To sum up,' he concluded, 'I am of the opinion that *Turandot* is the most normal and most human of all Gozzi's plays.'[1]

In the autumn of 1920, Puccini travelled to Vienna for the Austrian premières of *La rondine* and *Il trittico*. Shortly after he returned to Torre del Lago, he wrote to Sybil Seligman:

> I'm not yet working [on *Turandot*] because they haven't given me the libretto yet. If they wait much longer I shall have to get them to put pen, paper and ink-pot in my tomb! What a cheerful idea! That's how I feel – just like that. In a few days' time I go to the Maremma to get far away from everyone – there I hope to find solace. I spend my time unprofitably – and sometimes stupidly, shooting.
>
> Why do you tease me about Vienna? You don't know the Viennese, because if you did you would change your opinion of them. They're the nicest people in the world – after Sybil. That's all.[2]

On Christmas Eve, 1920, Puccini wrote to Adami asking him to hurry with alterations for *La rondine* and begging him also 'not to forget the cruel Princess' (Turandot). By the end of January, 1921, the composer had begun to sketch the first act of the opera. But *Turandot*'s struggle towards birth was not an easy one. The shape and structure of the libretto underwent several changes before Puccini was completely satisfied with it. In April he reported to Adami that all was going well, and that he had made great strides. 'But', he added, 'what about Act II? And Act III? For God's sake, don't wear me out with waiting.' In mid-September he attempted to persuade Simoni that the opera should be in only two acts, but did not pursue the idea.

He worked slowly, beginning the orchestration of Act I in March, 1922, and completing it in November. By this time, he had received a

[1] *Carteggi Pucciniani*, op. cit.

[2] Seligman, op. cit.

revised draft of the second and third acts. In October, he had written to
Adami:

Let us hope that the melody which you rightly demand will come to me, fresh
and poignant. Without this, there is no music. I am working, but I have so
much before me to do! I am appalled, too, when I think of the burden of
years that I carry. But – forward without trembling or fear! Send the stanzas,
especially those for the aria . . . What do you think of Mussolini? I hope he
will prove to be the man we need. Good luck to him if he will cleanse and give
a little peace to our country![1]

That Puccini was not in his usual ebullient state of health is suggested
by the letter he wrote to Adami on 11 December:

I have no good news about *Turandot*. I am beginning to be worried about my
laziness. Can I have had enough of China because I have composed one
entire act and nearly finished a second? I am certainly failing to write
anything else that is good. Also I am old! Of that there is no doubt.

If I had found the sort of subject I was looking for, and am still hoping to
find, I should have it staged by now. But this Chinese world! I shall certainly
come to a decision of some kind in Milan. Perhaps I shall return the money to
Ricordi and cancel the contract . . . I have tried again and again to write the
music for the introductory scene of Act II, and cannot. I don't feel comfortable in China.[2]

The visit to Milan which Puccini referred to was in connection with a
new production of *Manon Lescaut* at La Scala, to commemorate that
opera's thirtieth birthday. Toscanini conducted the first performance on
1 February, 1923, and a magnificent testimonial dinner was given for
Puccini. It was on this occasion that the composer and his great interpreter renewed their friendship, agreeing to forget their old quarrels.
The morning after the anniversary performance, Puccini wrote to 'dear
Arturo':

You have given me the greatest satisfaction of my life. In your wonderful interpretation, *Manon* became a far better work than I had thought in those far-
off days – you performed this music of mine with such poetic feeling, such
souplesse and irresistible passion.

Last night I truly felt the greatness of your soul, and all your affection for
your old friend and companion of those early struggles. I am happy because
you showed, above all, such an understanding for the spirit of my passionate
youth of thirty years ago! My beloved creature in the hands of Arturo
Toscanini! I thank you from the depths of my heart.[3]

[1] Adami, op. cit.
[2] Ibid.
[3] Leopoldo Marchetti, *Puccini nelle immagini* (Milan, 1949).

Toscanini is said to have replied that, if only Puccini would refrain from rushing to see so many terrible performances of *Manon Lescaut*, he would not be so overwhelmed by a decent performance!

Early in 1923, Puccini completed his first draft of Act II of *Turandot*. When he came to work on Act III, he found that he was still not happy with the libretto, and asked Adami for more changes:

> It is quite impossible. Perhaps – and maybe there's no perhaps – I too am no longer possible! But about this Act III there is no doubt at all. I am not quite at the stage of crying 'Muoio disperato' [I die despairingly],[1] but very nearly.
>
> I wonder if you could take it and make something out of it with the help of the old Act III. Is it possible? And shall I be able to do my part? I am very, very much afraid! . . . I am a poor, unhappy man, discouraged, old, abject, nothing! What am I to do? I don't know. I'll go to bed and sleep to escape the torture of thinking.[2]

Towards the end of 1923, while he was at work on the orchestration of Act II, Puccini began to complain of a sore throat and a persistent cough, but since he had been a heavy smoker all his life, and accustomed to occasional throat ailments, he thought little of it, and worked at *Turandot* with an ever-increasing intensity. By 22 February, 1924, he had finished Act II, and during March he managed to complete the orchestration of Act III up to and including the death of Liù. As his throat was now causing him acute discomfort, Puccini consulted not only his local doctor but also a Milan specialist. Both doctors diagnosed rheumatic inflammation of the throat, and advised Puccini to take the cure at Salsomaggiore, a health resort near Parma. From Salsomaggiore, he wrote to Sybil Seligman on 1 June: 'I go back to Viareggio on Saturday; my throat is just the same – the cure hasn't made any difference. They say that I shall be better later – we'll see.' This was the last letter Puccini wrote to his old friend, for six months later he was to die after an operation for throat cancer: it is a sad irony that he ends his letter by assuring Mrs Seligman, 'I'm smoking your Abdulla cigarettes with great enjoyment.'[3]

The previous year, Puccini had been his usual worldly and competitive self. He was delighted when Mussolini made him a Senator: perhaps he thought it put him on the same level as Verdi, who had been elected to the first Italian Parliament in 1861. And he hinted to Sybil Seligman that he would not be averse to receiving an honour of some kind from King George V:

> I see that for many years I have reigned over Covent Garden, and I am glad of it. But now that I am an old man I think I might have received some form of recognition from your great country. The father, no less than the son, the present King, loved and love my music; I know that, whether at the opera or

[1] From Cavaradossi's Act III aria in *Tosca*.   [2] Adami, op. cit.   [3] Seligman, op. cit.

at court, they wanted and they want songs from *Bohème*. But never once have they thought of that author who, too, has reigned for so many years in their home on the throne of music of the theatre.[1]

Puccini accepted honorary membership in the Fascist Party, and sought an audience with Mussolini, ostensibly to discuss a grandiose cultural propaganda plan but more probably because he simply wanted to be able to boast of having shaken hands with the great leader. But, by the summer of 1924, Puccini seemed to be a changed man, interested only in completing the opera he was finding such difficulty in writing. He must have known that he was seriously ill, for he certainly appeared to realize that he had no time to lose.

Early in September, by which time he had composed everything except the Act III love duet and the finale, Puccini was visited by Toscanini, who wanted to hear some of the music and discuss details of the Scala première which had been arranged for the spring of 1925. Puccini wrote to Adami:

Toscanini has just left. We are in perfect agreement, and I breathe at last. A weight has been taken off my mind which has oppressed me since April.[2] We discussed the duet, which he does not much like. What is to be done? I don't know . . . I see no light at all. I have already reduced myself to a state of stupidity over this duet. Speak also to Renato about it. We must find a way out of this difficulty, because I'm at my last gasp . . . P.S. The little that I played to Toscanini made an excellent impression.[3]

In October, Puccini and Toscanini met again in a rehearsal room at La Scala with Renato Simoni present, and Puccini played to the conductor those parts of the opera which Toscanini had not already heard. The pain in his throat had now increased to such an extent that Puccini, even though he feared having it confirmed that he was seriously ill, was persuaded to consult another specialist, in Viareggio, who advised him merely to stop smoking, and to rest. Unknown to his family and friends, Puccini now sought another opinion, in Florence, and this time a growth was discovered in the composer's throat, under his epiglottis. Further tests revealed that he was suffering from cancer of the throat in so advanced a stage that it was probably incurable.

The true nature of Puccini's illness was kept from him. His son Tonio arranged for yet another examination, in which two Florentine surgeons were joined by a colleague from Naples; the earlier diagnosis was confirmed, but it was hoped that X-ray treatment might arrest the rapid

---

[1] Ibid.

[2] Having made up their differences in February, 1923, Puccini and Toscanini had quarrelled again in April, 1924, over Boito's *Nerone*, whose première Toscanini was then about to conduct.

[3] Adami, op. cit.

progress of the cancer. Of the two clinics in Europe known to have had some success with this kind of treatment, one in Berlin, the other in Brussels, the Brussels Institut de la Couronne was chosen, and Tonio made arrangements for his father to be treated there. On 22 October, Puccini wrote from Viareggio to his 'caro Adamino':

> What am I to say to you? I am going through a terrible time. This trouble in my throat is giving me no rest, although the torment is more mental than physical. I am going to Brussels to consult a well-known specialist. I am setting out very soon. I am waiting for a reply from Brussels and for Tonio's return from Milan. Will it be an operation? Or medical treatment? Or sentence of death? I cannot go on any longer like this. And then there's *Turandot*. Simoni's verses are good, and I think he has done just what was needed and what I had dreamed of. All the rest of Liù's appeal to Turandot was irrelevant, and I think your opinion is correct that the [text of the] duet is now complete. Perhaps Turandot has too much to say in that passage. We shall see – when I get to work again on my return from Brussels.
>
> Let us hope that I shall get over this![1]

Before setting out for Brussels, Puccini had one further meeting with Toscanini to discuss the progress of the opera and its proposed production the following spring in Milan. According to Puccini's biographer Arnoldo Fraccaroli, it was on this occasion or shortly afterwards that Puccini is supposed to have said, 'My opera will be staged incomplete, and then someone will have to come onto the stage and say to the public: "At this point the composer died!"'[2]

On 4 November, Puccini set out for Brussels, accompanied by Tonio and by a friend, Carlo Clausetti, a minor composer who was now managing the firm of Ricordi. Puccini took with him to Brussels his sketches of the love duet and the finale of the last act of *Turandot*. Elvira, who was unaware of the real nature of her husband's illness, remained in Viareggio suffering from bronchitis. Her daughter Fosca (Puccini's step-daughter) joined Puccini in Brussels on 23 November, the day before the crucial operation on his throat was due to take place.

Puccini described the earlier part of the treatment in a letter to a Viareggio friend, Angiolino Magrini:

> I am crucified like Christ. I have a collar round my throat which is a very torture. External X-ray treatment at present – then crystal needles into my neck and a hole in order to breathe, this too in my neck. But say nothing about it to Elvira or anyone else.
>
> The thought of that hole, with a rubber or silver tube in it – I don't yet know which – terrifies me. They say that I won't suffer at all and I must just put up with it for eight days so as to leave undisturbed that part of the throat which is to be treated. For to breathe in the normal way would upset it. And so I must breathe through a tube! My God, what horror! I remember that an

---

[1] Ibid.   [2] Fraccaroli, op. cit.

uncle of Tabarracci's went about with a tube all his life. After eight days I shall breathe through my mouth again.

What a calamity! God help me. It will be a long treatment – six weeks – and terrible. But they assure me that I shall be cured. I am a little sceptical about it and am prepared for anything. I'm thinking of my family, of poor Elvira. From the day of my departure my malady has grown worse. In the mornings I spit mouthfuls of dark blood. But the doctor says that this is nothing serious and that I ought to calm myself now that the treatment has started. We'll see.[1]

On 24 November, Puccini underwent an operation in the course of which his throat was punctured, and seven radioactive crystal needles were inserted into the cancerous growth. During the entire three and a half hours the patient was conscious, for only a local anaesthetic was administered, so as not to overtax his heart. For the next three days, Puccini was unable to speak or to swallow food. After the operation he wrote on a scribbling pad: 'I feel as though I have bayonets in my throat. They have massacred me.'

On the fourth day it seemed to his physicians that the patient would recover. Dr Ledoux, who had performed the operation, even announced: 'Puccini en sortira' (Puccini will pull through). The composer's step-daughter Fosca wrote to Sybil Seligman:

Everything is going well, and the doctors are more than satisfied. Our adored papa is saved! *Saved* – do you understand? Certainly he has suffered a good deal, but from now on this terrible part of the cure is over, and he will only have to submit to the boredom of convalescence . . . His throat is no longer swollen; the radium has destroyed the tumours. I believe that on Sunday or Monday they will remove the needles and then this ghastly week will be over. It's true that he is reduced to a shadow, but the doctors assure us that he will very quickly recover; he has a strong constitution, his heart is absolutely sound, and his diabetes has given no cause for anxiety. But how painful it is, Sybil dear, to see him with that hole in his throat, and being fed by the nose through a syringe . . .[2]

Fosca's letter was neither sent nor even finished. While she was writing it, at about 6 p.m. on 28 November, Puccini suddenly collapsed in the armchair in which he had been resting: the radium treatment had, after all, affected his heart. The needles were removed from his throat at once, and he was given an injection, but it was too late. For the next ten hours, he fought a losing battle, but was still conscious when the Papal Nuncio arrived to administer the last sacrament. Puccini died at four o'clock on the morning of 29 November 1924.

A funeral ceremony was held in Brussels on 1 December, after which the composer's body was taken by train to Milan where another

[1] Reprinted in Carner, op. cit., from Don Pietro Panichelli's memoir, *Il 'Pretino' di Giacomo Puccini racconta*.

[2] Seligman, op. cit.

ceremony was held in the Duomo, at which the chorus and orchestra from La Scala, conducted by Toscanini, performed the Requiem from *Edgar*, and Hina Spani sang Fidelia's phrases, 'Addio, addio, mio dolce amor.' In pouring rain, the coffin was conveyed to a provisional tomb in the Milan Cimiterio Monumentale, and two years later the composer found his last resting place in a mausoleum at his villa in Torre del Lago.

On the day of Puccini's death, Mussolini issued a statement on behalf of the Italian government, in the course of which he said:

> This is not the hour in which to discuss the worth and the nobility of his creation. It is certain only that, in the history of Italian music and in the history of the Italian spirit, Giacomo Puccini occupies an eminent position. I wish to remind you in this moment that a few months ago this renowned musician requested admission to the National Fascist Party. He wished to express with this gesture his adherence to a movement which is being discussed, which is being disputed, which is disputable, but which is the only living thing today in Italy.[1]

As Puccini had left *Turandot* unfinished, the première of the opera had to be postponed from its proposed date in April, 1925, until a year later. Toscanini recommended that Riccardo Zandonai be engaged to complete the opera, but this was opposed by Puccini's son Tonio on the grounds that Zandonai was too well established a composer. The name of Franco Alfano was then suggested, and apparently approved by Toscanini. Alfano (1875–1954) was then in his fiftieth year. His first opera had been produced in 1898, and he had composed a further seven before working on *Turandot*; his final opera was written in the 1940s and staged in Rome in 1949. It took Alfano six months to write the final pages of *Turandot*: the opera eventually reached the stage of La Scala on 25 April, 1926.

Alfano's task was not made easier by Toscanini, who first asked him to expand the finale beyond the version he had originally presented to the conductor, and then rejected much of the expanded version. Toscanini's biographer states that, after the dress rehearsal, Alfano approached the conductor and asked him, 'What do you have to say, Maestro?', whereupon Toscanini replied, 'I say that I saw Puccini approaching from the rear of the stage to clout me.'[2] The rehearsal period was more than usually stormy, and shortly before the first night Toscanini informed the company that he proposed not to perform Alfano's ending at the very first performance. So the famous laying down of the baton at the point at which Puccini finished writing may have been, on Toscanini's part, an act not only of piety towards Puccini but of vindictiveness towards Alfano.

As Mussolini was in Milan for a few days in connection with the Fascist

[1] Quoted in Marek, op. cit.   [2] Harvey Sachs, *Toscanini* (New York, 1978).

Party's celebration of Empire Day, a holiday which he had invented, the management of La Scala invited him to attend the première of *Turandot*. Mussolini accepted the invitation, on condition that the Fascist hymn, 'Giovinezza', be played at the beginning of the performance. The staunchly anti-Fascist Toscanini made it clear to the Scala management that if they wanted Fascist anthems they would have to find another conductor for the opera. The management informed Mussolini accordingly, and Il Duce did not attend the première.

Toscanini conducted what was by all accounts a superb performance; the principal singers included Rosa Raisa (Turandot), Miguel Fleta (Calaf), Maria Zamboni (Liù), and Carlo Walter (Timur). Gaetano Cesari described the work and the occasion in the Milan evening newspaper, the *Corriere della sera*:

> How extraordinary is the power of evocation possessed by music which bears in itself the clear imprint of the composer's personality! Last night at the Scala, Puccini was with us. He was with the great public who had admired and applauded him in the days of his most splendid triumphs. He was in the theatre which, if it gave him some pain in the days of his striving, was not less generous with praise and homage, as on that occasion in particular when its genial conductor brought before the public again, in new beauty and freshness, the composer's most vigorous opera [i.e. the thirtieth-anniversary performance of *Manon Lescaut*].
>
> Until last night's performance, Puccini's vision of the tale of *Turandot* had remained a secret. Like the beautiful and cruel princess whose name it bears, the opera had kept closed within itself its own enigma. The mysterious prince, although perhaps foreseeing his success, had awaited his trial like the other, hiding in his heart the trepidation which he must have felt. Yet a few beats from the firm baton of Toscanini sufficed to bring before the great assembly the living spirit of the sweet singer of Manon, of Mimi, and of Butterfly. The exotic colour and the unfamiliar setting lessened in no degree the sense of his presence felt from the first notes of *Turandot*.
>
> The artist was among us yesterday with the sadness of his own tragedy. 'If I do not succeed in finishing the opera,' he had said one day, with a presentiment of his approaching death, 'someone will come to the front of the stage and say "Puccini composed as far as this, then he died."' The opera stopped yesterday at the point where Puccini had had to leave it. Thus *Turandot* ran its course like a living symbol of the life of its creator: a brief story, interrupted by a pause which is of eternity. The performance, punctuated by frequent applause, ended with a moment of silence, when the little, mangled body of Liù disappeared behind the scenes followed by the procession of the mourning populace, and a shrill E flat from the piccolo seemed to tell once more of the fleeting soul and of the far-off and forever impenetrable mystery, to which alike great passions and obscure loves like little Liù's come at last and are lost. Then, from where he stood as conductor, Toscanini announced in a low voice full of emotion that at that point Puccini had left the composition of the opera. And the curtain was slowly lowered on *Turandot*.
>
> This moment of intense emotion will not be repeated. For at the second

performance the opera will be given with the addition of the last duet and the short final scene of which Puccini had merely outlined the music.

The *Corriere* also told its readers that the absence of Mussolini was because 'the Prime Minister did not want his presence to distract the public in any way: their attention had to be entirely devoted to Puccini.'

Eight performances of *Turandot* were given at La Scala before the end of the season, most of them conducted by Toscanini but at least one conducted by Ettore Panizza, who was responsible for all fourteen performances when the opera was revived at La Scala in the autumn.

Two months after its Scala première, *Turandot* was given its first production outside Italy, at the Teatro Colón in Buenos Aires, with Claudia Muzio as Turandot and Giacomo Lauri-Volpi as Calaf. The following month, it was heard in Germany for the first time, at Dresden, and in October the Vienna production with Lotte Lehmann and Leo Slezak on the first night, and Maria Nemeth and Jan Kiepura the following evening, was given a sensational reception. In November, *Turandot* reached the Met, with Maria Jeritza and Giacomo Lauri-Volpi, and Tullio Serafin conducting, and on 7 June 1927, it was heard at Covent Garden, with Bianca Scacciati replacing an indisposed Jeritza as Turandot, and Aroldo Lindi as Calaf. (At the three subsequent performances, Florence Easton sang Turandot.) The conductor was Vincenzo Bellezza.

The response of the Italian critics to *Turandot* was, in general, enthusiastic, though some of them were perplexed by parts of the opera which did not sound like the old Puccini, the Puccini of *La Bohème* and *Tosca*. For many years, *Turandot* was distinctly less popular with the public than those two works and *Madama Butterfly*, but over the years its popularity has increased. The famous Covent Garden performances of George VI's Coronation year, 1937, with Eva Turner and Giovanni Martinelli, firmly established *Turandot* in English affections, while it was Birgit Nilsson and Franco Corelli who persuaded Metropolitan Opera audiences to reassess the work in 1961. In Italy, *Turandot* has always retained its place in the repertory: Maria Callas was an admired interpreter of the title role in the early part of her career in several Italian towns and in Buenos Aires, but relinquished the role in 1949, returning to it only once for a 1957 recording.

II

The opera is set in the Chinese Imperial City of Peking, in legendary times. Act I takes place outside the Great Palace, at sunset. A Mandarin reads to the assembled crowd a proclamation which refers to the decree that the Princess Turandot will become the bride of whichever royal suitor succeeds in answering her three riddles. Unsuccessful suitors lose not only the Princess but also their heads. Turandot's latest suitor, the

Prince of Persia, has failed to answer the riddles, and the Mandarin announces that he is to be beheaded when the moon rises. The bloodthirsty crowd howls its approval and its impatience.

As the crowd is pushed back by guards, a young slave girl, Liù (soprano), cries out that the old man she is accompanying has been knocked down. A handsome youth goes to their aid, and discovers that the man he is helping to his feet is his father, Timur (bass), the deposed Tartar king. The blind old king is overjoyed to be reunited with his long-lost son, Calaf (tenor), who is travelling, like his father, incognito, for both are being pursued by the usurper of the Tartar throne. Liù, the slave girl, is also moved to see Calaf again, for she has loved him from afar for years. Timur explains to his son that Liù helped him to escape, and has proved a faithful guide. When Calaf asks Liù why she chose to share the king's anguish, she replies, 'Because one day, in the palace, you smiled at me.'

A group of the executioner's assistants now enters, preceded by the bearers of the hone, to sharpen the executioner's great scimitar. This excites the crowd of citizens to fever pitch and they sing an incantation to the moon, comparing its white disc with a severed head, and urging it to show itself. As the moon dutifully rises, the young Prince of Persia is led to the scaffold. The fickle crowd is now moved to pity, though it is also aroused by the look of ecstatic joy it discerns in his eyes. Calaf curses the cruelty of the Princess Turandot but, when the Princess appears on a balcony, he is suddenly struck by her beauty. The crowd prostrates itself, only the Prince of Persia, the Unknown Prince (Calaf) and the executioner remaining on their feet. Turandot gives the signal for the execution to proceed, and the condemned man is led off.

Resolving that he will attempt to win the hand of Turandot, Calaf is deaf to the pleading of Timur and Liù. He is about to strike the great gong as a signal of his intention when his way is suddenly blocked by three curious figures, Ping, Pang and Pong, the Emperor of China's three chief Ministers, who are respectively Grand Chancellor, Grand Purveyor and Grand Cook. They too attempt to dissuade Calaf from what they consider to be a suicidal course. 'We don't want any more mad foreigners!' they exclaim, pointing out that, after all, Turandot is only a woman with a crown on her head. If you strip her naked, she's simply raw flesh. Calaf is unimpressed by their arguments.

A group of Turandot's maids appears on the balcony demanding silence, for the Princess is sleeping. Ping, Pang and Pong continue their attempt to appeal to the Unknown Prince's reason, and now the phantoms begin to appear, the spirits of unsuccessful suitors, proclaiming their love for Turandot from beyond the grave. Undeterred by the phantoms, by the executioner who now appears bearing the head of the Prince of Persia, by the tears of Timur and Liù, or by the arguments of Ping, Pang and Pong, Calaf in an ecstasy of love and desire rushes to the gong, seizes the hammer, and strikes it three times. 'Let him go,' the three Ministers say to one another. 'It's useless to shout either in Sanskrit, Chinese or Mongolian. When the gong is sounded, death rejoices.' And they run off, snickering, as the curtain falls.

Act II is in two scenes. Scene i takes place in a pavilion where Ping, Pang and Pong discuss the wretched condition to which the country has been reduced by the law which requires the slaughter of Turandot's unsuccessful suitors. In the Year of the Mouse there were six executions, in the Year of the Dog eight, and in the current year, the Year of the Tiger, already thirteen, if one counts the latest contender, the Unknown Prince. The three Ministers think longingly of their homes in the country, far from Peking and its bloodshed. They recall such 'mad lovers' as the Prince of Samarkand, the Prince of the Kirghiz, and others from India, Burma and Tartary, all beheaded when they failed to answer Turandot's riddles, and they imagine how happy China could become if only a suitor could be found to solve the riddles. The trumpets announcing the beginning of the ceremony in which Calaf will be tested recall them to the present and they go off to enjoy what they refer to as 'l'ennesimo supplizio', the umpteenth torture.

Scene ii takes place in a vast square inside the Palace walls. In the centre is a great marble staircase, with the Emperor's throne at its summit. A crowd of citizens watches the arrival of the Mandarins, the Eight Wise Men each of whom carry three sealed silk scrolls containing the answers to Turandot's riddles, and finally Ping, Pang and Pong. The aged Emperor Altoum appears at the top of the stairs and takes his place on the throne, as the crowd prostrates itself. The Unknown Prince, Calaf, enters and stands at the foot of the staircase. The Emperor addresses Calaf. A dreadful oath, he says, forces him to keep faith with the horrid ruling by which Turandot can be won only by risking one's life, but he begs Calaf not to undergo the test. Three times he attempts to dissuade Calaf from his undertaking, and three times Calaf answers, 'Son of Heaven, I ask to undergo the trial.' The conditions having been announced by a Mandarin, the Princess Turandot advances to stand beside the throne of her father. She explains that, thousands of years ago, her ancestress the Princess Lo-u-Ling was ravished and killed by a foreign invader. She, Turandot, feels herself to be the avenging reincarnation of her ancestress. No man will ever possess her: her enigmas are three, but death is one, she warns Calaf, who replies, 'No, the enigmas are three, and life is one.'

Turandot poses her first enigma: 'What is the name of the phantom which spreads its wings at night over the black infinity of humankind, which is invoked by all, but which disappears at dawn? What is this thing which is born every night and which dies every day?' Calaf answers confidently, 'Hope!', and the Wise Men open their first scroll to confirm that the answer is correct. Turandot now proceeds to her second enigma: 'It flickers like flame, but is not flame. Sometimes it rages, sometimes it is languorous. When one is defeated, it grows cold, when one is victorious it is hot.' After some moments of hesitation, Calaf answers, 'Yes, Princess, it both flames and languishes in my veins when you look at me. It is "Blood".' Again, he is correct, and when the onlookers make encouraging noises Turandot angrily orders the guards to flog them. Descending the staircase, she bends over the Unknown Prince who has fallen to his knees before her, and urgently poses her third enigma: 'Ice that sets you on fire, but which becomes icier from your fire. One who, setting you free, makes a slave of you. One who, taking you as a slave, makes you a King. What is this frost which gives off fire?' There is an even longer pause this time, after which Calaf leaps to his feet with the answer: 'Turandot.'

The Wise Men again confirm that he has answered correctly, and the crowd acclaims the Unknown Prince. Turandot, however, makes an agonized appeal to her father not to throw her into the arms of a stranger. 'The oath is sacred,' replies the Emperor, but Turandot insists she will not be possessed by anyone. 'Do you want me in your arms against my will, and in fury?' she asks her successful suitor, who replies, 'No, proud Princess, I want you ardent with love.' He reminds her that he has answered her three questions, and he now puts one question to her: What is his name? If Turandot can discover his name before dawn, the Unknown Prince is willing to die. Turandot signifies her assent, the Emperor expresses the hope that at sunrise he will have gained a son, and the crowd affirms its homage and devotion to the Emperor.

Act III is also in two scenes, the first of which takes place in the garden of the Palace, shortly before dawn. The voices of heralds can be heard proclaiming Turandot's decree, 'Tonight no one in Peking must sleep,' for all must help her discover before dawn the name of the Unknown Prince. Resting on the steps leading to Turandot's pavilion, Calaf awaits the dawn which he is confident will bring him victory and the Princess's love. Ping, Pang and Pong approach, offering Calaf wealth, beautiful maidens and precious jewels if he will leave Peking, for they fear the wrath of Turandot should she fail to discover his name.

A group of guards enters, dragging with them Timur and Liù from whom they have been attempting to extract the name of the Unknown Prince. Calaf tries to persuade the crowd which now gathers round that neither Timur nor Liù knows him, but Turandot appears and begins to question Timur. Liù steps forward saying that only she knows the stranger's name, and the crowd howls for her to be tortured until she reveals it. Calaf tries to protect Liù, but Turandot orders her guards to seize him. Liù is tortured, but says she would rather die than reveal the Prince's name. Turandot asks what has given her such strength, to which Liù replies that it is love, her love for the Prince. She predicts that, before dawn, Turandot will come to love him also. Then, fearing that under torture she may be forced to reveal Calaf's name, Liù quickly seizes a dagger from one of the guards, and stabs herself. She stumbles over to Calaf, who is still restrained by guards, and falls dead at his feet.

The crowd of citizens fears that, since Liù has died the victim of an injustice, her spirit may return as an avenging vampire. They bear her body away, tenderly and respectfully, as Timur and Calaf lament her death and even Ping, Pang and Pong are affected. Left alone, Calaf confronts Turandot, whose face has been veiled by her handmaidens to protect her from the disagreeable sight of Liù's dead body. Angrily, Calaf tears the veil from her, accusing her of the direst cruelty in her responsibility for the death of Liù. Icily, Turandot refers to herself as the Daughter of Heaven, whose spirit is aloft, beyond his reach. Calaf replies that her spirit may be beyond his reach, but her body is not. In a passionate frenzy he kisses her, and Turandot, bewildered and softened, finds herself weeping for the first time in her life. She confesses to Calaf that she feared him from the moment she first saw him, for the light of heroes was in his eyes. She begs him to go, and take the mystery of his name with him. Calaf tells her he no longer has a mystery, for he has conquered her. She can destroy him if she wishes, for he will give her his name: he is Calaf, son of Timur. The trumpets are heard summoning all to the new trial, and Calaf goes off confidently with Turandot.

The brief final scene takes place outside the Palace. The assembled crowd greets the Emperor, and Turandot announces that she has discovered the name of the stranger. His name is Love! She and Calaf embrace, and the crowd rejoices.

Puccini was by no means the first composer to base an opera on Carlo Gozzi's play, *Turandot*. The play appeared in 1762; during the nineteenth century at least seven composers wrote operas about Gozzi's cruel Princess, among them Danzi (in 1817), Reissiger (1835), Vesque von Püttlingen (1838), Bassini (who had taught Puccini at the Milan Conservatorium and whose opera *Turanda* was produced in 1867) and Rehbaum (1888). Weber and Lachner, amongst others, composed incidental music for productions of Gozzi's play, which was frequently staged in the German-speaking countries in an adaptation by Schiller. In the twentieth century, Busoni's opera, *Turandot*, was produced nine years before Puccini's; Busoni also composed music for a Berlin production in 1911 of Gozzi's play as translated and adapted by Karl Vollmoeller.

Count Carlo Gozzi (1720–1806) was the author of a number of charming and witty plays, many of them based on fairy stories, or *fiabe*, which were sometimes morbid as well as fantastic. Such a play was *Turandot*.[1] This 'fiaba chinese tragicomica in cinque atti' (tragicomic

---

[1] One sometimes hears the heroine's name pronounced without the final 't' (Turando). This is incorrect. In Gozzi's play, the name is sometimes spelt 'Turandotte',

chinese fairy story in five acts) underwent a number of changes at the hands of Adami and Simoni, who tightened up its action considerably, compressed it into three acts, and in the process altered the balance between tragedy and comedy. In Gozzi's play, when Calaf answers the three riddles successfully Turandot refuses to accept the situation, claiming that the riddles were too easy because she had not sufficient time to prepare really difficult ones. When her father insists that she abide by the rules, Turandot replies that if she is forced to marry she will stab herself to death, for she will never be possessed by any man. It is then that Calaf makes his chivalrous offer to die if she can discover his name, and that of his father. By a series of intrigues, Turandot does so, and is able to announce the next day that her unknown suitor is Calaf, son of Timur. However, since she feels drawn to him despite herself, she spares his life, telling him to depart from Peking for ever. In despair at being unable to win her love, Calaf attempts to kill himself, and it is this proof of his devotion which softens Turandot's heart. The play ends with a speech by Turandot in which she asks forgiveness for her former cruelty towards the male sex ('Ciel, d'un abborrimento sí ostinato, / Che al sesso mascolino ebbi sinora, / Delle mie crudeltà perdon ti chiedo!') and then steps forward to assure the audience that she loves all these amiable people in the play ('Sappia questo gentil popol de' maschi, / Ch'io gli amo tutti').

Into his Chinese fable, which he derived either from *The Arabian Nights* or from *Le Cabinet des fées*, a collection of Persian tales, Gozzi inserted four of the traditional figures of the Italian *commedia dell'arte*: Pantalone, who becomes the Emperor Altoum's Secretary; Tartaglia, who is the Grand Chancellor; Brighella, Master of the Pages; and Truffaldino, the chief of Turandot's slaves. Puccini and his librettists retained the idea of using these Italian *maschere* (masks) in a Chinese milieu, but reduced their number to three, suppressed their *commedia dell'arte* names and characteristics, and introduced them as Ping, Pang and Pong. An important character in Gozzi's play who does not appear in the opera is Adelma, a former Tartar princess who has become the favourite slave of Turandot. Adelma is in love with Calaf, and, by informing him that the cruel Turandot intends to have him killed, tries to persuade him to flee with her. It is Adelma who, in the play, reveals Calaf's name to Turandot. Adami and Simoni introduced a new character into the plot: Liù, who dies rather than disclose the identity of Calaf to the Princess Turandot.

Puccini's correspondence with Simoni and, in particular, Adami reveals the great pains the composer took over a period of more than

---

and one of Puccini's immortal couplets, addressed to Simoni, advises: 'Bevi una tazza di caffè di notte; / Vedrai, non dormi e pensi a Turandotte' (Drink a cup of coffee at night; / You'll see, you won't sleep, you'll think of Turandot instead).

four years to get the libretto of *Turandot* exactly as he wanted it. In the spring of 1920 he mentioned to Adami that he intended to procure not only some old Chinese music but also descriptions and drawings of Chinese instruments 'which we shall put on the stage – not in the orchestra', and added, 'But at the same time you two Venetians must give an interesting and varied modern form to that relative of yours, Gozzi.'[1] In another letter written to Adami in the spring of 1920, he again urged his librettists to build upon Gozzi:

> Make Gozzi's *Turandot* your basis, but on that you must rear another figure; I mean – I can't explain! From our imaginations (and we shall need them) there must arise so much that is beautiful and attractive and gracious as to make our story a *bouquet* of success. Do not make too much use of the stock characters of the Venetian drama – these are to be the clowns and philosophers that here or there throw in a jest or an opinion (well chosen, as also the moment for it), but they must not be the type that thrust themselves forward continually or demand too much attention.

How much importance the *commedia dell'arte* characters were to be allowed in the opera was a question which required especially careful consideration, and Puccini vacillated for some time over it. Further instructions and advice were showered upon Adami:

> Immediately on the receipt of your express letter today, I wired to you on a first impulse, advising the exclusion of the masks. But I do not wish this impulse of mine to influence you and your intelligence. It is just possible that by retaining them *with discretion* we should have an Italian element which, into the midst of so much Chinese mannerism – because that is what it is – would introduce a touch of our life and, above all, of sincerity. The keen observation of Pantaloon and company would bring us back to the reality of our lives. In short, do a little of what Shakespeare often does, when he brings in three or four extraneous types who drink, use bad language, and speak ill of the King. I have seen this done in *The Tempest*, among the elves and Ariel and Caliban.

In a letter to Adami on 10 November, 1920, Puccini spoke of 'the large bundle of melancholy' which he carried through life – 'I have no reason for it, but so I am made, and so too are made all men who feel, and are not fortified by stupidity' – and voiced his fear that the opera would never be finished:

> It is impossible to work like this. When the fever abates it ends by disappearing, and without fever there is no creation; because emotional art is a kind of malady, an exceptional state of mind, over-excitation of every fibre and every atom of one's being, and so on *ad aeternum*.

In December, 1920, Puccini sent Simoni an outline for a proposed

[1] This and subsequent letters to Adami in this section are from Adami, op. cit.

revision of Act II (the present Act III). He began by recommending that the action press forward rapidly, except for those necessary moments of lyrical repose, and continued:

Entrance of Turandot, nervous;
Nessun dorma – Peking, romanza for the tenor;
Temptations: drink, women, no banquet. The masks are the ones who offer them to him, and they are the protagonists of the scene.
Invitation to *tell his name* to save their lives. Calaf:*No, I lose Turandot*. Invitation to flee – *no* – then a little plot aside and a threat of death. *No incubi.* Turandot arrives – *duet shorter – torture shorter.* The three announce their hearts are broken – *I have lost her*, my heart, why are you beating? Liù says she wants to remain, to tempt Turandot to pity.
Darkness – Scene in a room with draperies, slaves and Liù. Turandot on the point of jealousy. *Not a long scene*. Darkness.
Final scene: large white palace – *Pegonie*, all already present including the Emperor, in their places. *Rising sun.* Calaf: farewell to the world, to love, to life. His name? I don't know, *terse*.
Big love phrase with modern kiss and all present start to sing lustily![1]

'*Turandot* is groaning and travailing, but pregnant with music,' Puccini announced to Adami in the middle of 1921, but a month or two later the libretto was still giving trouble:

Why not have an original scene after Calaf's cry, 'I have lost her'? A scene *à la* Shakespeare in front of a special curtain in which they would sing – standing still if you like – a hymn to the risen victory? Or else a dance, and add an epilogue with Liù, slaves, and Turandot? And then the final scene? In short, I do not think we should delay long after the riddles. Delay here means weakening the opera. Even the incidents of the second act [the present Act III] are not important apart from the duet and the torture. The importance lies in the threat of death to the Prince and the suggestion of flight which precedes it.

On 11 November, Puccini wrote to Adami from Rome, presumably in answer to a letter which complained of the slow pace of the opera's progress and perhaps hinted that Puccini was bored with the project:

I am grieved by your letter. Do you think that I am doing this because I am weary of the subject? God knows it isn't that! But I think that with a more convincing and effective second act our ship will sail safely into harbour.

I feel that this act as it is does not convince me and cannot convince the listener. There are certain laws which a theatrical composition must observe: it must interest, surprise, stir, or move to laughter. Our act must interest and surprise. Leave Gozzi alone for a bit and work with your own logic and imagination. Perhaps you could develop it differently, more daringly? One never knows. By myself I cannot find the way. But if you attack it with a will, I think that you will arrive at something good. I am the one of the three of us

[1] *Carteggi Pucciniani*, op. cit.

who least of all should give up. I have already written the music for Act I, and, good or bad, the act is there. Therefore don't tell me that you see *Turandot* fading away! That would be a shame! I do not know, but it seems to me that all your will to work with me is dying out. And I am grieved about it. You have said to me so often, 'If it is not right we shall do it again, but we must finish it.' You will have received a letter of mine from Torre del Lago in which I discussed the duet and was even returning to the idea of one single act, closely packed with incident, to finish the opera. I am still of this mind, although the general opinion is that two acts are not enough for an evening's performance. What does it matter, if the opera turns out more convincing and conclusive in this form?

By July of the following year, 1922, the three-act form had been decided upon, but Act III was still not satisfactory:

I have reread Act III. I find much in it that is good. *Much* – but we shall have to make cuts – *many* – and the duet too, good at the beginning and in some of the rest, must, however, be touched up in the concluding section. I have some ideas. I am in favour of uniting the first and second parts, but in rather a different way. I should like the icy demeanour of Turandot to melt in the course of the duet, or, in other words, I want a love passage before they appear *coram populo* – and I want them to walk together towards her father's throne in the attitude of lovers and raise the cry of love while the crowd looks on in amazement. She says 'I do not know his name,' and he, 'Love has conquered . . .' And the whole ends in ecstasy and jubilation and the glory of the sunlight. Get rid of the Mandarin and the Emperor. The finale should follow on from the duet without a break.

But four months later, in November, Puccini and Adami were still chipping away at the intractable material of the last part of the opera:

I am so sad! and discouraged too. *Turandot* is there with the first act finished, and there isn't a ray to pierce the gloom which shrouds the rest. Perhaps it is wrapped forever in impenetrable darkness. I have the feeling that I shall have to put this work on one side. We are on the wrong track for the rest of the opera. I think the second and third acts are a great mistake as we have envisaged them. I am coming back, therefore, to the idea of two acts, and getting to the end now in only one more act.

In March, 1923, 'I am working – I don't say full steam ahead, but I've got started again, and God grant me good going!', Puccini wrote to Adami. The opera by now had achieved its final three-act form: 'I may need that wretched Act III at any minute. *Turandot* is proving a frightful bore to me, so we can imagine what it will be to the public.'

Some progress was made in the summer and autumn of 1923, and on 12 November, Puccini was clearly in a creatively active state, despite the gloomy opening of his letter to Adami:

I am accomplishing nothing or next to nothing. Poor, neglected *Turandot*! Now that I have at last settled down to write a bar or two, I find that I have no lines for the death of Liù. The music is all there; it is a case now of writing words for music which is already made. It is only an outline, of course; it is impossible to develop the sad little scene satisfactorily until I get the words.

In January, 1924, Puccini was extracting verses from his librettists, while attempting to orchestrate the first part of Act III, and as late as July he was still waiting for pieces of text. A letter of 4 July to Adami began in the usual way:

I am bored. I must get this *Turandot* finished. Please send me the verses – I shall take the work up again, and it will do me good. Idleness does not suit me. Try to send me the *final version*, including the lines for the priests at the end of the march for the Persian prince – the 'Hymn of Confucius'. I have the score here and will put them in. See that you give me a good *finale* in the metre given.

The duet and finale were never to be written. In September, Puccini was still asking for the words of the duet:

It must be a great duet. These two almost superhuman beings descend through love to the level of mankind, and this love must at the end take possession of the whole stage in a great orchestral peroration. Well, then, make an effort. Come!

In October, the composer received the words of the duet and found them 'very beautiful'. He thought that perhaps Turandot had been given too much to say, but his letter of 22 October to Adami ended, 'We shall see – when I get to work again on my return from Brussels.' Alas, Puccini was not to return alive from Brussels.

III

If one were to ask 'What is the most recent Italian opera to have achieved world-wide popularity?', the answer would have to be 'Puccini's *Turandot*'. The answer would probably still be '*Turandot*' even if one omitted the qualifying adjective 'Italian' from the question; for, despite the fact that other operas have won international approval, among them Strauss's *Arabella* and *Capriccio* and Britten's *Peter Grimes*, none is performed as frequently as *Turandot*. Yet *Turandot* is the least 'Puccinian' of Puccini's operas. It is also a work which the composer left unfinished, and the scene which he did not live to write was the one which he had intended should be the musical and dramatic climax of the entire work.

The fiercely dramatic phrase of four notes with which the opera begins [Ex. 63] is one which will recur throughout Act I. A few bars later, the curtain rises on the exotic scene of ancient Peking, while the

Ex. 63

orchestra immediately lets us know that we are in for some exotic sounds as well, for the announcement of the Mandarin is punctuated by Chinese gong and by xylophone. Even with the more conventional western instruments of his orchestra in *Turandot* Puccini produces a more arrestingly foreign sound than the pretty *japonaiserie* with which he invested *Madama Butterfly*.

The chorus bursts in upon the Mandarin's mention of the executioner with its quickened-up version of Ex. 63 in which it calls for blood. Throughout *Turandot*, the chorus is to play a much more active dramatic role than in any other Puccini opera, with the possible exception of *La fanciulla del west*. The actual writing for the chorus is somewhat less complex than in many of the composer's earlier operas, but the crowd plays a large and important role in the unfolding of the action, not only commenting on the events but helping to shape them. For this reason, perhaps, there are no choral passages which sound effective out of context (with the possible exception of the invocation to the moon early in Act I); instead, the chorus is integrated into the musical and dramatic fabric of the work in a manner which recalls not Puccini's Italian predecessors of the nineteenth century but the Russian Mussorgsky.

As a short, passionate theme bursts forth from the orchestra [Ex. 64],

Ex. 64

the crowd is pushed back by the guards, and the individual figures of Liù (soprano), Calaf (tenor) and Timur (bass) emerge from the mass. Ex. 64, whose passion was fierce at its first appearance, is now heard in more tender vein as Calaf recognizes his long-lost father. Their scene of reunion is briefly interrupted by the excited crowd, calling for death to the Prince of Persia and exulting at the appearance of the executioner and his assistants. Then, while a funereal drumbeat is heard in the orchestra, Timur narrates his story to Calaf, and a lyrical mood is introduced as the old King speaks of Liù's devotion to him. Liù remembers the day, years ago, when Calaf smiled at her, in a meltingly soft B flat which she sustains over descending chords in the orchestra.

Liù's tender moment is abruptly shattered by the huge and exciting choral ensemble ('Gira la cote': Turn the whetstone) which develops as the executioner's twelve assistants, all basses, sharpen the sword, urged on by the crowd.

The chorus of invocation to the moon which follows immediately upon the ferocity of 'Gira la cote' is a delicate and mysterious sequence, unlike anything else in Puccini in its exquisite orchestral colouring, its wispy fragments of melody, its Debussian harmonies, its curious little arabesques for clarinet, and exotic figures for harps and flutes. The impressionistic delicacy of the ensemble gives way to *fortissimo* cries of 'Pu-Tin-Pao' (the executioner), which in turn fade as a chorus of boys' voices, off-stage, is heard in a melancholy dirge whose theme [Ex. 65]

Ex. 65

will be heard, transformed in various ways throughout the opera, but always associated with the awesome figure of Turandot. This theme is the first of several pieces of authentic Chinese music to be made use of by Puccini in *Turandot*. It is a folk-tune, entitled 'Moon-Lee-Wha', which first became known in Europe at the end of the eighteenth century and, according to Mosco Carner, is quoted in an English travel book as well as in a German volume of musical history.[1] Puccini probably heard it played by an ancient Chinese musical box in the possession of a friend of his.

The boys' chorus leads directly into a funeral march for the Prince of Persia. The march proceeds inexorably in the orchestra while above it the crowd now calls for pity. Calaf's solo phrases, embedded into the fabric of the march, call down curses on the Princess whom he has not yet seen. The pace of the march quickens, and Ex. 65 rings out in pompous splendour as, acclaimed by the crowd, Turandot now appears. Calaf's curses are changed to cries of ecstasy at the beauty of the Princess, but are still uttered to the rhythm of the solemn march at whose conclusion Timur and Liù attempt to persuade Calaf to come away with them. But the love-besotted Calaf can only repeat the name of Turandot, emphasizing it the third time with his high B flat. His cry of love is echoed a semitone lower, off-stage, by the Prince of Persia as he meets his death.

Ping (baritone), Pang and Pong (tenors) now make their first appearance. As their leader, Ping is, throughout the opera, given more

[1] Carner, op. cit.

solo lines to sing than the other two, but the three are not individually
characterized, their musical utterance combining as, so to speak, one
unit of musical-dramatic character. The mood of the scene and the
nature of Puccini's orchestration undergo a sudden and startling change
as Ping, Pang and Pong begin to warn Calaf against competing for the
hand of Turandot. Triangle, celeste, glockenspiel and xylophone are
greatly to the fore in the accompaniment to the Masks' oddly jaunty
'Chinese' tunes, the very first of which quotes from the modern (1912)
Chinese Imperial Hymn, interrupted by Calaf's irritable responses.
Several of the short, pentatonic phrases derive from Chinese folk-song.

The Masks are interrupted by a chorus of nine sopranos, two of them
given solo phrases, who gently request a little quiet, as the Princess is
sleeping. Calaf utters a dreamily lovesick phrase, and the Masks make a
final chattering attempt to dissuade him from his suicidal pursuit of
Turandot. The ghosts of the Princess's past suitors, four contraltos and
four tenor voices, are heard off-stage, protesting their love from beyond
the grave, in a fragmentary chorus of an unearthly sweetness and
mystery. Ping, Pang and Pong continue to warn Calaf, and Timur now
adds his voice. The first solo passage in the opera long enough to be considered an aria is Liù's 'Signore, ascolta' (Signor, listen to me), so
typically Puccinian in its delicate sentimentality that it comes as a
surprise to learn that its pentatonic melody is based on another of the
genuine Chinese folk-songs which Puccini incorporated into his score in
so masterly a fashion. This one was originally a song called 'Sian Chok'.
Again, Liù ends on a softly floated B flat, which is a kind of musical
signature for her.

Calaf immediately responds to Liù with his first aria, 'Non piangere,
Liù' (Do not weep, Liu), a tender, somewhat lachrymose melody which
leads into the magnificent finale of the act, an ensemble in which the
voices of Liù, Calaf, Timur, Ping, Pang and Pong are soon joined by the
chorus. The first climax is provided as Calaf repeats the final phrases of
'Non piangere, Liù', the second as he strikes the gong, and the great
'Turandot' theme [Ex. 65] resounds in a *fortissimo* orchestral tutti in D
major. An orchestral peroration brings the curtain down as Calaf stands
transfixed in ecstasy.

The first scene of Act II is an extended trio (lasting about twelve
minutes) for Ping, Pang and Pong. Scherzo-like in character, this
'Pavilion' scene with the slightly exaggerated elegant *chinoiserie* of its
light and delicate instrumentation as well as its writing for the voice
provides welcome light relief from the surrounding grimness. The
tempo is generally lively at the beginning of the trio, the opening *allegro
moderato* slowing only marginally to an *allegretto*. In a delightful *andantino
mosso* sequence, the three Masks led by Ping recall their idyllic homes in
the country [Ex. 66]. In this nostalgic central section of the trio, some of
the Chinese trimmings drop away, and Ping, Pang and Pong appear to

Ex. 66

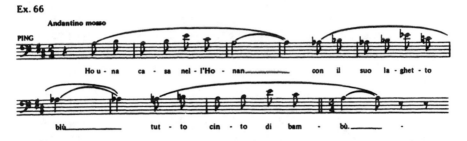

speak with what is, for them, an unusual sincerity and wistful sadness. Soon after the tempo has quickened again to *allegretto*, an off-stage chorus is heard repeating its bloodthirsty cries from Act I.

There is no break in the music between scenes i and ii. The sound of drums, trumpets and trombones awakens the three Masks to present reality, and they hurry off as the scene changes. The music develops into a processional march based on pentatonic Chinese motifs, and the general effect is one of great pomp and splendour as the crowd acclaims the Princess Turandot. When the aged Emperor Altoum addresses the populace, it is in a thin, frail tenor, weary with age. Spike Hughes has irreverently pointed out that the phrase for off-stage trumpets and trombones which precedes the Emperor's announcement is identical with the beginning of the song 'I am Chu Chin Chow of China' from Frederick Norton's *Chu Chin Chow*, a musical play which Puccini saw when he visited London in 1919.[1] What is most likely is that both Norton and Puccini lifted their tune from the same Chinese source.

The Emperor's words are unaccompanied, but punctuated by tremolo chords in the orchestra, while Calaf's confident replies are echoed with equal firmness by the orchestra. The entrance of Turandot is heralded by choral and orchestral references to motifs already heard, a shortened version of the mandarin's announcement from the beginning of Act I, and the off-stage voices of children singing their song of praise to the Princess [Ex. 65].

Turandot begins her great aria, 'In questa reggia' (In this palace) [Ex. 67], without orchestral preamble. In a firm, tense arioso she explains the

Ex. 67

reason for her hatred of all who would try to possess her. Twice the crowd adds its comment, but quietly. When Turandot reaches the dramatic phrase 'quel grido e quella morte' (that cry and that death), a new and stirring theme [Ex. 68] is heard in the orchestra, and the second,

Ex. 68   Largamente ♩ = 56

broader section of the aria is launched. Ex. 68 is heard three times, the pitch rising a major third with each repetition, and it is only at its third statement that Turandot sings the entire phrase. The device of heightening tension by raising the pitch is repeated as Turandot now proclaims 'Gli enigmi sono tre, la morte è una' (The enigmas are three, but death is one). Calaf responds by changing the words to 'The enigmas are three, but life is one' (una è la vita) and hurling the phrase back at the Princess in a higher key. The key-progression continues: the third time, Turandot and Calaf sing in competition with each other, both holding their high C at the climax of the phrase. The rock-like aria which has become a duet ends as an ensemble, for the chorus now bursts in, to the tune of Ex. 68, urging Turandot to proceed to the questioning of the stranger.

Trumpets call the crowd to attention, and Turandot asks her first question, unaccompanied except by thumps of punctuation from woodwind and percussion, and a lamenting figure from two solo cellos. Puccini makes superb use of silence in this sequence of riddles: there is only a brief pause before Calaf, to the same tune in which the riddle was asked, answers it confidently, his answer confirmed three times by the eight bass voices of the sages. Turandot accepts the answer with an ill grace, and proceeds to the second question. Tension mounts as Calaf this time hesitates before answering, while the Emperor and the crowd offer him encouragement. It is only when Liù too implores him, for the sake of love, to persevere, that Calaf arrives at the second correct answer. The third time, a semitone higher than before, Turandot asks her question, and the agonized silence which follows it is portrayed in the orchestra by the falling figure of lament. But Calaf finally produces his third correct answer and the crowd bursts into the hymn of praise for Turandot, [Ex. 65], now directing it to Calaf.

When Turandot's pathetic appeal to the Emperor is unsuccessful, she turns angrily on Calaf. Twice in the ensuing ensemble she rises icily to her high C in her haughty defiance of the stranger who has conquered her. In Calaf's phrase in reply, there is an optical top C which is a temptation to most tenors, though the alternative ending of the phrase, rising no higher than G, is musically to be preferred. To the music of the riddles, Calaf now asks his question, and gives Turandot until dawn to answer it. At his words 'Il mio nome non sai' (You do not know my name), we hear, anticipated by the orchestra [Ex. 69], a theme which we

Ex. 69

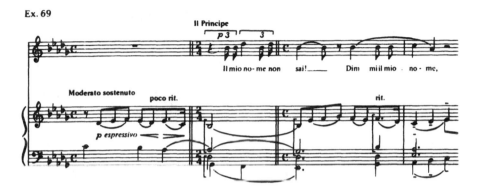

shall encounter in Calaf's great aria, 'Nessun dorma', in Act II. The Emperor is briefly heard again, above an exotic accompaniment, before the act is brought to an end with the populace singing the tune of the Imperial Hymn.

The haunting, nocturnal beginning of Act III contains some of Puccini's most powerfully evocative music, conjuring up the mystery of the night, and the tense expectancy of the morrow. The composer's impressionistic scoring contributes to musical scene-painting of a high order. Off-stage, the voices of the heralds (eight tenors) proclaim that none shall sleep ('Nessun dorma') in Peking that night, for the stranger's name must be revealed before dawn. Answering echoes from groups of citizens grow fainter and die away. Over a muted accompaniment of rich harmonies, now in a quiet but confident G major, Calaf begins his aria by declaiming the words of the heralds, 'Nessun dorma' [Ex. 70]. This

Ex. 70

aria, one of Puccini's most beautiful, consists of two melodies, the first somewhat austere, the second the exalted and passionate tune already adumbrated at the end of Act II [Ex. 69]. The second theme, sung by Calaf to the words 'Ma il mio mistero è chiuso in me' (But my mystery is enclosed in me), is followed by a truncated reprise of the first theme. Then, off-stage, a female chorus laments, to the tune of Ex. 69, that all must die tomorrow if the stranger's name be not known. Calaf takes over

the melody, crowning it with a thrillingly confident coda. 'All' alba
vincerò' (At dawn I shall be victorious) he sings, lightly touching a high B
natural as he sings the word 'vincerò' for the third time. At least, that is
what the score instructs him to do. Most tenors who have a B natural,
and even those who do not, and who transpose the aria down, prefer,
having reached the heights, to dwell there awhile in order to prove that it
was no fluke! Though I am not generally in favour of what one might
call 'high note hogging', I cannot honestly say that the tenor who holds
his top B on 'vincerò' does any damage to the music. He may even
enhance the drama.

The orchestra repeats Calaf's final phrases in passionate accents, and
then Puccini achieves an abrupt change of mood as Ping, Pang and Pong
burst on to the scene, accompanied by 'shadowy figures' who turn out to
be beautiful semi-nude girls whom the Masks thrust at Calaf, the *allegro*
of their arrival slowing to a seductive *lento* as the girls display their charms
to an unresponsive Calaf, and quickening again to a bustle of *chinoiserie*
when the girls are rejected and the Masks, now supported by the chorus,
change their tactics. With an oddly melancholy theme of distinctly
Chinese flavour [Ex. 71], Ping launches an ensemble in which he warns
Calaf of Turandot's cruelty.

Ex. 71

The crowd now assumes a threatening tone, and the scene of the
torture and death of Liù begins. Torture always exercised an odd attraction for Puccini: this time the musical description of it is less graphic
than it was in *Tosca*, although the means he uses are similar. The guards
(eight basses) enter, dragging Liù and Timur with them, the Princess is
called upon and enters to the sound of her theme [Ex. 65], reinforced
off-stage by trumpets and trombones. Turandot's theme continues in
the orchestra as the Masks prostrate themselves before her. Rather oddly
choosing the passionate tune first heard in the orchestra in Act I (Ex. 64),
Turandot addresses Calaf, who uses the same theme in his reply. It is
developed and distorted until its mood is violently dispelled by the
crowd calling for Liù to be bound and beaten. The quiet beauty and
simplicity of Liù's little aria, 'Tanto amore segreto' (So secret a love), is
abruptly shattered by Turandot, and Ping leads the crowd in calling for
the executioner.

'Tu che di gel sei cinta' (You who are girdled with ice) |Ex. 72|, Liù's final aria, is surely the most moving solo in the score, and its words are,

Ex. 72

in fact, not by his librettists but by Puccini himself. He had composed the music before the text was ready, and composed it to his own words which Simoni and Adami were unable to improve upon. The aria's rhythmical subtlety and the skill and effectiveness of its orchestration do not force themselves upon the attention, but are as responsible for its emotional impact as the beauty of the melody. Writers on Puccini generally comment upon the composer's compassion for poor little Liù, and amateur psychiatrists among them like to equate Liù, the faithful slave who loves Calaf, with the servant girl Doria Manfredi who was driven to suicide by the Turandot-like figure of Elvira Puccini. The relationship between art and life is, however, a more complex affair, and a superficial analysis of Puccini's personal relationships is of little help to a discussion of *Turandot*.

The orchestra thunders out Ex. 72 as Liù stabs herself, while the crowd demands of the dying girl that she reveal the Prince's name. Calaf and Timur lament Liù's death to the same theme which becomes a threnody for her. Liù's body is borne away as the crowd murmurs its prayer of propitiation to the spirit of the dead girl in a passage of great harmonic beauty. The theme of 'Tu che di gel sei cinta' |Ex. 72| returns as the funeral procession moves off, Timur continuing his lament in broken phrases and the chorus, now off-stage, providing the final statement of the theme. As their voices fade away, the sound of the piccolo's high E flat is sustained in the accompaniment for two bars, before it, too, fades into silence. It was at this point in his composition of the opera that Puccini had arrived when he broke off to enter hospital in Brussels. Liù's funeral procession was the last music that he wrote. And it was at this moment in the first performance of *Turandot* that Toscanini laid down his baton, with the words, 'Qui finisce l'opera lasciata incompiuta dal Maestro, perchè a questo punto il Maestro è morto' (Here ends the opera left incomplete by the Maestro, who died at this point).

The remaining pages of *Turandot*, approximately fourteen minutes of music, were composed by Alfano. Are they necessary, or should performances of the opera end where Puccini left it, at the death of Liù? Surely the answer is that, dramatically, the concluding pages *are* necessary and that, musically, Alfano has performed his task well enough to avoid anti-climax. Puccini agonized over the duet which he did not live to write, producing a number of sketches for it, and hoping to make it 'like Tristan'[1] by which he surely meant not that he intended to write a pastiche of Wagner's *Tristan und Isolde* love duet but that he must somehow find a way to produce the same effect of catharsis and transformation, a musical means of lifting the nature of Calaf's love for Turandot on to a higher spiritual level. Alfano can hardly be blamed for having failed to do this; he deserves, rather, to be praised for the professional manner in which he musically carried the action to its conclusion.

Alfano based his conclusion to the opera on Puccini's pencil sketches, a total of 36 pages of notes. His opening bars for the duet are often criticized for their un-Puccinian brashness, yet Calaf's lines and their supporting harmony are to be found in Puccini's sketches. The sketches continue up to the beginning of Turandot's aria, 'Del primo pianto' and, in more fragmented form, even further. Where Alfano had no guidance from Puccini's sketches, he resorted to themes from earlier in the opera. His duet is workmanlike, and effective in performance. After its climax, Turandot's theme [Ex. 65] is heard off-stage.

Turandot's aria, 'Del primo pianto' (Of my first tear) is frequently omitted in performance, but ought always to be included, for it is clear that Puccini wanted an aria at this point, in order to reveal the psychological change in his heroine, and Alfano was able to incorporate into the aria several phrases intended for it by Puccini. The important passage of twelve bars at the conclusion of the aria, from Calaf's 'Il mio mistero?' (My mystery) to Turandot's 'So il tuo nome!' (I know your name) exists in Puccini's sketches. It includes the unfortunately banal phrase to which Calaf cries 'Io son Calaf, figlio di Timur' (I am Calaf, son of Timur); a 'legend', mentioned by Spike Hughes, which attributes this phrase to Toscanini[2] has no basis in fact.

The short final scene which follows without a break is disappointingly perfunctory. After the chorus has sung a few bars of the Imperial Hymn, Turandot announces that the name of her unknown suitor is Love ('Il suo nome e Amor!'), and with a choral restatement of the theme from Calaf's 'Nessun dorma' the opera ends: not altogether appropriately, since Calaf had used that phrase to declare that his mystery remained locked within him, but there can be no guarantee that Puccini would not, in any case, have chosen the same phrase to bring the curtain down. He was not very particular in these matters!

---

[1] 'Poi Tristano' (literally 'Then Tristan') is scribbled on one of his sketches for the duet.

[2] Hughes, op. cit.

IV

Puccini was the last of the popular composers of Italian opera. He is often spoken of as Verdi's true successor; though he encompassed a narrower range than his great predecessor, he succeeded in composing a number of operas which, in the words of Giulio Gatti-Casazza in a speech shortly after the composer's death, 'speak above all to the emotions of the public, and speak in a voice that is original, moving, penetrating and sincere'.[1]

Lacking Verdi's stature as an artist, Puccini, it must be admitted, also lacked it as a man. His will, bequeathing a very large sum of money to Elvira and to Tonio, was thought distinctly ungenerous by many because, unlike Verdi's, it left nothing to charity or to his community. More to the point, surely, is the lack of generosity of spirit Puccini revealed in his lifetime. His character was neither philosophically reflective nor especially attractive in any way. He was self-centred, and his principal interests outside his music appear to have been sex, fast cars, and the shooting of birds. But he shared with Verdi at least one characteristic: a vein of melancholy. Most of Puccini's verse consists of comic doggerel, but among his papers was found a page, dated 3 March, 1923 (about eighteen months before his death), on which he had written a non-comical poem. It is of no value as poetry, but it tells us something about the composer. (Puccini's minimally punctuated Italian is reproduced without alteration.)

> Non ho un amico
> mi sento solo
> anche la musica
> triste mi fa.
> Quando la morte
> verrà a trovarmi
> sarò felice
> di riposarmi.
> Oh com' è dura
> la vita mia
> eppur a molti
> sembro felice
> ma i miei successi?
> passano e . . . resta?[2]

---

[1] The text of Gatti-Casazza's speech is preserved in the archives of the Metropolitan Opera, New York.

[2] I have no friend, / I feel alone, / even music / makes me sad. / When death / comes to find me / I shall be happy / to rest. / Oh how hard is / my life / though to many / I seem happy, / but my successes / pass, and . . . what

ben poca cosa –
Son cose effemere
la vita corre
va verso il baratro
chi vive giovane
si gode il mondo
ma chi s'accorge
di tutti questo?
Passa veloce
la giovinezza
e l'occhio scruta
l'eternità.[1]

[1] remains? / it's worth little / They are ephemeral things. / Life runs on / towards the abyss. / He who lives and is young / finds the world enjoyable / but who is aware / of all this? / It passes quickly, / one's youth, / and the eye scrutinizes / eternity. (The page in Puccini's handwriting is photographically reproduced in Marchetti, op. cit.)

Some Books Consulted

(This list contains titles of general interest. Details of other volumes are to be found throughout the text, in footnotes.)

Adami, Giuseppe: *Puccini* (Milan, 1935)
Ashbrook, William: *The Operas of Puccini* (New York, 1968)
Carner, Mosco: *Puccini* (2nd edition, London, 1974)
Hughes, Spike: *Famous Puccini Operas* (London, 1959)
Marchetti, Leopoldo: *Puccini nelle immagini* (Milan, 1949)
Marek, George R.: *Puccini* (New York, 1951)
Puccini, Giacomo: *Epistolario*, edited by Giuseppe Adami (Milan, 1928), translated as *Letters of Giacomo Puccini* (London, 1931)
Seligman, Vincent: *Puccini among Friends* (London, 1938)
Specht, Richard: *Giacomo Puccini* (Berlin, 1931)

Index

CPSIA information can be obtained at www.ICGtesting.com
Printed in the USA
LVOW06s1731160116

470247LV00004B/483/P